✔ KU-284-425

Understanding Cooking

Donald E. Lundberg, Ph.D.

Head, Department of Hotel and Restaurant Administration,
University of Massachusetts, Amherst, Massachusetts, U.S.A.

Lendal H. Kotschevar, Ph.D.

Formerly Professor, School of Hotel, Restaurant and Institutional Management,
Michigan State University.

British edition edited by
Victor Ceserani MBE

Head of Department, School of Hotel Keeping and Catering, Ealing Technical
College, London.

Mandy Hodgkins
129, Manchester Rd
Ramsbottom
Bury
Rams 2417.

Edward Arnold

© Donald E. Lundberg, Lendal H. Kotschevar and
Victor Ceserani 1970

First published in Great Britain 1970 by
Edward Arnold (Publishers) Ltd.
25 Hill Street, London W1X 8LL

Reprinted: 1973, 1974, 1976

ISBN: 0 7131 1550 5

All Rights Reserved. No part of this publica-
tion may be reproduced, stored in a retrieval
system, or transmitted in any form or by any
means, electronic, mechanical, photocopying,
recording or otherwise, without the prior
permission of Edward Arnold (Publishers) Ltd.

*The oven in the cover photograph is
by Smith and Wellstood (G. & G.) Ltd.*

Printed by Offset Lithography by
Billing & Sons Limited
Guildford and London

Foreword

The authors do not presume to imply that reading this book will guarantee comprehensive understanding of cooking, for that requires knowledge of physics and chemistry and a lively appreciation of French culinary history to say nothing of a wide experience in the kitchen.

This book, however, should greatly improve the reader's understanding of cooking principles and of cooking in general.

The material is programmed, meaning that as new words or ideas are presented they are at once reinforced in the reader's mind. This is done by immediately asking the reader to use the information or by asking him to play back the new information in some manner. Opinions differ as to the proper length of items in programmed instruction. Items in this book vary in length depending upon the complexity of the idea and how it relates to other ideas. Other programmers no doubt would present the same material differently.

Professor Kotschevar, who is well known as an expert in food preparation and service, has been primarily responsible for the content of the book, while Professor Lundberg, as a psychologist, has been more concerned with the presentation.

Several persons have been kind enough to criticize the content of the book. Professor Leslie I. Bond of Cornell Hotel School and Dr. Robert V. Decareau of Litton Industries were especially helpful on the section dealing with radiation cooking.

Foreword to the British Edition

Having practised, studied and taught professional cookery at various levels for many years I found that meeting Donald Lundberg was an interesting experience. Hearing him talk in 'workshops' using 'Understanding Cooking' as his text and having the opportunity to study the book, opened my mind to fresh areas of thought. I welcomed, therefore, the invitation to edit a British edition and have found the task enjoyable and informative, it has stimulated me to think more deeply of the principles and practice involved in cooking and catering.

It is my hope and belief that in this book teachers of cookery will find information and stimulus to assist them in a fuller understanding of their work and that students at all levels will find beneficial areas of study.

Practising chefs and caterers may also gain knowledge that could assist in a deeper understanding of their profession and help to achieve a more efficient and economic job operation.

Information based on American practice has deliberately been left in as it is considered to be a useful broadening of knowledge.

I am grateful to my colleagues Ronald Kinton, Linda Formesyn and Stanley West for their help and advice in the preparation of this British edition.

V. C.

Metrication

Teachers and students will be aware that this book is being published at a time when there is great discussion within the industry of the implications of the 1971 changeover to decimal currency and the adoption by Britain in 1975 of a metric system of measurement, the Système International d'Unites (S.I.).

Our enquiries have led us to the view that the new systems are more readily assimilable if the student is not given the old unit alongside the new one. For the most part, therefore, the text is completely metric. Exceptions have been made, for example in steam cookery, where we have been unable to obtain metric sizes and pressures from the manufacturers. In these instances approximate equivalents have been given.

NB: All temperatures are shown as 100C (212F). We have retained the Fahrenheit equivalent as there is so much machinery in use based on this scale. The degree symbols (°) have been omitted for space-saving and clarity but should be used by the student in *all* written work (100°C).

To the Student

This textbook is put together differently from most textbooks you have seen. The material is written in the form of 'programmed' instruction, which is designed to make learning easier and faster for you. Instead of reading an entire chapter and trying to digest the whole of it, ideas or pieces of information are presented one at a time. You are then asked to respond to this information so that learning is almost automatic. Ideally, one piece of information builds on the next.

The cover board provided with the book should be used to cover the answers which appear on the right hand margins. By not looking at the answer until you have thought about what is called for, your learning is increased. In some cases, the material in the margin adds to the information presented in the item itself.

Contents

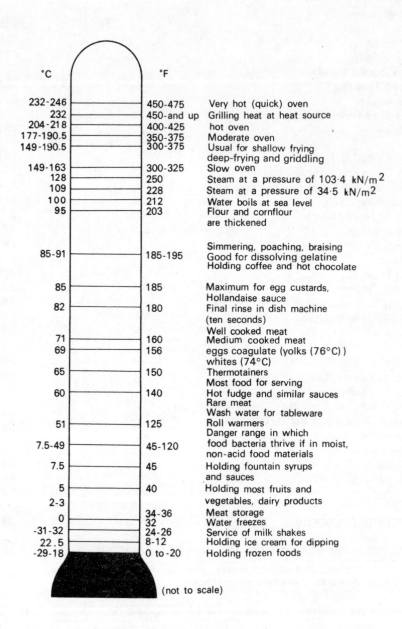

°C	°F	
232-246	450-475	Very hot (quick) oven
232	450-and up	Grilling heat at heat source
204-218	400-425	hot oven
177-190.5	350-375	Moderate oven
149-190.5	300-375	Usual for shallow frying deep-frying and griddling
149-163	300-325	Slow oven
128	250	Steam at a pressure of 103·4 kN/m²
109	228	Steam at a pressure of 34·5 kN/m²
100	212	Water boils at sea level
95	203	Flour and cornflour are thickened
85-91	185-195	Simmering, poaching, braising Good for dissolving gelatine Holding coffee and hot chocolate
85	185	Maximum for egg custards, Hollandaise sauce
82	180	Final rinse in dish machine (ten seconds)
71	160	Well cooked meat Medium cooked meat
69	156	eggs coagulate (yolks (76°C)) whites (74°C)
65	150	Thermotainers Most food for serving
60	140	Hot fudge and similar sauces Rare meat Wash water for tableware
51	125	Roll warmers Danger range in which
7.5-49	45-120	food bacteria thrive if in moist, non-acid food materials
7.5	45	Holding fountain syrups and sauces
5	40	Holding most fruits and vegetables, dairy products
2-3		
0	34-36	Meat storage
-31-32	32	Water freezes
22.5	24-26	Service of milk shakes
-29-18	8-12	Holding ice cream for dipping
	0 to -20	Holding frozen foods

(not to scale)

The Cooking Process

WHAT IS COOKING?

1   Cooking is the application of heat to food for the purpose of making it more digestible, safer to eat, more palatable, and to change its appearance. To cook food, ... must be introduced into the food.

heat

●

2   In the cooking process, what is it that breaks down the cellulose in plant foods, softens some of the connective tissue of meat, breaks down and gels starches present, changes and blends flavours within the food, destroys bacteria, and makes food more acceptable to humans and to human digestion?

Heat

●

3   Cooking may include a process of extraction, leaching and steeping by which soluble materials are removed from a food for use as flavouring medium.

When bones are simmered to produce stock, for example, the soluble compounds in the bones are extracted and pass into the simmering water. The stock can then be used in soup and sauce making. Is coffee brewed by the drip method another example of cooking by extraction?

Yes, the boiling water passes through the ground coffee at between 93C (200F) and 99C (210F), extracting the coffee flavours.

●

4   While the application of heat to food materials is the principal action taking place in cooking, other things are done to enhance the flavour and spices, sauces, and seasonings are added. Monosodium glutamate is added

1

to some food materials to bring out flavours already present. The food may be marinated (soaked) before cooking; it may be cooked in wine. Fat may be added before, during or after cooking. Flavours and colours may be added. Different foods are blended together to produce new flavours and appearance.

Strictly speaking, for cooking to take place, heat must be added to a food material. But the term 'cookery' has been extended to include many of those things done to food to improve it for eating. 'Food preparation' is another broad term which includes all of the things done to make food edible and flavourful.

True or False: The terms food preparation and cookery are broader and more inclusive than the term cooking.

True

●

5   Are you cooking when you season foods by adding salt, pepper and other spices and herbs?

No, since heat transfer is not involved. However, seasoning of foods is very much a part of food preparation. Salt is a food and in the mouth stimulates hundreds of taste buds. Added to liquid food such as beer, salt releases odour compounds which increases the flavour greatly. Monosodium glutamate and other salts also greatly increase flavour in some foods.

●

6   Some foods such as raw fish are made palatable by marination in lime juice, lemon juice or vinegar. The acid in the juice breaks down the connective tissue of the fish and inhibits bacteria. Can this be called cooking?

Not if we stand by our stipulation that heat must be applied if cooking is to take place.

●

7   Is salad making an aspect of cooking?

No. It is usually considered to be a part of the broad term 'cookery' which has come to include most of the things done to prepare food for eating.

8   The baking of pies, cakes, biscuits and various doughs is also cooking in the sense that heat is applied to food materials. In most baking an aerating action takes place. Air, steam or carbon dioxide stretch the gluten in dough to expand it. Baking is a more precise process than cooking in that once the leavening process is set in motion, adjustments are not possible as is true in cooking most other food materials. The aerating agent used must be in exactly the right quantity for the desired effect on the other ingredients present. The balance or proportion of ingredients must also be precise. This is not as true as practised in cooking many items in the kitchen but it should be.

True or False: Cooking and baking are similar processes except that baking calls for more precision in formula than the usual recipe requires and baking often involves an aerating action.   True

●

UNDESIRABLE EFFECTS OF OVER-COOKING

9   Cooking—especially over-cooking—has undesirable as well as beneficial effects on food. Seven adverse effects in food caused by over extended cooking or by the use of excessively high heat are:

(a) The proteins in such food materials as meat, eggs, fish, and birds are denatured, toughen or become stringy, or all three. Or, with too long a cooking a flesh food may become over-cooked and disintegrate.

(b) Vitamin C (ascorbic acid), thiamine (B_1), and other nutrients are destroyed or leached from the food. Ascorbic acid is found in a good supply in most fruits and vegetables. Thiamine is found in some vegetables, and in protein foods. Riboflavin (B_2) is more heat stable than ascorbic acid and thiamine, but is very easily destroyed by light.

(c) The texture of some foods is softened to the extent that the food lacks palatability.

(d) Flavours may be lost, changed, or destroyed.

(e) Red, green, and white colours in vegetables are changed; red colours may turn a dirty blue or purple, chlorophyll (green) turns a drab green, and white colours may turn grey or yellow.

(f) Sugars and other compounds may over caramelize or burn and result in off-flavours.

(g) Food may become excessively dry and hard.

What two vitamins are most likely to be lost or inactivated by cooking and especially by overcooking?

Vitamin C and thiamine.

●

10   Overcooking results in the loss or changing of vitamin C, riboflavin and thiamine in some foods and in change in flavour, form and texture and . . . . in some foods.

colour

●

11   Overcooking also results in excessive loss of water in many foods. Most foods have a surprisingly high water content, 50—95% water. Extended cooking or high temperatures evaporates the juices in such foods as meat, vegetables and fruits. In meats, fish and fowl, heat also melts some of the fat present allowing it to escape.

Overcooking usually results in loss of nutrients, flavour, form, texture, colour and . . . .

juices or water

●

12   We must be careful to distinguish between long, slow cooking and overcooking especially as regards to meat. Meat studies show that long cooking at low temperatures gives the most tenderness and juiciness. The white connective tissue called collagen turns to gelatine and the muscle fibres become tender. Using oven temperatures of less than 93C (200F)* requires

---

*All temperatures are shown as 100C (112F). We have retained the Fahrenheit equivalent as there is so much machinery in use based on this scale. The degree symbol (°) has been omitted for space-saving and clarity but should be used by the student in all written work (100°C).

as long as 30 hours to cook beef roasts but the meat is juicy and tender.

'Overcooking' must be interpreted in terms of the food to be cooked and the . . . . used.

temperature

●

COOKING TEMPERATURES

13 At what temperature can we say 'cooking' takes place? The answer depends upon the food material and the reaction desired. Most bacteria are killed if subjected to 60C (140F) for a period of time. The common way to cook vegetables is to drop them into boiling water. Egg whites coagulate at 65C (149F), yolks at 70C (158F). Most proteins in solution denature or lose moisture at around 63C (145F) and final coagulation occurs somewhere between 74C (165F) and 79C (175F). Shrinkage occurs with coagulation. Coagulation is a process of adjacent protein molecules joining together by means of side-chain hydrogen bonds. Extended heat at around 79C (175F) is required to change collagen in meat to gelatine in the presence of moisture proteins begin to cook at about . . . .

63C (145F); gelatine formation requires a little higher temperature.

●

14 Starch cookery may involve higher temperatures. Starch does not dissolve in cold water, but on heating, water enters the starch granules, causing swelling. At the same time, the starch paste becomes very thick and on further heating, the grains burst, giving a gel of starch in the water. With lower heat and insufficient water only some of the starch granules open and a poor gel occurs.

Regular starch such as that from cereals, rice, potatoes, arrowroot, tapioca, and sago begin to thicken at 62C (144F) and finish their first stage of thickening at about 72C (162F). At this point the novice may think cooking is completed but it is not, for the thickened mixture will have a grainy texture from unexploded starch granules and an uncooked starchy flavour. Final thickening of this type starch occurs around 193C (200F), when the paste is completely smooth and the uncooked flavour disappears.

Waxy maize or modified starches thicken at around 68C (155F) to 75C (167F) and no second thickening occurs. Above 91C (195F) these starches may thin slightly. Waxy maize and modified starches are as thick hot as they are cold but the regular type starches set slowly as they cool and become quite firm.

Cereal starch starts to thicken at 62C (144F) but final thickening does not take place until about . . . .

93C (200F)

●

15   Starch cooking requires higher/lower heat than protein cooking.

usually higher

●

16   Fairly high heat and water are needed in starch cooking so that the starch will burst open, take on water and form a paste. This process is known as . . . .

gelatinization

●

17   Waxy maize or modified starches can be processed so that the addition of a cold liquid such as fruit juice, milk or other liquid will cause them to set or thicken, e.g. instant pudding. This type of starch is best for fruit or berry pies where a minimum of cooking is desired to maintain a fresh flavour. Cooking a cold setting starch does not destroy its thickening power.

Pastry flour—high in starch—is used for thickening gravies, sauces and soups; cornflour or arrowroot is effective in thickening puddings and fruit juices.

True or False: The thickening power of all starches depends upon the temperature at which the starch is cooked.

False. Not 'all', for some of the processed starches need no cooking at all in order to set. They are merely mixed with water.

●

18   As starches cook they swell by taking in water and gelling; as sugars cook they darken and caramelize; as flesh foods cook the protein coagulates or firms, changes

colour and the connective tissue softens; as vegetables cook they become tender and may change flavour. Each process takes place at a different temperature.

True or False: A 'correct' cooking temperature depends upon the nature of the food material being cooked.

True, keeping in mind the objective of retaining juices, nutrients, texture and flavour.

●

19   Heat applied in cooking destroys bacteria dangerous to man such as those causing dysentery, salmonellosis, and streptococcus food infection. A temperature of 60C (140F) applied over 30 or more minutes kills most pathogenic germs. However, some spores and the toxin produced by staphylococcus aureus—a common cause of food poisoning—are not destroyed by the usual cooking temperatures.

High acid foods which include most fruits and berries do not support these germs. Low acid foods such as milk, corn, beans and peas require longer or higher heat to make them safe for eating.

Would you expect that a longer application of comparatively low heat would destroy most food bacteria as effectively as high heat for a shorter time.

This is usually the case. Milk, for example, can be pasteurized at 62C (144F) for 30 minutes or at 72C (161F) for 15 seconds.

●

TIME AND TEMPERATURE

20   Cooking usually involves a decision concerning time and temperature. Thick solid food materials such as roasts require lower heat and longer time to cook than do thin pieces of meat, which can be grilled or fried at relatively high temperatures in a short time. Less tender meat can be braised, stewed, steamed or simmered. The time necessary for heat to penetrate into the food material partly determines the method of cooking and the best cooking temperature.

Temperature in cooking is usually related to what other important factor?

Time

21   Browning of flesh foods is done to develop a favourable surface appearance and to develop flavour by bringing the salts to the surface. The problem in browning is to expose the flesh to heat high enough or long enough to cook it, but not so high or so long as to burn the surface or overcook the interior. Continued heat application to protein foods dries the food material, denatures and toughens the protein, destroys the vitamins and detracts from the appearance of food. Meat and flesh foods are often browned at high heat and finished at low heat, e.g. roast beef and grilled mutton chop.

Browning flesh foods is a good example of the necessity of cooking for the right time and at the right . . . .   temperature

●

22   Time and temperature are particularly important factors in cooking thin pieces of meat, fish, or fowl. Thin, tender pieces of meat are grilled or roasted at high heat to avoid excessive evaporation even though low heat would be preferable as regards tenderness.

Following this reasoning would it be better to use comparatively high temperature in roasting small birds?

Yes, their surface area is comparatively large. If cooking time is extended, the birds will dry out excessively.

●

23   With some foods a higher heat means less cooking time and the cook has a choice of using high heat for a short cooking time or a lower heat for a longer cooking time. A leg of lamb weighing 2 kg can be cooked in $1\frac{1}{2}$ h using high heat or lower heat can be applied for a . . . . . .
cooking time.   longer

●

24   The method of heat transfer affects the time of cooking. As seen later, heat is transferred to food principally by three means: conduction, convection, and radiation.

Heat transfer is quickest by means of radiation. Cooking methods reflect the means of heat transfer taking place in a particular piece of cooking equipment and method of cooking. These methods, equipment used, and their effects on food material are covered later in this chapter.

True or False: Time required for cooking and the temperature desired for cooking is related to the method of heat transference employed.

True

●

25 The cooking of fresh vegetables offers a dramatic example of the importance of time and temperature as it affects vitamin C retention. The time required to bring the vegetables to the boiling point, or close to it, is critical for the reason that the enzymes in the vegetables are activated by heat up to a point and destroy the vitamin. (Vitamin C may also be destroyed by oxidation or by the presence of alkaline substances, e.g. bicarbonate of soda.)

From the above, would you say that the cooking water for vegetables should be brought to the boil before adding the vegetables?

Yes, indeed. This reduces the time required to inactivate the enzymes, thereby saving the vitamin C.

●

26 Starchy foods which contain much water are usually cooked at relatively high temperatures. For example, pizza pie, a dough shell covered with tomato paste, cheese and other foods, requires 288C (550F) or higher temperatures in the oven to brown it rapidly. The tomato paste is dried by the high heat and the dough shell is quickly browned. Crispness of the bottom crust is achieved by this high temperature.

Potatoes, another high starch and water food, are baked at an oven temperature of 204–232C (400–450F). However, the same vegetable will cook when boiled at 100C (212F).

How can these wide differences in temperature be explained?

The temperature in the food itself is the one that counts. Starch gels at about 93C (200F). High oven heat does not mean high food temperature when the food contains water that can evaporate, cooling the food.

9

ACIDITY AS RELATED TO COOKING

27 The degree of acidity of a food material—its pH value—affects the reactions which take place in cooking. The acidity or alkalinity of a substance is compared with that of pure water which is given a value of a pH of 7 or neutrality.

pH

0	10 000 000	*High acid*, pH 2·0—3·7:
1	1 000 000	Limes, lemons, vinegar, plums,
2	100 000	gooseberries, pickles, rhubarb,
3	10 000	grapefruit juice, sauerkraut,
4	1 000	most fruits, gingerale
5	100	*Acid*, pH of 3·7—4·5: Or-
6	10	anges, cherries, pears, apple-
7	0	juice, tomato juice, butter-
8	10	milk
9	100	*Medium*, pH 4·5—5·3:
10	1 000	Bananas, figs, asparagus,
11	10 000	pumpkin, spinach, beets,
12	100 000	carrots, coffee
13	1 000 000	*Low acid*, pH 5·3—7·0:
14	10 000 000	Butter, milk, sweet peas,

most vegetables, shrimp, salmon, meat

Alkaline, Over pH 7: Ripe olives, cream crackers, egg white, hard water, or water softened by sodium exchange

The pH numbers indicate the hydrogen ion concentration and are stated in logarithms. The lower the number below 7 the more acid, the higher the number above 7, the more alkaline or base is the substance. For example, a pH of 4 is 1000 times more acid than water with a pH of 7.

Judging from the chart are many foods alkaline in nature?

No, very few foods are alkaline, and they vary widely as to their degree of acidity.

●

28 Could you have guessed that cream crackers would be alkaline in nature?

Yes, the soda in them is definitely alkaline.

29   The degree of acidity of foods must be controlled in some cooking processes to achieve a certain effect. For example, a pH between 3·0 and 3·4 is necessary for the production of an acceptable sugar jelly. At a higher pH the gel is soft; at a lower pH it is tough.

Vegetables containing orange or yellow pigments— carrots, peaches, cantaloupes, corn and sweet potatoes— appear lighter in colour when in an acid media and duller in an alkaline media.

Would it be a good idea to cook carrots in gingerale? (look at the chart to learn the pH of gingerale.)

The ginger ale is highly acid because it contains citric acid and will make carrots appear a bright yellow.

●

30   Vegetables containing the water soluble red colours called anthocyanins—beetroots, red cabbage, rhubarb, blueberries, strawberries, raspberries, plums, and radishes—are bright red in an acid, blue if in an alkaline medium.

To achieve maximum redness we can add vinegar to the cooking water of beetroot or red cabbage. Why would you not need to add acid to rhubarb or strawberries to retain their red colour?

Because they are acid already.

●

31   Vegetables containing oil soluble red pigments— tomatoes, watermelon and red peppers—are little affected by pH. If anything, they brighten in acid, become duller in a basic medium.

Will we lose the red colour in tomatoes if we cook them in something containing an acid such as vinegar, lemon juice or cream of tartar?

No

●

32   Green vegetables are something else again. Chlorophyll, the green colouring matter, turns brighter in an alkaline medium and dull olive in an acid.

From this information could one add a little lemon juice to green peas?

No, the chlorophyll is degraded by the acids.

33 Green salads become limp if salad dressing is poured on them very long before serving. Salad dressings are acid in reaction. Will green salads left very long with salad dressing lose colour?

Yes, the acid destroys the chlorophyll in any green vegetable. However, since there is no heat the reaction takes longer.

34 Why do salad greens to which dressings are added go limp?

The acid and seasonings in the dressing draw the moisture from the greens. The oil may also be absorbed making the green limp.

35 Fresh milk has a pH of 6·6. As it ages, the milk sugar, lactose, begins changing to lactic acid and at a pH of 6·4 the change in pH along with other changes can be detected in taste. We say the milk is sour at a pH of between 4·5 and 5·0 when the coagulation of the protein takes place and the milk has curdled. Buttermilk has a pH of between 4·5 and 5·0.

Milk is most likely to curdle at a pH of about 4·6. Tomato juice has a pH of 4·29. What danger is there in adding tomato juice to milk?

The tomato juice may reduce the pH of the milk to the point where it will curdle.

36 In light of the above information, would adding bi-carbonate of soda (a base) to tomatoes before making tomato soup prevent curdling?

Yes, but this is not recommended because soda adversely affects flavour and destroys the ascorbic acid (vitamin C).

37   We are also concerned with pH in a number of other cooking reactions. Adding an acid such as cream of tartar to egg white makes the protein in the egg more tender and able to stretch, gives the white more stability and lightens the egg pigments. Yeasts can stand an acid limit to about a pH of 2·5, an alkaline limit of 8. Bread doughs have their maximum diastatic activity (starches best converted into sugars) at a pH of about 5. The degree of acidity in cooked fondant (a sugar mixture) controls the firmness of the product by determining the amount of the sucrose which is inverted (changed to simple sugars). A high degree of acidity detracts from the taste of sweetness in sugars.

True or False: We can see that while we do not have to be a chemist to understand cooking, a knowledge of the acidity of a food material may help to control its cooking.

True

●

37a   Table wines have a pH of between 3·0 to 3·5, beers 4·0—5·0. Would you have to be careful in adding wine to dishes containing milk?

Yes. The pH of the milk could be lowered to the point where it will curdle.

●

38   The pH or hydrogen ion concentration is also important in starch cooking. As starches are heated their granules absorb water and become firm (gelatinize). Starch mixtures with both high and low pH values gelatinize more rapidly than those with intermediate pH values (4—7). These same high or low pH value mixtures also break down starch more rapidly by destroying the starch cell.

Would you think that a lemon pie filling is likely to gel more quickly and break down more quickly than a banana cream pie filling?

Yes, the lemon pie filling has a low pH (high acid); the banana cream pie filling is in the intermediate pH range.

●

39   The pH factor in cooking occurs in the oddest places. The colour of chocolate cake is related to the pH of the cake. In a series of experiments chocolate cakes were yellow at pH of 5·0, brown at an intermediate pH, and reddish at a pH of 7·5.

The colour of chocolate cakes depends in part on the amount and type of chocolate or cocoa used, but also in part on the pH, cakes tending to be on the acid side are what colour?

Yellowish

●

40   To review: A pH of 2 indicates high/low acidity?

high

●

41   A pH of over 7 is common/uncommon in food materials?

uncommon

●

42   Colour in green vegetables brightens/dulls when placed in an acid medium?

dulls

●

43   Curdling in milk takes place when the acidity is raised/lowered?

raised (a lower pH)

●

44   With some foods pH is an indication of its freshness. The pH of egg whites rises to $9 \cdot 0$ after they have been stored a few days.

The pH of living muscle is about neutral but becomes acid after death owing to formation of lactic acid from glycogen present. As the meat decomposes, the pH level rises markedly. Bacteria associated with putrefaction grow best in an alkaline medium.

True or False: In practical cookery pH is not measured but it could be used as measure of age in egg whites and meat.

True

●

45   A glance at the pH chart shows that milk and shrimp are about neutral in pH, and we have learned that meat too is about neutral. All of these foods are subject to food poisoning if not refrigerated or kept

heated. None of the acid foods or medium acid foods are favourable media for food poisoning bacteria.

True or False: Acid foods are not as subject to the development of food poisoning organisms as are those foods which are only slightly acid.

True

●

SELECTION OF A COOKING METHOD

46 Cooking times, temperatures and equipment are selected to maximize flavour, develop appetizing appearance, and retain as much as possible of the colour, nutrients, vitamins, and water in the food material.

Do you suppose that custom also plays a large part in the selection of the cooking method?

Yes, both regional and national customs can have distinctive effects, which can be reflected in the selection of the cooking method.

●

47 The selection of a cooking method often represents a compromise. Cooking meat in water breaks down the connective tissue but the water also leaches out some of the vitamins and minerals and produces a different texture than if the food were cooked by dry heat.

In cooking green vegetables a pinch of bicarbonate of soda brightens the colour but may destroy the vitamin C. Cooking mutton to a medium degree gives greater yield of edible meat, but the fat often has a pasty texture. Low temperature cooking of meat is usually desirable but sometimes takes more time than the cook has available.

True or False: In selecting a cooking method, custom, nutrition, time available, the amount of water in the food, tenderness of the food and other factors bear on the decision.

True

●

48 In cooking vegetables, cutting them into pieces reduces cooking time which is desirable and saves the colour, but at the same time increases the loss of soluble

nutrients. (refer to vegetable section pages 266–284.) When cooking green vegetables, keeping the lid on the cooking utensil reduces cooking time, which is desirable, but retains the volatile acids retarding their escape in steam. With the cover on, these acids condense and drip back on to the vegetables, turning them olive green.

In vegetable cooking, one action may be favourable in one respect, ... in another.

unfavourable

●

49   With some foods the amount of fat present largely determines the cooking method. It may be desirable or necessary to add fat to the food during cooking. One purpose of frying is to add fat to a food. Young chickens, or broilers, for example, are a low fat food, containing only about 5% of their weight in fat. Deep frying them adds another 5–10 per cent fat. The fat adds flavour and 'lubricates' them for easier chewing and swallowing. Vegetables and other foods are often fried for the same reason.

Ordinarily what kind of foods are deep fried—foods high or low in fat?

Low fat foods

●

50   Sometimes the choice of cooking is dictated by the food material. Usually tough flesh foods are cooked in steam or liquid, so called moist heat, the moisture and heat together serving to soften the connective tissue. However, recent research suggests that all cuts of beef can be cooked by low heat satisfactorily. More tender flesh foods are usually cooked by dry heat or fried. Choice of cooking methods for fish is largely determined by the fat content. Poultry is usually cooked according to age and size. Green vegetables are cooked so as to retain the green colour (chlorophyll) and the vitamin C.

True or False: In some cases there is a best way to cook a food material; in other cases the cook has a choice of methods.

True

51   The cooking method also determines the amount of vitamin loss. In meat cookery, for example, frying results in less thiamine, riboflavin, and niacin loss. Grilling is next most favourable, followed closely by roasting. In stewing, the meat loses the most B vitamins, but most of them are retained in the stock.

Why would more vitamins be lost by stewing?

Because the meat is cut into relatively small pieces with large surface areas exposed to liquid with consequent leaching of the vitamins into the liquid.

●

52   Since frying results in the least loss of the B vitamins, why not cook all meat by frying?

Frying being a fast method of cooking, the connective tissue is not exposed to the heat long enough to be broken down and made tender and is therefore not used with less tender meat. Also we want a range of flavours and textures which can be had only by using a variety of cooking methods.

●

THE NATURE OF CONDUCTION, CONVECTION AND RADIATION HEATING

53   Heat is transferred to food from a heat source by three principal methods: conduction, convection and radiation. Induction and dielectric heating are also possible but are used rarely or only experimentally in cookery.

To better understand what takes place when conduction, convection and radiation heating are used in cookery, consider how they apply to a person in a room sitting in front of a fireplace. The bricks are hot. Heat has been transmitted to the bricks by means of conduction, one brick heating the next; by convection, hot air circulating past the bricks; and by radiation, heat transmitted directly by wave energy. Should the person stand a few feet away from the fireplace, he still feels warm even though the air within the room may be cool.

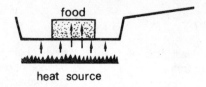

Cooking by conduction.

The reason for this is that he receives heat directly from the fire by means of radiation, electromagnetic energy transmitted by short waves directly to the body. The electromagnetic waves strike the flesh and are transformed into heat by agitating the molecules on the surface of the flesh and for a short distance under the flesh, depending upon the wavelength of the energy.

The room itself is heated mostly by means of convection, air which has been heated by the combustion of oxygen with the fire. The heated air rises, cooler air falls and air circulation takes place throughout the room.

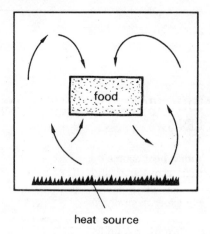

Convection currents carry the heated air to the surface of the food.

18

Radiation heating can be seen in action if you have ever gone skiing on a sunny day. Even though the thermometer reads zero you may be quite comfortable being heated by the sun's radiated energy, as long as you stand in the sun and the wind is not blowing. The infra-red waves from the sun strike you and turn to heat. (About 60% of the sun's rays are infra-red, the balance is made up of visible light and ultra-violet waves.)

A room which is heated by a fireplace has heat reflected from the bricks by means of . . . .

radiation

●

54   Heat is circulated within the room by means of . . . . currents.

convection

●

55   Once the radiated or convected heat reaches a person within a room, heat is carried from the surface of his body inward by means of . . . .

conduction

●

56   To see how conduction heating takes place, apply a lighted match to one end of a small metal rod, holding the other end. Soon the fingers holding the end of the rod will get hot, because heat has been conducted along the length of the rod, molecules having agitated those adjacent to them in passing the 'heat' along. Some metals are better conductors of heat than others. Copper is one of the more prominent metals used in cooking equipment because of its high conductance, which is nearly twice as great as aluminum. (Copper cooking utensils are usually lined with tin or stainless steel because copper reacts unfavourably with some foods.) Aluminum conducts heat about twice as fast as stainless steel. Teflon lined pans probably slow heat flow, but are widely used because they prevent foods from sticking to the pan and are easily cleaned.

Heat is passed from the stove top up through and around the cooking utensils, on into the food materials. Heat passes by conduction from the surface of the food into the food by conduction.

How is heat transferred within the food?

By conduction unless radiated directly into the food.

57   All food which is cooked involves some heat transference by means of conduction, especially within the
food itself. Consider the process of frying. Food is placed
in fat or oil. The oil or fat is heated and circulated by
means of convection currents. The food comes in contact
with the oil and the heat is transferred into the food
by means of . . . .   conduction

•

58   In simmering, water moves by convection currents,
then gives up some of its energy to the food contained
within it, again by means of . . . .   conduction

•

59   In steaming, the steam surrounds the food and as
it changes from steam to water, gives up its heat to the
food by means of . . . .   conduction

•

60   Convection heating refers to heating which is   movement or
brought about by . . . . of hot liquids or gases.   circulation

•

61   In the usual oven, air is heated by the combustion
of gas or by electrical heating elements. The heat cir-
culates throughout the oven by means of convection: hot
air currents rise by means of convection, cool air drops,
and there is a circulation within the oven. The hot air
surrounds the food that is being baked or roasted and
finally the heat is transferred from the hot air to the food
by means of . . . .   conduction

•

62   If food rests on the bottom of an oven in a pan, heat
passes through the bottom of the oven into the pan, then
into the food again by means of . . . .   conduction

63   To hasten transference in ovens, fans or blowers have been introduced. The fans agitate the air rapidly, passing the hot air over the food being cooked. Although *forced convection* ovens have been used for some 30 years in heavy baking, their use in restaurants did not appear until the late 1950's when such an oven was introduced. These forced convection ovens reduce cooking time by about 0—50 per cent, depending upon the food being baked or roasted and its position in the oven. Meat shrinkage is also reduced; however, in at least one of these ovens large temperature variations exist within the oven, and foods bake at different rates depending upon which rack they are placed on.

The fast movement of air in a forced convection oven causes more rapid . . . . of the air and more rapid conduction of the heat from the air to the food.   convection

●

THE NATURE OF HEAT AS RELATED TO COOKING

64   Stated in physical terms, heat is determined by the speed of molecular action within a substance. Heat is a relative term. Rapid action means high heat. Cold is the absence of heat.

A faster/slower molecular action means less heat?   slower

●

65   In refrigerated or frozen food the molecular action is relatively . . . ., but far from being completely stopped. If a substance should reach −273·1C (−459·6F), it would be at absolute zero, and no molecular action would occur. Otherwise, molecules are in constant motion.   slow

●

66   The unit in which energy and work are both measured is the joule, symbol J. Approximately 4185 joules of heat energy are required to raise the temperature of 1 kilogramme of water through one degree Celsius.

As the joule is a very small unit, multiples of this such as the kilojoule (kJ) and the megajoule (mJ) are often used.

How many kilojoules of heat energy are required to raise the temperature of 1 kilogramme of water through one degree Celsius?

4·18 kJ

●

67　A typical burner on a commercial gas range is rated at 15·8 mJ. This means that the energy it produces is the equivalent of the burning of . . . . bars of an electric fire.

4

●

68　Cooking is done using either the Celsius or the Fahrenheit scales, and therefore it is sometimes necessary to convert one scale to the other.

On the Fahrenheit thermometer freezing is at 32, boiling at 212. To convert Celsius to Fahrenheit multiply the Celsius reading by 1·8 or 9/5 and add 32. To convert Fahrenheit to Celsius subtract . . . . and multiply by 5/9.

32

●

69　194 Fahrenheit is equal to . . . . degrees Celsius.

30 degrees Celsius is equal to . . . . Fahrenheit.

$(194 - 32) \times 5/9 = 90$

$(30 \times 1·8) + 32 = 86$

●

70　Two pieces of cooking equipment may create the same quantity of heat energy but the heat available or transferred to the food is different. Radiated heat is transferred more efficiently than convected heat and much heat that is generated in cooking equipment may escape or be exhausted out of the equipment without being transferred to the food.

From this information, we can say that a kilojoule of heat energy developed in one piece of cooking equipment is/may not be the same in effectiveness of cooking as a kilojoule of heat energy developed in another piece of cooking equipment.

may not be

●

71   Speaking generally as regards cooking effect, one kilojoule of heat generated by electricity is equivalent to about 1·6 kilojoules of heat generated by means of gas combustion. There is a logical reason for this difference.
    What is it?

Much of the heat is carried out of the exhaust which goes along with the noxious waste products of combustion.

●

72   *Electric* power equipment is rated in kilowatts (1000 watts). A deep fat fryer rated at ... kilowatts converts 5000J of electrical energy into heat energy every second.

5 kW

●

73   When two objects, or different parts of the same object, are at different temperatures, energy is transferred from the region of higher temperature to that of lower temperature. This transfer of temperature is called heat flow and the energy transferred is heat energy. Such a flow of heat will continue until the two objects concerned attain the same temperature. The greater the . . . . between two objects, the greater will be the flow of heat energy from the hotter to the colder.

temperature difference

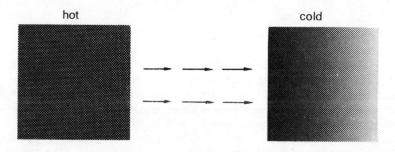

Heat energy flows from a region of higher temperature to that of a lower temperature.

74　Temperature differentials are created within food, higher temperatures being near the source of heat which is usually the surface. Will the temperatures tend to equalize even though the food is no longer exposed to the external heat?

Yes, equalization continues and so too does cooking even though food is removed from the heat source. That is why a large roast removed from the oven at an interior temperature of 60C (140F) will rise to 68C (155F) to 74C (165F) in the interior as it stands.

●

75　Even though taken from an oven or other cooking equipment, the internal temperature of food material is often high enough for cooking to continue. This continued cooking or *carry-over* cooking must always be considered in the cooking process.

Is it reasonable to remove food from a heat source even though it is not completely done?

Yes, we shall see later that this is usually necessary and is most important in radiation cooking and in roasting and grilling meats.

●

76　In meat cookery the methods of cookery are divided into those using moist heat and those using dry heat. Moist heat methods are those in which the meat is surrounded by hot liquid or steam while in dry heat methods the meat is exposed directly to hot air or radiated heat.

Strictly speaking, can heat be 'moist'?

No, heat is energy. Water or steam contain heat but the heat is not wet. In moist cooking, moisture is used to carry the heat to the food.

77   Water, steam, and oil conduct heat more readily than does air. Would you expect food to be cooked more quickly if placed at the same temperature in water or steam than in hot air as in an oven?

Yes, in one study, meat that required 23 hours to cook at 90C (194F) in an oven was cooked in three hours in water at the same temperature.

●

78   Would you think that the meat cooked in the water would be more tender than that cooked in the oven?

You might think so, but in meat cooking, slow cooking makes for tenderness.

●

79   At what temperature do you think the foods are when cooked in boiling water?

Maximum temperature that can be reached is 100C (212F) unless pressure is added, which increases the temperature.

●

80   If a roast is an oven which is 100C (212F), would you guess that eventually the internal temperature of the roast would reach 100C (212F)?

Yes, if all the water were evaporated. In practice, 100C (212F) cannot be reached because of the cooling effect of moisture evaporating from the surface.

B

81   The time required to cook food is a function of
temperature, specific heat and of the thermal conductivity of the food and of the thickness of the food.
The amount of water in bone and meat, fish and fowl
affects cooking time. Water conducts heat at one rate,
bone, fat, and muscle at different rates. The specific
heat capacity—the number of joules of heat energy
required to raise the temperature of one kilogramme
of a substance by one degree Celsius—varies from
substance to substance. Ice in frozen food has a
different thermal conductivity from the unfrozen
food around the ice.

Most foods have a high water content—much higher
than would be guessed. By weight, most meats contain
about 60% water, eggs about 74%, fish 65—80%, fruit
and vegetables 85—95%. A frying-chicken is about
75% water. Correct cooking time depends upon what
other important factors than temperature?

The thermo-physical
properties of food
especially the
amount of water
and its thickness

●

82   Most food material including meat is a relatively
poor conductor of heat. Would you expect faster cooking
if metal skewers or open ended tubes were inserted
into the beef?

Yes, metal conducts
heat faster than
bone, muscle, or fat.
Cooking time can be
cut by 30%—but
the appearance of
the meat is less
attractive and the
meat may be less
tender than if a
longer cooking time
is used.

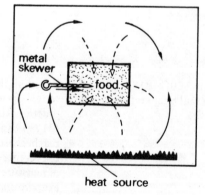

heat source

The metal skewer is a better conductor than the food.

83 Why do some meats, such as chicken, tend to cook last around the bone?

The bone is usually in the centre where cooking would occur last regardless of whether bone were there or not and chicken bone is a poor conductor of heat.

●

84 Two pieces of meat, each weigh the same, but one is flat and thin, the other round and thick. Which cooks the faster?

The thin piece

●

84a Melted fat transfers heat faster than bone or muscle. A layer of unmelted fat, however, acts to retard heat transfer.

Once muscle is dehydrated in cooking, heat transfer is slowed.

Will it take longer to raise the temperature of turkey muscle from 82C (180F) to 85C (185F) or from 85C (185F) to 88C (190F)?

It takes much longer to raise it to the higher temperature because it has been dehydrated and heat transfer is slower.

●

85 Ice in food poses an additional problem for whenever matter changes state, (i.e. solid to liquid, liquid to gas, liquid to solid etc.) a considerable quantity of heat energy is exchanged with the surroundings. *344 kilojoules of heat energy are required to convert one kilogramme of ice into water* even though the temperature remains unaltered. In cooking food from the frozen state considerable heat is needed merely to change the ice to water.

Conversely when freezing foods 344 kilojoules of heat energy must be drawn off a kilogramme of water merely to change it to ice. The heat involved in these changes is known as the *specific latent heat of fusion* of ice. Is it possible to add or subtract heat while not changing the temperature?

Yes, changing ice to water is such a case. Later we see that changing water to steam presents a similar instance.

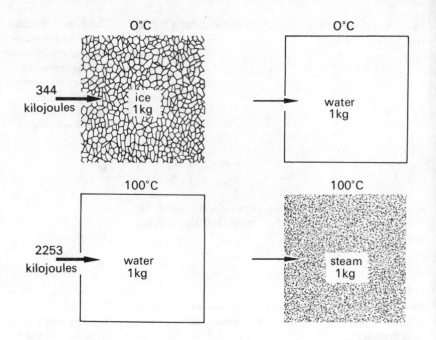

The specific latent heat of fusion is that amount of heat energy required to change the state of a unit mass of a substance without a change in temperature e.g. ice to water, water to steam.

PRESSURE AS RELATED TO COOKING AND EVAPORATIVE COOLING

Pressure is the force exerted on a substance. It is measured in newtons per metre squared (N/m^2) i.e. a newton is the unit of force exerted on a substance of 1 square metre.

86 Foods cooked under pressure cook faster than foods cooked at atmospheric pressure. Why? As pressure increases so too does temperature. Steam under $34 \cdot 5$ kN/m^2 (5lbf/in^2) of pressure has a temperature not of 100C (212F) but $109 \cdot 5$C (228F) and contains six times mòre heat than boiling water.

STEAM PRESSURE AND TEMPERATURE

Pressure		Temperature
(kN/m^2)	(lbf/in^2)	C
34·5	5	109
68·9	10	115
103.4	15	121
137·9	20	126

One reason cooking is faster under pressure is that steam is used and steam contains a lot more/a little more heat than boiling water.

a lot more

●

87   The creation of steam within or outside food may have the adverse effect of causing *evaporative cooling*. As steam forms it absorbs 2 253 kJ of heat for every kilogramme of steam formed. This is called the specific latent heat of vaporization of water.

Does steam formation act to slow cooking?

Yes, the formation of steam from water in the food requires heat which might otherwise be used to cook the food.

●

88   As pressure on the surface of water increases the boiling point of water increases:

Water boils at	if Pressure is
C	
100	atmospheric
116	68·9 kN/m^2 (10 lbf/in^2)
126	137·9 kN/m^2 (20 lbf/in^2)
135	206·9 kN/m^2 (30 lbf/in^2)

At 68·9 kN/m^2 pressure water does not boil until it reaches 116C (240F). At 137·9 kN/m^2 of pressure water boils at 126C (259F).

What would happen to the boiling point of water as pressure decreases?

The boiling point drops.

89   What happens when food is cooked by steam under pressure?

The extra heat required to raise the temperature to produce steam under pressure, plus the heat of vaporization plus the heat required to heat the water to boiling is all given off as the steam condenses on the cold food in the steamer.

●

90   Would you expect cooking to take longer at high altitudes where water boils at a temperature lower than 100C (212F)?

Yes, at Denver, Colorado with an altitude of about 1830 metres, water boils at 94C (201F). This means a lower temperature and longer cooking time for boiling food.

ALTITUDE AND BOILING POINT OF WATER

Altitude (metres)	Degrees	
	C	F
500	98·972	210·2
1500	96·82	206·3
2000	95·65	204·2
3000	93·25	199·8

●

STEAM COOKERY

91   Let's now look more closely at the way in which steam cooks. Why is steam so hot, as anyone can testify who has received a burn from steam. How does the heat get into steam?

At sea level water boils at 100C (212F). To change water at this temperature to steam it is necessary to add 2253 kJ to each kilogramme of water. This amount of heat or energy is known as the specific latent heat of steam; it is latent within the steam, ready to be released.

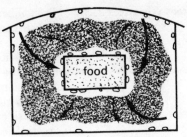

Steam surrounds the food and as it condenses gives off latent heat.

When the steam condenses on food or in a cooking vessel, changing back into water, the same amount of heat energy——2253 kJ/kg is given off and may be transferred to the food present.

The principle of physics involved is that a quantity of energy is given out or taken in whenever a substance changes its state although there is no temperature change involved.

One kilogramme steam contains 2253 kJ/kg of what kind of heat energy?

Specific latent

●

92   This latent heat helps to account for the relatively fast cooking action of steam. Steam which is at about 34·5 kN/m² (5 lbf/in²) pressure contains six times more heat than boiling water. As steam pressure increases so too does the heat contained in it. Pressure on any gas——and steam is a gas——increases the temperature of the gas. High pressures contain more/less heat.

more

●

93   Cooking by steam can be accomplished by equipment in which live steam surrounds the food material. It can be free venting, the steam escaping into the atmosphere.

In such a case the steam is at what pressure?

Atmospheric pressure

94   Low pressure steamers cook root vegetables such as whole potatoes, beetroots, turnips and parsnips more quickly than would boiling water. Why?

The temperature is higher than boiling water; the steam transfers its latent heat to the food. Yet the temperature is not so high that the outside of the vegetables are overcooked before the inside is done.

●

95   Pressure steam cooking equipment is common today.

At $103 \cdot 4$ kN/m^2 (15 lbf/in^2) pressure the temperature of the steam is 121C (250F) and the cooking will proceed more/less quickly.

more

●

96   When we cook in a casserole or other covered vessel, e.g. braised steak, peas, French style, are we likely to be steaming the food?

Yes, liquid may be added and the water in the food changes into steam. The casserole in effect becomes a steamer.

●

97   Another way in which steam is used for cooking is by directing it into a shell enclosed kettle. Steam jacketed kettles ranging in capacity from 4 to 900 litres have an outside shell in which steam can be introduced—the steam changes to water giving up its . . . . heat and the heat is then conducted through the metal into the food inside the kettle.

Specific latent

32

98   Food within a steam jacketed kettle is heated by conduction of heat from the shell where the steam is to inside the food. In cooking many foods—particularly vegetables—once the food has reached the desired state of doneness, the cooking process must be stopped to avoid overcooking and consequent loss of vitamins, structure and flavour.

It is possible with some steam jacketed kettles to rapidly cool food by replacing the steam in the jacket with cold water. Heat then flows from the food to the . . . .

cold water.

●

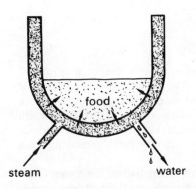

Steam in the jacket changes to water, giving up its latent heat energy to the food.

99   A disadvantage of using a large steam jacketed kettle comes in the fact that food materials in the centre of the kettle are likely to be undercooked while those adjacent to the sides of the kettle are overcooked. The only solution to this is to . . . .

stir and mix the foods frequently.

●

100   Braising of meat—browning and partially steaming it—can be done well in steam jacketed kettles since the steam pressure in the kettles range from about 34·5 to 103·4 kN/m² (5—15 lbf/in²) above the outside atmospheric pressure and the resultant temperatures range from about 105C (220F) to 120C (250F). (Some kettles go much higher).

To steam the food in a steam jacketed kettle is it necessary to cover the kettle?

Yes, the steam produced in the equipment is enclosed in the jacket and does not reach the food directly.

101   Boiling can take place in a steam jacketed kettle but few foods—except some starchy foods and vegetables—should be cooked by boiling because the temperature is too high and toughens proteins being cooked. Also the rolling of the water breaks up the form of the food being cooked.

Rather most food is simmered—accomplished at about 85—88C (185—190F). Bubbles form but do not break as in boiling, or as the French say, the surface 'smiles'.

Simmering usually has what two advantages over boiling?

It allows the food to retain shape and does not toughen the proteins to the same degree.

●

102   In steam pressure cookers the cooking utensil is sealed and some of the liquid within the food after being heated changes to steam. Steam pressure in some cookers builds up to $103 \cdot 4$ kN/m^2 (15 lbf/in^2) which results in a temperature of 120C (250F) which breaks down the cellular structure of vegetables making them more tender.

In some high pressure steam cookers live steam under pressure is introduced directly into the food from outside the cooking vessel.

Cooking is also speeded by increasing the pressure and introducing the steam to the food in jet streams. The steam is broken by nozzles of small size and develops a speed of about 300 kilometres per hour. The jet streams are said to penetrate most vegetables and reduce the cooking time. So far the jet streams have not been a particular advantage in cooking leafy vegetables such as spinach. The purpose of the so-called jet stream is to . . . . the vegetables and carry the steam into them.

penetrate

●

103   Food which has been cooked by steam applied directly to it results in a comparatively moist/dry surface.

moist

104　Would you expect food cooked in steam or water to show less shrinkage and other weight loss?

Less evaporation takes place provided the cooking time is not extended or the temperature too high.

●

105　Moist heat, as the heat caused in hot water or in steam is called, is usually used rather than dry heat for cooking fleshy foods which are high in connective tissue since the moisture helps to soften such tissue.

Simmering is cooking in water at 85—88C (185—190F) for fairly long periods. Poaching is the same process but the term is usually applied when shorter cooking periods are used.

Simmering and poaching are examples of moist heat cooking in which the heat in the water passes to the food contained in it by *what means* of heat transference?

Conduction

●

106　What is the difference between simmering and poaching?

Very little, the term poaching being used for short simmering times.

●

107　Since moist heat offers advantages why not use such heat for all cooking?

A moist surface results, and the higher heat may toughen the proteins. The taste and texture of foods cooked by moist heat is different than when dry heat is used.

COOKING BY INFRA-RED RADIATION

108   Grills using dry heat are excellent for cooking meat, fish, and other items which are fairly tender to begin with. The food is placed a few inches above or below the heat source. Some of the heat which is given off by the heat source is carried to the food by means of convection, the rest by means of radiation. The radiation is in the form of infra-red rays. Infra-red rays are a form of radiation which are just a little longer than those waves which are seen as red, shorter than radio waves and shorter than microwaves.

heat source

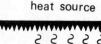

Infra-red waves penetrate food slightly.

Infra-red wave lengths are small and range in length from about 0·07 to 1000 millionths of a metre.

Infra-red waves are energy waves just a little longer/ shorter than light waves.

longer

●

109   Even within the range of wavelengths designated as infra-red, much of the radiated energy is not effective in cooking because it will not pass through the water vapours created around high water content foods when they are heated.

Wavelengths of from 1·4 to 5 millionths of a metre are the most effective for cooking food, because they pass through the vapours and act on the food and the moisture contained in the food. Shorter wavelengths are not absorbed well by the water in the food.

Cooking equipment which relies on infra-red waves for energy transfer should produce infra-red waves of what length?

1·4 to 5 millionths of a metre

●

110   As temperature increases in a heat source, the energy radiated shifts to shorter wavelengths. As the temperature is doubled, the radiated energy maximum shifts to half the wavelength (known as Wien's Law).

A temperature of 649C (1200F), for example, produces a maximum-energy wavelength of 3 millionths of a metre effective in infra-red cookery.

However, the surface of foods cannot stand temperatures much above 260C (500F) without burning (unless they are very moist). With high temperatures food must be placed some distance from the heat source. High temperatures are desirable to produce infra-red waves of maximum cooking effectiveness but are so hot that if food is placed near this heat source it will . . . .

burn

●

111   Infra-red heating is fast because the energy is transmitted from the heat source to the food almost instantaneously, not having to be carried by means of hot air to the food as in the case of convection heating. The infra-red rays penetrate the blanket of vapour surrounding the food and enter the food a few millimetres, which also speeds up the cooking process. Some of the new grills produce a great amount of infra-red energy and, hence, are much faster than the old style grill which produced less infra-red energy.

It would be expected that the closer the food is placed to the source of radiation, the . . . . it would cook.

faster

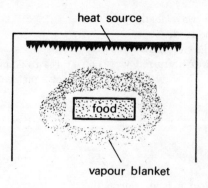

heat source

food

vapour blanket

Radiant heat energy is transmitted directly to the food passing through the vapour blanket.

112   The amount of energy which reaches food from an infra-red source varies geometrically to the distance the food is away from the source.

A steak placed 5 cm away from a heat source will cook . . . . times as fast as the same steak 10 cm from the source.

four

113   Infra-red rays travel in straight lines in all directions from the emission source. It would be expected that if something like aluminum foil were placed on the food being cooked by infra-red, there would be much/ little advantage in using infra-red.

Little, except that higher temperatures may be involved.

114   Infra-red lamps are also used to keep food hot and to give them a rich red colour on buffet tables and cafeteria lines. Infra-red lamps transmit heat instantaneously to food exposed to them and make the food appear more . . . . in colour.

red or brown

115   The amount of heat 'absorbed' by food from an infra-red source depends upon the reflectivity of the surface of the food; the darker the colour of the surface of the food, the . . . . the rate of absorption.

faster, greater

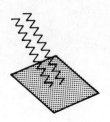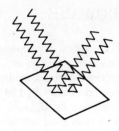

Dark surfaces absorb wave energy; white or shiny surfaces reflect it.

116 Most light and heat sources give off some energy in the infra-red wave band. Infra-red lamps and infra-red grills are designed so that most of the energy emitted is infra-red. Some gas-fired grills and ovens make use of a German invention, the Schwank burner for producing infra-red energy. One such grill cooks a 340 gramme steak in about six minutes, less than half the time required for grilling using a conventional grill. Infra-red energy is produced by electric cooking equipment and by . . . . cooking equipment as well.

gas

●

117 A recent invention, the 'Ultra-ray' grill, is gas-fired and produces almost 100% infra-red radiation. It consists of three layers of Incaloy metal screens sandwiched together. Air and gas readily pass through the screens, produce a blanket of flame about 1 cm in thickness. Temperatures vary from 621C (1150F) to about 815C (1500F). The device has an additional advantage of reaching maximum capacity within six seconds.

With such a grill, time required for grilling is a function of the distance from the energy source and its . . . .

temperature

COOKING BY MICROWAVE

118   During World War II, the Allies developed radar which utilizes electromagnetic waves to detect objects at a distance, which cannot be seen visually, and to see objects at night and those behind clouds. In 1947 this same wave energy known as microwaves, because of the short wave length, was used to cook food in a specially designed oven.

The microwaves region is generally considered to correspond to frequencies between 300 and 30 000 mHz, that is wavelengths between about 1 metre and 1 centimetre. In other words the higher the frequency, the shorter the wavelength.

Compared to the wavelengths which comprise light and infra-red rays, microwaves are long. Light waves and infra-red rays are measured in wavelengths of a thousandth of a centimeter. However, compared to the wavelengths found in radio waves, which are sometimes miles in length, microwaves are indeed short.

The Federal Communications Commission allocated seven frequencies for industrial, scientific, and medical uses (so called ISM frequencies). Microwave ovens now available use 915 mHz and 2450 mHz (wavelengths equal to 33 cm and 12·2 cm). Penetration into food materials is somewhat greater at the lower frequency.

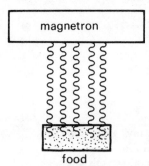

Microwaves penetrate food up to 7.5 cm.

Microwaves are electromagnetic waves, longer than light waves and infra-red waves and shorter than radio waves, which have the unusual power to penetrate food materials and to heat them. Within the microwave band of wavelengths, the longer wavelengths penetrate less/ more than the shorter wavelengths.

more

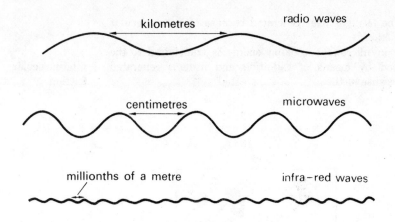

kilometres · radio waves

centimetres · microwaves

millionths of a metre · infra-red waves

118a   Which has the shorter wavelength microwave or infra-red?

Infra-red

•

119   Microwave energy is generated at specific frequencies and wavelengths. It can be sent through free space and directed within wave guides. It can be focused, diffused or shaped into patterns and can be generated almost instantaneously.

It can be controlled and directed better than the usual thermal energy which includes multiple wavelengths and has no specific wave patterns.

The usual kitchen which is not air conditioned is a hot, humid place in which to work because of the wild heat and moisture which escapes into the room from the cooking equipment.

Would you expect less heat and humidity where microwave ovens have been substituted for some of the conventional cooking devices?

Yes, less heat and humidity since the microwave energy is directed into and absorbed by the food materials. Present kitchens, however, must use some conventional cooking equipment.

•

120   Microwave energy strikes food placed in the chamber in the microwave oven. Since the food is a non-conductor of this energy the molecules in the food are driven back and forth (oscillate) at the frequency of the microwaves themselves, e.g. a frequency of 915 mHz means a vibration rate of 915 million times per second.

The result is heat generated because of intermolecular friction.

In microwave cooking energy is transferred to the food by means of radiation and heat is generated because of the .... created.

intermolecular friction

●

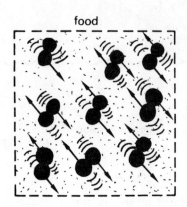

food

Microwave energy causes the molecules to oscillate, and sets up friction between them.

121 The distance microwaves penetrate into food materials depends upon the nature of the food and the wavelength used. Food material is dielectric; that is, it is a poor conductor of electricity and of microwaves. Food materials which are poor conductors absorb more of the microwave energy near their surfaces. Those food materials which are partial conductors allow the energy to penetrate more deeply. Penetration is infinite in perfectly transparent substances, and microwaves easily pass through some glass and ceramic materials with little heating effect.

Reflective materials, such as metal in pots, pans and aluminum foil, allow almost no penetration of microwaves.

Could you bake a potato wrapped in aluminum foil in a microwave oven?

No. The microwaves are reflected rather than absorbed. Similarly, metal containers delay the cooking of food in them.

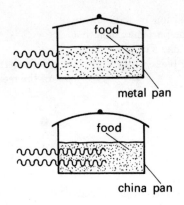

Microwaves bounce off metal but penetrate china or paper.

122   Various food materials absorb microwaves at different rates. In a 2450 mHz frequency oven, pure water absorbs one half of the intensity of the microwave energy within a depth of 1·2 cm. In a 915 megacycle oven, this half-intensity depth is about 7·6 cm. Another way of stating the same thing is to say that half of the energy produced by microwaves in the 12·7 cm wavelength is absorbed after it has penetrated only 1·2 cm in pure water, but that the 33 cm wavelength microwave has one half of its energy absorbed at a depth of 7·6 cm.

In other words, the longer wave penetrates more/less deeply than the shorter wavelength.

more

●

123   Microwave heating occurs at vastly different rates within a food. In other words, the different materials within a food absorb microwave energy at vastly different rates. According to one research report water is heated at about ten times the rate of ice. Fat is heated four times as fast as lean meat. Marrow heats faster than the bone surrounding it.

From the above would you say that the part of a frozen food which thaws first is cooked much more than a part which thaws later?

Yes, this is one of the problems of cooking frozen foods by microwave

123a   Differences in the composition of food within a frozen meal may be large and one part may melt first when exposed to microwave heating. This part heats rapidly creating a 'hot spot' and boils while the rest of the meal is still frozen.

So what?

So in defrosting part of the meal may be overcooked.

●

124   The density of a food affects the rate of conduction of heat. Bread is less dense than beef muscle. Therefore, the bread heats faster than the meat.

The rate of heating food by microwave energy depends upon the amount of water present. The more water present in a food, the more heat required to raise the temperature of the food.

Which requires more energy to heat, a kilogramme of potatoes containing about 80% moisture or a kilogramme of minced beef containing about 50% moisture?

The potatoes since they contain more moisture.

●

125   In cooking most foods by microwave, heat piles up just below the surface where much of the energy is absorbed. With larger pieces of food, time must be allowed for this piled up heat to reach the interior of the food by means of conduction. This carry-over or equalization cooking time is especially important in cooking larger pieces of meat by microwave.

To obtain a roast cooked to a rare state of 60C (140F) internal temperature, the roast is removed from a microwave oven when the internal temperature is only 32C (90F) to 38C (100F).

The heat near the surface is conducted inward giving a 'rare' pattern and very little shrinkage. Most roasts require a carry-over cooking time of 30—50 minutes after the power in the oven is shut off.

From the above, would you think that carry-over cooking must be allowed for in cooking such foods as potatoes in a microwave oven?

Yes, carry-over cooking must be considered in any sizeable, dense food. For potatoes, carry-over cooking time, time for the heat to equalize, is about five minutes.

126   When larger pieces of frozen meat are heated in a microwave oven, the edges and corners thaw first and liquid forms. These areas brown and eventually over-

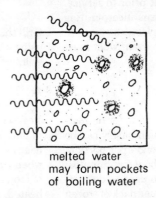

melted water
may form pockets
of boiling water

Microwaves may heat frozen foods unevenly.

cook before the centre of the meat is cooked. The reasons for this happening, we learned, is that microwaves are absorbed preferentially by . . . . and microwave energy piles up just under the surface of many foods.

liquids

●

127   Oddly enough, the surface of some foods, such as bread and rolls, baking in a microwave oven are relatively cool while their interior is hot. Two reasons for this strange phenomenon exist: the microwaves pass through the surface and are absorbed in the interior of the bread; and the oven itself, being cool draws off the surface heat of the food.

Is it logical to develop a brown crust in the bread by prebaking it at a higher than normal temperature in a conventional oven to develop a brown crust, then finish baking the interior by microwave?

Yes, in an industrial bakery this is reasonable and is being done in England in at least one bakery.

●

128   The problem of how to brown or crust a food surface is a major one in microwave cooking, and this is one reason why microwave ovens are not more widely used. Steaks cooked entirely by microwave lack the

charred, crusty appearance usually preferred. To overcome this shortcoming, steak and chops are usually
grilled by conventional means, refrigerated or frozen,
then finished in a microwave oven just prior to service.
Research is being carried out into ovens incorporating
both microwave and convection principles.

When cooking chops in a microwave oven, what must
be done in order to brown them?

Grill them quickly,
using a conventional
grill.

●

129   A major use for microwave heating is for defrosting foods. Frozen doughnuts and Danish pastry can be
defrosted and heated in 10 to 20 seconds per portion.
A dozen doughnuts can be heated in about two minutes.

Microwaves are extremely fast when used in defrosting frozen fruits. For example, a consumer pack of frozen
strawberries is defrosted by microwave in three minutes,
which allows the individual berries to be separated for
intermediate use.

Do you think that a few seconds of overheating a
filled pastry will boil the filling?

Yes, seconds count
in microwave
heating especially
when single portions
of food are being
heated. If bread or
rolls are overheated,
the taste is the same
as occurs in staling.
In the case of a
frozen doughnut,
the jam inside can
be very hot while
the outside
is cool to the
touch.

●

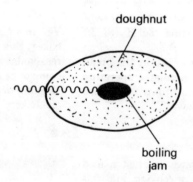

doughnut

boiling
jam

*In heating a jam doughnut by microwave the jam will boil while
the outside is cool.*

129a   A 1kW microwave oven heats 28 grammes of the usual food material in about 8 seconds. More energy could be introduced into the food in the same time but steam will form from water within the food and burst open the surface of a solid food.

Is this bad?

You must admit it is unsightly.

●

130   Cooking frozen vegetables by microwave is fast when done in small quantity. Frozen corn, for example, can be cooked quickly because it has already been almost completely cooked in the blanching stage before being frozen. Frozen cauliflower is also quite fast when cooked by microwave. The microwave oven offers an advantage in cooking vegetables which contain much water, such as marrow and eggplant, because no water needs to be added.

When vegetables—or other—foods are to be cooked in quantity, conventional cooking equipment is faster.

Are microwaves useful in cooking vegetables or other foods in which surface crispness is desirable?

No, hot air or hot fat is necessary for such crisping to take place. For this same reason, microwaves are not effective in heating fish sticks, fried fish, or shellfish—or any breaded item.

●

131   Food material in a microwave oven is heated from all sides provided the food is not shielded by metal or other material which absorbs or reflects the microwaves.

Would you expect microwave penetration into the bottom of food that is resting on the deck of the oven?

No; however, the food can be raised off the bottom by resting it on a nonconducting or glass material, and penetration from the bottom does take place.

●

132   Food can be cooked by microwave when placed in china or glass containers which are nonconductors. Metal utensils or dishes with metallic trim should not be used. Electrical arcing occurs across small gaps between the utensil and the oven and between pieces of metal. The trim will burn off, and the metal will shield the microwaves from entering the food. Plastic ware such as Melmac is not suitable.

However, aluminium foil is used to wrap small parts of meat such as shank on a leg of lamb to slow its cooking so that the shank is not overcooked.

Would you expect arcing to occur between the ragged edges of the foil when so used?

Yes, fold the foil so that there are no ragged edges.

●

133 In baking cakes by microwave, cake containers should be made of porous paper. The paper transmits the developing vapours which would otherwise collect and condense on the cake itself as it cools if a glass or other non-porous utensil is used.

What's wrong with vapour condensate on a cake?

The texture of the cake surface is undesirable, and the application of the icing is made difficult.

●

134 Foods can be cooked by microwave while they are in plastic bags. Is it wise to puncture such plastic bags which contain wet food?

Yes, otherwise the steam generated explodes the bag. Eggs cooked in their shell are also likely to explode if not punctured. Potatoes for baking should also be pricked by a fork at their ends.

●

135 Microwaves are generated in special tubes called magnetrons, which are built in various capacities, to produce between 800 and 2000 watts of energy (high power tubes which generate over 400 kilowatts are being built, but not for kitchen use). Unlike most electrical heating elements and gas burners, the magnetron produces a fixed amount of energy which in cooking is an advantage/disadvantage.

A disadvantage if we think of the ability to raise or lower heat level at will, as can be done within limits using gas or conventional electric cooking equipment.

●

136 Since the magnetron gives off a fixed amount of energy, control of the amount of heat transferred to a food item in a microwave oven must be done as a function of . . . . and . . . .

time, shielding

137 What device generates the microwaves in a microwave oven?

The magnetron tube(s)

●

138 Presently available microwave ovens have relatively small cooking capacity because the microwave energy is limited. One of the 1kW ovens bakes one potato in $2\frac{1}{2}$ minutes, two potatoes in 4 minutes, and 13 potatoes—its capacity—in 13 minutes.

As more food is added to a microwave oven the time required to cook the food increases rapidly/remains the same.

Increases rapidly

●

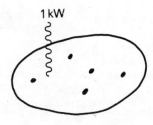
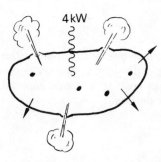

Too much microwave energy may explode the food by changing the water content to steam too quickly

139 Because of the fixed amount of energy, the microwave oven of the usual size is not useful as a heavy production piece of equipment and is, therefore, used primarily to cook items to order, to defrost small items, or to reheat foods quickly.

If a microwave oven is used in a home or commercial kitchen today it is likely to be a basic/supporting cooking device.

supporting

49

140   Some microwave ovens are energized by two magnetrons which may be operated singly or together, which permits some control in the speed of heating.

Other microwave ovens incorporate standard grilling or conventional oven heating elements to provide surface heating and browning of food, while the magnetrons cook the interior of the food.

Incorporating two magnetrons into an oven or combining microwave with conventional oven heating elements is done to provide more/less flexibility in cooking.

more

●

141   One way to control the amount of energy which is put into food via microwaves is to have a number of magnetrons and control the movement of food under them. The slower the food moves on a conveyor belt under the magnetrons, the more/less energy it will receive.

more

●

142   Since energy is applied within, as well as on the surface of food in a microwave oven, control of what factor in cooking is more important than with other cooking devices?

Time

●

143   Energy produced within a microwave oven bounces around within the chamber and must be absorbed. Otherwise, it will be reflected back to the magnetron and may damage it. For this reason, the microwave oven must not be operated unless something is in it which will . . . . the microwaves.

absorb

●

144   The energy field created by the magnetron in the microwave oven is not evenly distributed. To overcome this, food is placed on a turntable in one oven or the energy is 'stirred' by some means in some of the other ovens. The stirrer or the turntable has the effect of . . . . the energy evenly over the surface of the food.

distributing

145 Since time is the only control factor in most microwave ovens, it must be controlled precisely. To do it automatically, in one oven the operation of the magnetron is controlled by the steam generated in the food which actuates a temperature sensing device, and by the weight of the food. These two variables are considered together in controlling what important factor in cooking?

Time

●

146 One big advantage of microwave heating is that there is no *wild* heat given off by the oven. All of the microwaves are contained within the oven itself, and no/some heat escapes the outside of the oven.

No. The magnetrons themselves must be cooled, but their heat is relatively unimportant.

●

147 Microwave cooking produces greater yield (what is left after cooking) in some foods, less in others, depending upon the composition and size of the food.

Yield and juiciness in pork chops, for example, is greater when they were cooked in a conventional oven or by frying. If they are slightly overcooked, objectionable dryness results; and this holds true for other thinly-cut meats. Roasts and meat patties give about the same yield or less yield when cooked by microwave or by other means; but in the case of the roast, some say that the meat is less juicy when cooked by microwave.

In cooking large pieces of meat by microwave, there is some/no yield or juiciness advantage as compared with cooking them completely with conducted heat.

No

●

REVISION

1. When food is being cooked, more than one means of heat transference is in use. A conventional grill with the heating element located over the rack holding the food has heat transferred to the surface of the food by means of . . . . and . . . .

convection, infra-red radiation.

2. Food which is griddled, placed upon a flat griddle, has heat transferred to it by means of . . . . . .   conduction

3. A piece of meat turning on a spit would have heat transferred to it by means of . . . . and . . . .   convection, radiation

4. A piece of meat in an oven has the heat transferred to the inside of it by means of . . . .   conduction

5. Increasing the pressure on water does what to its boiling point?   Raises it.

6. Increasing the pressure of steam increases its . . . .   temperature

7. Food cooked under pressure may show less shrinkage primarily because of . . . .   reduction in cooking time

8. What disadvantages are there in cooking under pressure?   The high heat generated toughens proteins present.

9. An acid condition does what to chlorophyll?   Degrades it.

10. What happens to milk at a pH of 4·6?   It curdles.

11. A high pH in starch hastens/delays gelatinization.

hastens

●

12. The pH of egg whites rises/lowers with storage.

rises

●

13. Frying meat results in good/poor retention of vitamins.

good

●

14. Heat of fusion refers to the energy necessary to . . . . matter such as ice and water from one form to another.

change

●

15. Proteins, starches and sugars 'cook' at the same/different temperatures.

different

●

16. Most harmful bacteria are destroyed if heated to . . . . for thirty minutes.

60C (140F)

●

17. Starch found in flour gelatinizes completely at about what temperature?

93C (200F)

●

18. In cooking we are concerned chiefly about the loss of which three vitamins?

C (ascorbic acid)
B_1 (thiamin)
B_2 (riboflavin)

●

19. Cooking involves a number of things but one process is always involved and must be taking place if we are to have cooking. What is this process?

Transfer of heat to the food material.

20. Most food materials have high water content. In much of cooking we are concerned about retaining as much as possible of the water. Why?

Because it contains most of the flavour and many of the nutrients.

●

21. When using steamers or microwave ovens, how is browning usually accomplished?

By use of grills or other conventional equipment.

●

22. The problem in much of cookery is to achieve a browned surface with a desirable texture and flavour inside. The surface of food can absorb only so much heat in a given period of time without . . . . . .

burning

●

23. In a forced convection oven, the movement of air is increased by means of a . . . .

fan or rotor

●

24. Is radiated energy more efficient in terms of heating effect than energy carried by air currents?

Yes, since the wave transmission is almost instantaneous and penetrates the surface of the food.

●

25. Are infra-red waves of various lengths equally effective for cooking food?

No, those of 1·4— 5 microns in wavelength are most effective.

●

26. In what kind of cooking is knowledge of the thermophysical properties of a food most important?

In cooking by microwave energy.

27. Carry-over cooking means the cooking which takes place after food is removed from a heat source. How do we compensate for carry-over cooking?

By undercooking the food initially, waiting for carry-over heating to complete the cooking.

●

28. Carry-over cooking is especially important in using what kind of energy for cooking?

Microwave

●

29. When steam changes to water it gives off 2257 kilojoules per kilogramme of steam which is known as what kind of heat?

Specific latent heat

●

30. Two wavelengths are used in available microwave ovens. Which wavelength—the 12·7 cm or the 7·6 cm—would be more likely to cook or reheat a half-inch steak the quickest?

The 7·6 cm since it penetrates less deeply; it gives up more of its energy in a shorter penetration.

●

31. Microwaves give up their energy preferentially to water. Is this an advantage or disadvantage?

A disadvantage since liquids are likely to boil before other food materials are done or reheated to the desired temperature.

●

32. Why is glass a good material for a cooking utensil to be used in a microwave oven?

It is relatively transparent to the microwaves, and does not heat up when exposed to them.

33. Would you expect the bottom of a glass utensil to be cool when food in it is heated by microwave?

No since some heat is transferred to it from the hot food by means of conduction.

●

34. Of what value is aluminum foil in microwave cookery?

It can be used to shield sections of the food to retard cooking there.

●

35. Would it be wise to wrap potatoes for baking by microwave in aluminum foil?

No, the foil prevents the microwaves from penetrating to the potatoes.

●

36. Equalization time or carry-over cooking time is important in cooking foods by microwave. Why remove a roast from a microwave oven before it has reached the desired internal temperature?

To allow the heat 'piled up' near the surface to move into the roast and finish the cooking.

●

37. Since microwave ovens do a relatively poor job of browning any food or giving it a crust, how can we achieve a browned chop and still take advantage of microwave cookery?

Develop the brown surface by means of a conventional grill or griddle, cook the inside of the chop by microwave.

38. Foods can be completely or almost completely cooked by conventional equipment and frozen until needed. Individual orders can then be quickly reheated by microwave. Can this be done while the food remains in a plastic bag or pouch?

Yes, the plastic is relatively transparent to microwaves. The bag, however, should be punctured before heating to allow the steam which is formed during heating to escape, otherwise the bag may burst.

●

39. Why is it necessary to puncture an egg in its shell before cooking it by microwave?

Again, the steam will build up rapidly and explode the egg if the shell is not punctured.

●

40. It is wise to cook food by microwave on a dish which is etched with metal?

No, the metal etching will cause arching and will burn.

●

41. Which will boil faster, a litre of water placed on a high output range top or a litre of water placed in a microwave oven?

The water on the range; the microwave oven has only a fixed amount of energy available which can be directed into the water and it is not as great as the energy produced by a heavy duty range top.

C

42. Which will boil faster in a microwave oven, a cup of water contained in a metal pan or a cup of water in a glass container?

The water in the glass; the metal acts to prevent the waves from reaching the water.

●

43. Which is more efficient in terms of energy utilization, gas or electric heating elements, or microwaves?

The microwaves are by far the most efficient—their transmission is almost instantaneous, can be directed more accurately.

●

44. Why is it necessary to have something in a microwave oven before turning on the energy?

The waves bounce back on the magnetron and overheat them if some material is not present in the oven to absorb them.

●

45. Radiant energy is stated in terms of its wave length or . . . .

frequency

●

46. Infra-red and . . . . energy are transferred through space without the use of an intermediate agent.

microwave

●

47. Vitamin B_1 is also known as . . . .

thiamin

48. Vitamin B_2 is also known as . . . .   riboflavin

●

49. Vitamin C is also known as . . . .   ascorbic acid

Sauce Cookery

DEFINING SAUCES

1 Sauces are liquid or semi-liquid mixtures which are added to meat, poultry, fish vegetables and desserts to give moisture or richness, to garnish or to otherwise enhance the appearance and, in some cases, the nutritional value, but, more importantly, to enhance the flavour. The principal purpose of a sauce, then, is to . . . . the flavour of a food.

add to or enhance

●

2 Butter, margarine, suet, chicken fat, oil or other fats are used in the roux.

To make a blond or white roux the fat should be hot but not sizzling. Add the flour and cook at moderate or high heat, until the roux is frothy and leaves the bottom of the pan easily and has hazelnut or pale gold colour. The texture should be some-what gritty. For a brown sauce use moderate heat and cook the roux just until it takes on a light brown colour. Overcooking results in poor texture.

In view of the time required to make roux and the ingredients used is it reasonable to make it in quantity and hold it until needed?

Yes, if you have the need for it since it can be refrigerated for several days.

●

3 Sometimes sauces are used to add a contrast in taste to another food. An accompaniment such as cranberry sauce with turkey provides contrast or tartness to an otherwise bland food. Apple sauce with fresh roast pork serves the same purpose. Some sauces are used to add sharpness or tanginess to a bland food.

A remoulade sauce served with shrimp is an example of a piquant sauce which contrasts or balances nicely with a bland food.

Sauces, in addition to being used as enhancers of flavour, are also used for the purpose of providing .... to bland foods.

contrast, balance, or piquancy

●

4 Sauces may add to the appearance of food, sometimes as a coating which is poured or brushed over the food to give a pleasing appearance to an otherwise uninteresting item. The chaud-froid sauce, made with a cream sauce or mayonnaise and gelatine, is used to coat various food items. The use of this sauce is a good example of a sauce enhancing appearance.

Sauces are used to add to the flavour, to contrast with flavours and to add to the .... of a food.

appearance

●

5 Sauces such as a barbecue sauce are used to modify the original flavour of a food, blending the sauce flavour with the flavour of the food. Some sauces are used to disguise or mask the original flavour of a food. Today's use of sauces to disguise or change the flavours of poor quality food is considered undesirable.

In addition to sauces serving to complement or enhance flavour, to add to its appearance and to serve as contrast or piquancy, sauces are also used to .... original flavours.

Modify

●

6 Sauces should never be used to change the flavour of a food material, only to enhance or complement the flavour of the food. As the French use the word *mask* in regard to sauces, masking a food with a sauce or jelly is to completely cover it physically hiding its appearance.

True or False: In culinary language, masking a food with a sauce means to change its true flavour.

False

7　Broadly speaking, any condiment or mixture of food which serves to contrast with or complement another food can be termed a sauce. In this broad sense, a peanut butter and jelly mixture would be a sauce to a piece of bread if they were served together. Salad dressings such as French dressing and mayonnaise could also in this sense be considered sauces. However, sauces are usually considered those mixtures served with meats, entrees, desserts and other major foods as a complement or contrast to their flavour. Sauces may be classified several ways; here is one system:

1. By serving temperature: warm or cold
2. By flavour: blandness or piquancy
3. By acidity
4. By sweetness
5. By colour
6. By base: neutral or meat

True or False: A sauce must always be a liquid and must be hot.

False; sauces can be solids such as a hard sauce or a compound butter; they are either hot or cold.

●

8　The warm or hot sauces are such items as gravies, hollandaise, demi-glace base sauces and so forth. Items such as gravies or demi-glace sauces are served at temperatures above 60C (140F). A hollandaise is served warm 49C (120F) but usually not at 60C (140F) which might break the emulsion. Hot in this instance does not refer to a sensation of taste from seasonings, vinegar, etc. but to the temperature of the food. If a sauce is cold, it is usually refrigerated but there are exceptions, some may be called cold if at room temperature.

Most warm sauces are served above a temperature of . . . . C.

49C (120F)

●

9　A bland sauce would be one which has a mild, smooth flavour such as a béchamel sauce (white sauce). If seasonings or acid liquids are added to a sauce to give it a tangy flavour the sauce is termed piquant. These give a sharp flavour to the sauce which may be described as burning or hot. Vinegar, or lime or lemon juice and/or spices such as pepper, chili powder, tabasco, paprika or items such as horseradish, capers, chopped onion and so forth may be added to give this touch of piquancy.

A tangy, piquant sauce such as a barbecue sauce or mustard sauce will give a .... or .... sensation when eaten.

burning, hot

9a The typical French sauce includes wine which has a pH of about 3·0—3·5. The acidity and flavour of the wine add character to the sauce.

Before adding wine to a sauce the conscientious cook reduces the wine by heating so that it will not dilute the sauce too much and thin out the starch.

Does a wine sauce contain much alcohol?

Practically none since the alcohol in the wine vaporizes readily, and boils at about 93C (200F), (depending upon the percentage of alcohol).

10 A tartar sauce made of mayonnaise to which chopped caper and gherkin and other items are added is an example of a cold acid sauce. It could be used to complement the flavour and texture of soft bland foods such as shrimp and fish. Some sauces are strikingly acid such as a mint sauce used with lamb. Oftentimes, classifications of sauces may not be completely distinct such as indicated here. A sauce may be both hot and tart. It may also be classified by its colour. A hollandaise sauce for example, could be called a yellow sauce. Apple sauce is an example of a hot or cold sauce, sweet and yet acid or tart. Classifications of sauces are, therefore, easy/difficult to make.

difficult

11 Fruit and berry sauces are examples of sweet sauces. A tart apple sauce, cranberry or cherry sauce are examples. There are other types of sauces that may be classified as, sweet sauces such as sweet-sour sauce used with some meats, bigarade sauce (sour orange) used with duck, cumberland sauce with venison, brandy-peach sauce with pork, or a pineapple or raisin sauce with cured ham. These sauces for meat are made by

heating granulated sugar in a pan until it is caramelized and brown stock and vinegar are added. Often the sauce is thickened. The sweetness in the sauce is frequently balanced by an acid item in the sauce which provides contrast to bland or low-acid foods when served with them. Dessert sauces such as rum, vanilla or lemon sauce would be included in a classification of sweet sauces.

Could a sweet sauce, then, be both sweet and sour?

Yes, this is often the case.

●

12 Sauces are often classified according to their colour: brown, blond or white. A brown sauce results from using a browned roux and a brown stock. This sauce is also called espagnole sauce because it originated in Spain but was adopted as a basic sauce by French chefs many years ago. It may have a small quantity of tomato in it. A white sauce is a sauce made from milk. If cream is an added ingredient to give extra richness, it may be called a cream sauce. White or cream sauces may also be called a béchamel sauce. A béchamel sauce may also be made from rich veal or chicken stock, thickened with a white roux and thinned with rich milk or cream. Strictly speaking, however, this sauce is a type of velouté sauce, another basic sauce, because its base is not milk but a meat stock.

White roux + milk =
Blond roux + white stock =
Brown roux + brown stock =

béchamel, velouté, espagnole

●

12a A velouté sauce is made from a white stock and thickened with a white roux. It is called a blond sauce because it is whitish in colour. It should not be called a white or cream sauce. It derives its name because of its smooth texture; velouté is derived from the root from which the word velvet is also taken.

A brown sauce may be called an . . . . sauce, a white or cream sauce a . . . . sauce, and a blond sauce a . . . . sauce.

espagnole, béchamel, velouté

64

13 A béchamel sauce can be either a . . . .   white or cream
or if veal or chicken stock is used, it is more properly   sauce, velouté
a . . . .   sauce

●

14 We will also hear chefs speak of a neutral or a
meat sauce. Neutral means that the sauce is made from
a non-meat base. This could be a white sauce made
with milk, a wine sauce made with wine, a hollandaise
sauce made with egg yolks vinegar or lemon juice and
butter, a mayonnaise made with oil, egg yolks and vinegar, a tomato sauce made without meat stock, a butter
sauce and so forth. Some sauces may be made from
either a meat or a non-meat base. For instance, a tomato
sauce may be made from a meat base or it may be neutral. If a béchamel sauce is made from milk, it is a neutral
sauce. If it is made from a rich veal or chicken stock
and later thinned with rich milk or cream, it is not.
    A neutral sauce is one which is made from a . . . .   non-meat
base.

●

15 While the classification of sauces may seem con-
fusing and the categories do overlap, learning them
by class assists in remembering and being able to produce them. Based on the classifications of sauces, how
would you classify each of these sauces in column 1,
matching the characteristics listed in column 2?

Apple sauce	. . . .	1) Acid, sweet, warm or cold
Fish velouté (Sauce vin blanc)	. . . .	2) Warm, smooth or blonde
Espagnole sauce	. . . .	3) Brown, warm, meat base
Devilled sauce	. . . .	4) Piquant, cold, neutral
White sauce	. . . .	5) Warm, neutral, white
Mint sauce	. . . .	6) Warm, piquant

1, 2, 3, 6, 5, 4

16   There are literally hundreds of warm sauces, but most are variations of a few basic or *mother* sauces. There is no complete agreement as to what these mother sauces are, but most experts name them as béchamel, a basic white sauce; espagnole, a basic brown sauce; hollandaise, a basic yellow sauce; velouté, a basic blond sauce; and tomato sauce, a basic red sauce.

Mother sauces can be classified as to colour: white, blonde, red, yellow, and . . . .

brown

●

17   Most of the other warm sauces can be made from one of these five mother sauces. The variations are called *little* sauces or *secondary* sauces. Little sauces are derived from the . . . . sauces.

mother

●

18   The basis of a warm sauce, other than hollandaise, is a stock or liquid. The stock may be derived from animal or fish flesh and bones or it may be a neutral liquid such as tomato purée, milk or wine. Usually the stock is thickened with a roux—usually a 50—50 mixture by weight of fat and flour—but there are exceptions. Roast gravy, the drippings from roast beef and served with the beef, is unthickened. Some pan gravies may be unthickened.

A warm sauce is usually made from a stock or liquid thickened with a . . . .

roux

●

19   Does it make sense to use chicken fat when making roux for a sauce to be served with a chicken suprême (boned chicken breasts)?

Yes, good sense.

THICKENING AGENTS FOR WARM SAUCES

20   Sauces are usually thickened either with a starch, a roux, or with eggs, especially egg yolks.

    Roux usually is made up by weight of $\frac{1}{2}$ flour, and $\frac{1}{2}$ . . . .

fat

●

21   Roux is classified as to colour—white, blond or brown. The colour depends upon the amount of *roasting* of the flour and the colour of the stock used. For example, brown stock plus a brown roux gives a brown sauce, or as it is known by its French name, an . . . . sauce.

espagnole

●

22   For a brown roux, the flour may be first roasted and then combined with the fat. The browning action reduces the thickening property of the flour by one to two thirds. Two to three times as much heavily browned flour is required to provide the same thickening quality as unbrowned flour. When making brown sauces more/less flour will be needed than with a white sauce.

more

●

23   Flour is usually used in the warm sauces because it browns well and provides a full bodied texture to the sauce. Flour differs in clarity and thickening power. Pastry and cake flours have less gluten, more starch than bread flour, hence more thickening power. Bread flour with its high gluten content gives a stringy quality to the sauce.

    In choosing between bread and pastry flour for a sauce, which would you use—bread or pastry?

Pastry

24   Cornflour contains no gluten and gives a clear sauce which tends to thicken more as it cools. About $\frac{3}{4}$ of a tbsp. of cornflour has the equivalent thickening value of one tbsp. of cake flour. Tapioca also firms more when it cools and the two starches can be used together to produce a pleasantly clear sauce (or glaze) for fruits which is not rubbery when cooled. A paste made from the two will give a nice sheen to fruit, but waxy maize thickening agents have a superior sheen.

In warm sauces, cornflour is/is not usually used in thickening.

is not

●

25   Waxy cereal such as waxy maize (corn) flours and starches produce a clear, soft sauce and are best for sauces that are to be frozen, because the sauce will not break down in the freezing process or when reheated. Four ounces of waxy maize starch has the equivalent thickening power of 156 grammes of cornflour, 226 grammes of cake flour or 284 grammes of bread flour. It gives a very clear, soft paste and is excellent for thickening the fillings of fruit pies. It is as thick when hot as when cold.

Frozen meals containing sauces are likely to have what kind of flour or starch in the sauces?

Waxy maize

●

26   How long should a starch thickener be cooked and to what temperature? Prolonged cooking of starches is not necessary as was formerly believed. Most starches and flours require a temperature of at least 93C (200F) for maximum gelatinization to occur. This is the stage where nearly all of the starch granules have swelled by absorbing water and are touching one another. A few additional minutes of cooking are needed to remove any starch flavour remaining. White sauces are cooked only a few minutes but blond and brown sauces are cooked longer to develop colour and texture.

Most starch thickeners must reach a temperature of at least . . . . degrees Centigrade in order for maximum gelatinization to take place and then are cooked a few minutes longer to eliminate any starch taste remaining.

93C (200F)

27   Beurre manié or manié butter is also used for thickening sauces. It is made by mixing four ounces of softened butter with three ounces of sifted flour and by kneading the two until well combined.

When needed to thicken a sauce, pea-sized balls are pinched off and dropped into the sauce which is near the boiling point, then mixed smooth.

Manié butter is used to 'correct' a sauce which is too thick/thin.

thin

●

28   If a cream sauce is too thin, correct it by adding beurre manié; if too thick beat in more milk or cream, a tablespoon at a time. Logically what substitute could be used for the prepared beurre manié?

Flour and butter mixed together, the same ingredients as for beurre manie.

●

29   Another thickening agent used in the kitchen is a *liaison* of rich cream and egg yolks, three parts of cream with one part yolks. It is usually added as a finishing agent at the end of preparation. The product is never boiled to complete thickening when the liaison is added for this would curdle the mixture. The temperature is brought up to 88C (190F) and thickening of the eggs takes place. This liaison is used for thickening some very delicate cream or velouté sauces but is most often used as a thickening agent for delicate cream soups.

It is proper after adding the liaison for thickening to bring the mixture up to . . . . deg C to cook the eggs and complete thickening.

88C (190F)

●

30   Cream and egg yolks used as a thickening for sauces, and soups is known as one of the . . . .

liaisons

●

31   Another thickening agent used to thicken sauces is a *slurry, whitewash* or *jayzee*. This is a mixture of flour, starch, waxy maize or other starch thickener and water. The starch thickener is added to the water and

mixed with a rapid agitation until free of lumps. It is then added to the sauce or liquid to be thickened. Good agitation is necessary when the slurry is added so that lumping does not occur. As a rule, the best cooks avoid slurries for thickening sauces, preferring a roux which gives better assurance against lumping and gives a smoother, finer flavour to the sauce. Slurries are often used to thicken dessert sauces or for thickening sauces made with cornstarch, waxy maize, or arrowroot. These starches go into solution more easily than flour and are less likely to lump in the slurry.

Another term for a slurry made of a starch thickener and liquid is . . . .

'whitewash' or 'jayzee'

●

3 2 Thickeners are *divided* with liquid or with fat as in egg yolks, slurry, or roux. Dividing the thickening agent prevents lumping by encouraging better solution and a complete mix before thickening occurs. Another method of dividing a starch is to add it to the sugar that is to be used in a sauce for sweetening, such as in a blanc mange or other dessert sauce. The sugar-starch mixture is then poured into the liquid to be thickened, mixed well as it is added. The sugar divides the starch thickener into small particles so that lumping does not occur.

Dividing a thickener is done for what purpose?

To prevent lumping when it is incorporated into the product.

●

3 3 If a sauce shows lumps after thickening they can usually be removed by whipping with a whip wire. Straining the sauce through muslin is a more certain method.

If a liaison breaks because of high heat, little can be done to eliminate the curdling.

Lumping in a warm sauce that does not include a liaison can be removed by . . . .

whipping or straining

70

MEAT STOCKS

34   As previously noted, the two principal meat stocks used for many sauces are brown and white stocks. Both are similar except that a brown stock is made from well browned meat, bones and vegetables. A white stock comes from unbrowned products.

Would you think that the quality of the sauce would be affected by the richness and quality of the stock?

Yes, the final quality of the dish made from the sauce depends upon the quality of the stock used to make the sauce.

●

35   To make 5 litres of good stock, use two kilogrammes of bones and meat, 6 litres of water and about $\frac{1}{2}$ kilogramme of chopped vegetables such as onions, leeks, carrots, celery, etc. This chopped mixture of vegetables is called a mirepoix. A sachet or bouquet garni is added. This is a mixture of herbs spices tied in a small cloth and removed from the stock when the flavouring is correct.

The proportions to make 5 litres of good rich stock are . . . . of meat and bones, ... of water and . . . . of mirepoix.

2 kilogrammes, 6 litres, $\frac{1}{2}$ kilogramme.

●

36   For a white stock, avoid using highly coloured vegetables such as carrots which add a tinge of colour to the stock.

The mirepoix is better added after the bones and meat have been cooked for about half of the cooking period; otherwise, the vegetables may give a slightly bitter flavour to the stock because of overcooking.

Meat may be removed when cooked tender and the bones left in to continue to cook. This meat is used for other dishes such as boiled beef, or chicken.

What is the principal difference between a white and brown stock?

The meat, bones, and vegetables in a brown stock have been browned; those in a white stock have not.

71

37   Depending upon the size of the bones and the way they are cut, a stock from meat and bones is simmered from 4 to 10 hours; from poultry 2 to 6 hours; and from fish 20 minutes.

Starting a stock from a cold water start gives more/less flavour.

more

●

38   The meat and bones not only contribute flavour to the stock but also body. Body is largely made up of gelatine and other soluble products extracted from the meat and bones. If stock has extracted a proper amount of gelatine, it will gel when cold.

What other products in a stock contribute flavour besides meat and bones?

The vegetables (mirepoix) and the seasonings.

●

39   The best bones to use for a stock are those from young animals. These contain more gelatine and the marrow contains more flavouring ingredients. Shin and knuckle bones are best, with neck bones next. The bones are best cut into about four inch lengths and split. These can be washed off in cold water before using. Veal and beef bones are often mixed together. Chicken carcasses and veal bones make an excellent white stock. A white fish stock is made by using the bones, flesh scraps, heads, and skins of white lean fish. Special stocks can be made from lamb or mutton bones and from the bones of cured pork. Stocks from lamb or mutton are used for a sauce used with that type of meat. Stocks from cured pork likewise have restricted use.

Where in bones are the flavouring ingredients mostly found?

In the soft cartilage parts in young animal bones and in the marrow. Some flavour may come from bits of meat adhering on the bones.

●

40   When stocks are reduced by cooking to about a fourth of their original volume, the product is called a *glaze*. Glazes are used to heighten the flavour of stocks and dishes. They are usually strained and stored in containers. Because of their concentration, they contain

enough gelatine to make a very firm, rubbery gel and are highly concentrated in flavour. A glaze made from meat is called a *glace de viande*; from poultry, *glace de poulet*; from fish, a *glace de poisson*.

A stock that has been reduced to one-fourth in volume by evaporation in cooking, and has a sticky gelatinous consistency is known as . . . .

a glaze

●

41 Today some cooks utilize soup or food bases instead of preparing their own stocks or glazes. When preportioned meats are bought there are no by-products of meat and no bones to use for stock building. The time and labour required to make stocks seems excessive to many people. A wide variety of bases are available on the market so that almost any type of stock can be prepared quickly. Check the ingredients on the container carefully and note how much meat flavouring ingredients and how much monosodium glutamate and salt are in the product. The ingredients must be listed according to ingredient in greatest to least quantity.

If a food base has listed as ingredients: salt, hydrolyzed protein (monosodium glutamate), chicken fat, chicken meat, etc. what would you be paying for mostly in this base?

Salt and monosodium glutamate.

●

42 What is the difference between a stock, broth, bouillon and consommé? All start as a stock. Stocks themselves are divided into white, or brown. Stocks are incorporated into soups and sauces and receive further cooking. The consommé is clarified by use of egg whites, and strained.

A chicken consommé starts as a . . . .

white stock

43   Other meat stocks that can be used are meat drippings from roasts or sautéed items. Some of these require little additional preparation. For instance, roast gravy, is served over sliced roast beef. This is made from the pan drippings from the roast beef.

Could pan drippings be used to make a gravy?

Yes, the drippings are often made into a thickened sauce. The main difference between a gravy and a sauce is that a gravy has the definite flavour of the meat from which it came while a sauce is thickened and is a subtle blend of flavours with no specific flavour predominating.

●

44   *Deglazing* is a process used to extract tasty bits of drippings from meat which collect in a pan during sautéing or frying meat items. Liquid—water, stock, or wine—is added to the cooking pan. The pan is heated and the drippings brought into solution by stirring and scraping. This may be further reduced by evaporation to give a richer stock. After the drippings are extracted from the bottom of the pan, the liquid is then used as a stock to make a gravy.

Deglazing is a process of removing what from pans in which meat has been cooked?

The bits of drippings which adhere to the pan.

●

45   What is the minimal time for preparing stock using beef bones? (See item 37 if you have forgotten).

Four hours

●

46   What is a glaze called if made from fish stock?

Fish glaze or glace de poisson

47 Similarly, what would you expect a glaze to be called which was made from chicken stock?

Chicken glaze or glace de poulet

●

48 Instead of making a stock from bones and meat, is it reasonable to use canned beef bouillon as a substitute?

Yes, bouillon is a rich broth and saves much preparation time. Bouillon cubes— beef or chicken— also can be used since they in effect are condensed bouillon. Soup bases, as noted, come in the form of a paste can also be used.

●

49 Is it reasonable to use a meat glaze dissolved in hot water as a substitute for stock?

Yes, after all, meat glaze is concentrated stock. Soup bases can be used also but care must be taken not to use too much because of their high salt content.

●

50 If a 'quickie' espagnole sauce is needed, add to beef bouillon the following: browned minced onions, carrots, celery, wine, parsley, bay leaf, thyme, and tomato paste.
   Is such a practice a culinary sacrilege?

Depends upon your viewpoint.

THE BROWN SAUCES

51 Brown sauce, or sauce espagnole, is made from a brown stock or gravy—or from the boiled-down essence or glaze of these rich liquids plus a brown roux.

What other item could be used as the base for this sauce?

A manufactured food base.

●

52 Brown (espagnole) sauce is one of the most widely used basic or mother sauces. It is usually reduced for use in secondary or small sauces (demi-glace). Many sauces are derived from it. For instance, bordelaise sauce, often served with steaks and other red meats, is made from a demi-glace sauce. Red wine, minced shallots, pepper, thyme and bay leaf are added to the sauce and the sauce is cooked for a half hour. It is then strained, skimmed and finished with lemon juice and sliced or cubed beef bone marrow that has been poached in slightly salted boiling water.

Bordelaise, a well known example of a small or secondary brown sauce, is a demi-glace sauce and red wine, shallots, pepper, thyme, bay leaf and finished with . . . .

beef bone marrow

●

53 Other popular brown sauces are chasseur, Madeira (made using Madeira wine), piquante and poivrade (pepper). These are all secondary or small sauces. From these, still other sauces can be derived. For instance, a Madeira sauce is used to make a Perigueux sauce. A poivrade sauce can be used to make a grand veneur sauce and a Bordelaise sauce can be used to make a Rouennaise sauce. The extension of one sauce into the other from a mother sauce allows for wide variety and heightened interest in food.

The easiest way to organize the sauces in one's mind is to remember that most of them are variations of a basic or mother sauce.

Madeira sauce is a basic demi-glace sauce plus Madeira or port wine.

If chopped truffles are added to a Madeira sauce, we have a Perigueux sauce, named for the Perigueux district, in France, well known for its truffles.

A demi-glace sauce + Madeira wine = ...
sauce.

Madeira

●

54 Madeira sauce + truffles = ... sauce.

Perigueux

●

55 Another example: Robert sauce, one of the oldest of French sauces, is a rich demi-glace sauce with sautéed onions, white wine and French mustard. It is usually served with roast pork.

Robert sauce = demi-glace sauce + white wine + sautéed onions and . . . .

mustard

●

56 We see that brown sauces can be a fascinating study in themselves. Carême, the famous French chef active in Napoleon's time, stated that any chef who could not make from memory at least 100 of the most common sauces derived from the mother sauces was not fit to be a chef.

Are you prepared for such a test?

It is doubtful that many people in this country could pass such a test. The reader can consult the dozens of cook-books published each year if he wishes to keep up to date with sauces.

●

THE BLOND SAUCES

57 The velouté sauce is a basic blond sauce. It is made from white stock and roux. Vegetables, seasonings, white wine and other items may be added to give flavour. Like brown sauce, it is cooked for about an hour and

then strained. If any fat is on the surface it is skimmed off. If a white fish stock is used, the sauce would then be called a . . . . velouté.

fish

●

58   If a rich chicken stock were used to make a velouté what would you expect the sauce to be called?

A chicken velouté

●

59   Like a brown sauce, the velouté is a basic or mother sauce that has wide use for the preparation of secondary or small sauces. By adding rich milk or cream, a chicken velouté becomes a suprême sauce. Adding egg yolks as a final thickening agent to a suprême sauce creates an Allemande sauce (German sauce),—originally the Allemande was made using veal stock. Both suprême and Allemande sauces have wide use in the preparation of other sauces. For instance, an Allemande sauce can be used to make a poulette sauce, Villeroy sauce, regency sauce or a chaud-froid sauce, the latter used for preparing chaud-froid items for a cold buffet.
    Would you call a velouté a white or cream sauce?

No, these terms are used to indicate a béchamel sauce. The velouté is called the blond sauce or sometimes the velvet sauce.

●

60   A chicken velouté + cream = ... sauce.

suprême

●

61   Suprême sauce + egg yolks = ... sauce.

Allemande

●

62   Another basic velouté is the sauce made from fish stock using white lean fish. This basic velouté makes many other sauces. A Normandy sauce is exactly the same as an Allemande sauce, with the exception that a white fish stock is used instead of a white stock from meat. From this secondary sauce many other sauces are derived such as a Joinville sauce, oyster sauce, or diplomate sauce.
    With what would you use Normandy sauce or some of its derivatives?

Fish or shellfish

78

63   A white fish velouté + egg yolks + cream = ... sauce.

Normandy

●

THE WHITE SAUCES

64   A white sauce is made with a milk base. If cream is added as a part of the stock, then the sauce is called a cream sauce. As noted in item 11, another name for these sauces is béchamel sauce (named for the Marquis Béchamel, Lord Steward to Louis XIV). To make a good white sauce, milk is heated with seasonings in a double boiler, in a thick saucepan or in a steam-jacketed kettle. When properly seasoned, the seasonings are removed and the sauce is thickened with a roux. A roux of half butter (or margarine) and half flour by weight makes a good sauce. Rich cream may be added and the sauce strained to give a cream sauce.

A white or cream sauce (béchamel) is a basic/secondary sauce.

basic

●

66   In item 11 we noted that béchamel sauce can also be made from rich chicken or veal stock, thickened with roux and thinned with rich milk or cream. Escoffier, one of the best known of modern day chefs, made his béchamel sauce by adding seasonings and raw cubed veal to rich milk and heating this at a low temperature until the veal was cooked and the flavours extracted into the milk. He then thickened it with roux. To achieve a similar flavour but to simplify the processing, we today extract the veal flavour (or chicken) by first making a stock, then thickening this richly flavoured stock with roux and finish it with rich milk or cream.

Strictly speaking, however, if a béchamel sauce is made from chicken or veal stock and thickened with roux and thinned with rich milk or cream, it is what sauce?

It is a suprême sauce; the thickened chicken or veal stock is a basic velouté but with the addition of the rich milk or cream, the sauce becomes a suprême sauce.

67   Since a white or cream sauce (béchamel) is a basic or mother sauce, many secondary or small sauces are derived from them. A cheese sauce, mustard, egg or Mornay sauce and many others are made by merely adding respectively cheese, prepared mustard, chopped hard-cooked eggs or Parmesan cheese.

Could a parsley sauce be prepared from a white or cream sauce?

Yes, by the addition of chopped parsley.

●

68   Cream sauce + cheese = ... sauce.

cheese or mornay

●

69   Cream sauce + prepared mustard = ... sauce.

mustard

●

70   Bread sauce may have a stock base of wine, milk or stock, or a combination of any of the three. The stock is seasoned and thickened with fine fresh bread crumbs. It is used with roast chicken, roast game which is delicate in flavour.

Would you think that a bread sauce could be made using a suprême sauce or a béchamel sauce base?

Yes, this is done. If done the quantity of bread crumbs used for thickening is less.

●

71   One of the best known variations of the cream sauce is 'à la King' sauce, authentically American, having been originated by a chef working in a Long Island hotel and named for the hotel manager, a Mr King. It is a thick cream sauce to which is added chopped or cubed meat, hard-cooked egg yolks, pimentos, chopped green peppers, and often mushrooms. Some of the most popular dishes made from an à la King sauce are chicken or turkey à la King and eggs à la King. What sauce is the base for à la King sauce?

Cream

●

72   The richness and thickness of a cream sauce is partly determined by the kind of milk or cream used. Homogenized milk produces a richer thicker sauce than

80

does unhomogenized. Evaporated milk (homogenized milk that has had about 60 per cent of the water removed and sterilized) would logically produce a richer/less rich cream sauce than whole cream.

richer

73   When using milk in cooking there is the possibility of curdling—the milk proteins separating into lumps. Curdling is caused by excessive heat, the addition of very hard water containing excessive calcium salts, or the addition of acid or salt.
    Is there a danger of milk curdling when it is poured into tomato mixtures?

Yes, the tomatoes are acid. To avoid curdling the tomato mixture is added a little at a time to the milk while stirring.

74   Would it be well when making a cream sauce to add salt only before serving?

Yes, this helps to avoid curdling which may occur if the sauce sets for a time.

75   To avoid curdling and the formation of an insoluble surface scum or deposits on the sides and bottom of the container, use low temperatures and stir the sauces while preparing them. If the sauce is to stand for a long time, brush the top with butter to prevent a scum from forming.
    One reason for constant stirring when making a cream sauce is to avoid . . . .

curdling in the milk

HOLLANDAISE SAUCE

76   Hollandaise sauce, of which there are several variations, is an emulsion of butter or margarine in lemon juice or vinegar. Egg yolks are used as an emulsifier.

The sauce thickens when the emulsion forms much as mayonnaise.

The emulsifier in hollandaise sauce is . . . .

egg yolks

●

77   Usually hollandaise is cooked over water, but a simpler method of making a small quantity is to place 120 grammes of cold butter in a sauce pan over low heat, add 2 eggs yolks, $\frac{1}{2}$ t. lemon juice, $\frac{1}{4}$ t. salt, and a pinch of pepper. Stir with a wooden spoon and continue to cook until the hollandaise reaches the desired consistency. It can be made even faster by using a blender.

An alternative method is to make a reduction of vinegar and crushed peppercorns. Add egg yolks and a few drops of water and cook over gentle heat whisking continuously until a sabayon is formed. Remove from heat and gradually whisk in melted butter.

If hollandaise separates or 'cracks' or is too thick, beat in hot water a little at a time. If too thin, add a teaspoon of lemon juice to a tablespoon of the sauce in a warm . bowl and whisk until thick. Then add the remaining sauce a little at a time while beating each new addition.

Sometimes broken hollandaise will not reform using this method. If this happens, add an egg yolk or a few drops of hot water or vinegar to a clean bowl and whip with a wire whisk while adding the broken hollandaise slowly.

To get even low heat, hollandaise may be made in a pan over water which is hot but not boiling.

What would happen if the heating water boils?

The yolks coagulate and there is no emulsion.

●

78   Hollandaise sauce is served hot over grilled or baked fish, vegetables, and eggs. Probably its most popular use in this country is as an accompaniment to cauliflower, asparagus, broccoli, salmon and turbot. It is part of the classical breakfast dish, Eggs Benedictine (English muffin, ham, poached egg covered with hollandaise). It is the most delicate of all sauces as regards handling for the reason that it cannot be heated over 82C (180F).

Knowing that it contains egg yolks, why can it not be heated over 82C (180F)?

The eggs will coagulate and become lumpy.

79   Hollandaise can be refrigerated and then put over very hot foods, to melt and form a sauce over the food. Sometimes, this is squeezed while still warm through a pastry tube onto a clean surface into a rosette form. These forms are chilled and used in place of spooned refrigerated hollandaise sauce over a hot item.

By being placed on top of a very hot piece of grilled fish just before being served.

How might this be used?

●

80   The more a hollandaise sauce is beaten the thicker it becomes. What happens if the hollandaise is heated to about 88C (190F)?

The eggs coagulate

●

81   Mousseline sauce, which is served on cooked fish, vegetables or with soufflés, is made using $\frac{2}{3}$ hollandaise or mayonnaise and $\frac{1}{3}$ whipped cream. It is often put over fish or meat for glazing under a grill. (See 40 in Fish and Shellfish Cookery.)

Yes, the mousseline is light and fluffy like the soufflé.

Would you use mousseline sauce rather than hollandaise on a soufflé?

●

TOMATO SAUCE

82   Another basic or mother sauce is the tomato sauce. It may be a neutral sauce or it may be made using a meat stock. It is basically tomato purée seasoned with vegetables and seasonings and thickened with a roux. It can be the basis of many secondary sauces such as creole sauce, Spanish sauce, barbecue sauce, Italian sauce, or Milanaise Sauce.

Many of the Spanish, Portuguese and Italian dishes use tomato paste as a sauce base. Probably the best known example of Italian sauce in this country is spaghetti sauce which of course uses tomatoes.

We have already mentioned that the most widely used of all tomato sauces for meat in the United States is . . . .

ketchup

83   To further clarify our understanding of the mother warm sauces, here is a little chart showing the French and English equivalent names and the colours.

French:	English:	Colour:
1) Béchamel	1) Cream	1) White
2) Velouté	2) Velouté (velvet)	2) Blond
3) Tomate	3) Tomato	3) Red
4) Espagnole	4) Brown	4) Brown
5) Hollandaise	5) Hollandaise (dutch style)	5) Yellow

What basic sauce would you expect to use with a poached fish dish?

Fish velouté

●

84   What basic sauce would you start with in making a sauce for braised beef?

Brown sauce or espagnole

●

85   If you wanted a basic sauce for vegetables that had no meat taste to it, had richness and tartness, which basic sauce would you use?

Hollandaise

●

86   To serve with ravioli or spaghetti, you need a red sauce to offset the whiteness of the pasta and a sauce which has some piquancy to it; which sauce would you choose?

Tomato

●

87   What is the mother sauce from which is derived each of the following popular sauces?

1. Mornay	a. Béchamel or cream
2. Bèarnaise	b. Hollandaise
3. Tartar	c. Mayonnaise
4. Bordelaise	d. Espagnole (brown)
5. Suprême	e. Velouté
6. Allemande	f. Tomato
7. Ketchup	
8. Burgundy	
9. Bercy for meat	

1 a., 2 b., 3 c.,
4 d., 5 e., 6 e.,
7 f., 8 d., 9 d.

SIMPLE BUTTER SAUCES

88 Maître d'hôtel butter is butter combined with lemon juice, parsley and a pinch of cayenne. It is usually rolled in damp grease-proof paper and put in a refrigerator to harden. Then cut in thick slices and served.

Beurre à la meunière, is the same as maître d'hôtel butter except that the butter is lightly browned. Then the lemon juice, parsley and cayenne are added and this mixture is poured or brushed over the food.

What is the difference between beurre à la meunière and maître d'hôtel butter?

Maître d'hôtel butter is prepared cold while à la meunière is lightly browned.

●

89 Melted butter is *clarified* by heating it, allowing the solids to settle to the bottom and skimming off the butter fat. As butter is further heated, it changes colour from brown to black. *Beurre noisette*, hazelnut butter, or brown butter is used as a sauce poured over fish and vegetables.

Beurre noisette, if browned further, becomes dark brown and is called *beurre noir*, or black butter. Black butter is usually combined with vinegar or lemon juice, and parsley and used for variety meats, vegetables and scrambled eggs. Capers may be added to black butter for certain dishes.

What is the difference between beurre noisette and beurre noir?

Beurre noir is browner or blacker than beurre noisette.

●

90 A little known fact about butter is that pure butter fat does not brown. Instead, it loses colour and turns white when heated.

Butter is composed of roughly 80 per cent butter fat, 16 per cent water, 2 per cent protein, and 2 per cent salt and minerals. It is the proteins and other solids which brown when butter is heated. The carotene, the yellow-colouring material, is lost with the application of heat.

A brown butter sauce can/cannot be made from pure butter fat.

cannot

91   *Beurre Polonaise* is another closely related butter sauce to à la meunière sauce. It is excellent for cauliflower, asparagus or broccoli and is topped with a chopped, hard-cooked egg. À la amandine is meunière butter to which sliced or slivered almonds have been added during browning.

What is the difference between beurre Polonaise and sauce à la meunière?

Chopped, hard-boiled egg is added to the polonaise sauce.

●

92   Amandine sauce is meunière + ...

slivered almonds

●

COMPOUNDED BUTTERS

93   Compounded butters are simple sauces, butter which has been softened and various ingredients added, such as chopped shrimp, anchovies, capers, garlic and other spices. Some recipes call for 50—50 mixtures. One of the best known compounded butters is maître d'hôtel butter, which is a stick of butter softened, to which is added a tablespoon of chopped parsley, salt, pepper and a tablespoon of lemon juice.

Maître d'hôtel butter is an example of a . . . .

compounded butter

●

94   A piece of butter to which anchovy paste has been added would be known as . . . .

anchovy butter

●

95   A compounded butter to which garlic has been added is known as . . . . butter, or beurre Provencale—or butter in the style of the province of Provence.

garlic

●

96   Some compounded butters are more complicated to make. Lobster butter, for example, according to

some recipes is made by crushing lobster shells, frying them in butter. The flavour of the shell passes into the butter which is skimmed off and used for adding flavour and red colour to other sauces. The coral (lobster eggs) are also added sometimes.

Would lobster butter be good served as a sauce itself?

Yes, it complements boiled lobster.

●

WELL KNOWN SAUCES FOR MEAT

97   What sauces go well with grilled meats? Music has its three B's—Bach, Beethoven and Brahms. It might be said that sauce cookery has its five B's— Bercy, Béarnaise, Bordelaise, Burgundy, and barbecue. The first four are as distinctly French as barbecue sauce is characteristically American.

The French 'B's' are more easily remembered if the name is related to a region in which they originated. Bercy is a section of Paris; Béarnaise refers to Bearn, a southwestern region of France; Bordelaise refers to the Bourdeaux area along the Atlantic coast and, of course, Burgundy to the Burgundy area in Eastern France. Bercy contains white wine; Bordelaise and Burgundy, red wine.

Sauce	Place of origin	
a. Burgundy	1.	1. Burgundy
b. Bordelaise	2.	2. Bordeaux
c. Bercy	3.	3. Paris
d. Béarnaise	4.	4. Bearn

●

98   Bercy has three variations: Bercy butter, Bercy for fish or chicken and Bercy for grilled meats. All are made with white wine, chopped shallots, butter and chopped parsley. For fish, a fish velouté is used; for chicken a chicken stock is the liquid; for grilled meats, meat glaze or bone marrow is added to the white wine. Bercy butter is about the same as the meat sauce. Bordelaise and Burgundy are almost the same. Both start with a demiglace sauce and contain shallots and chopped parsley.

Burgundy sauce quite naturally contains Burgundy wine, while Bordelaise uses a dry wine. In French, Burgundy sauce is sauce Bourguignonne.

The principal difference between a sauce Bourguignonne and a sauce Bordelaise is the fact that the Burgundy sauce uses Burgundy wine as a stock while the Bordelaise has . . . . wine.

Bordeaux

●

99 Sauce Béarnaise is a thicker variation of hollandaise to which is added tarragon vinegar, white wine, shallots, parsley and tarragon. It is a popular accompaniment to grilled steaks.

Barbecue sauce is anybody's tangy sauce with a hundred variations, but all based on tomatoes, onions and usually brown sugar.

The herb used in Béarnaise sauce to give it a distinctive flavour is . . . .

tarragon

●

100 Hollandaise sauce is usually served with salmon, turbot, vegetables, poached fish or eggs. What variation of hollandaise made thicker which includes tarragon vinegar is popular with grilled meats?

Béarnaise

●

101 Bercy sauce made with meat glaze goes well with what kind of food items?

Grilled meats

●

102 Bercy sauce is made using white wine while Burgundy sauce uses what kind of wine?

Burgundy, usually a red Burgundy

88

103   Barbecue sauce is used to 'barbecue' beef, pork, chicken or even fish. Is it necessary to cook out to barbecue food?

No, but the idea of barbecueing usually includes cooking outside with meat being grilled over an open fire. The sauce, however, is what gives food its 'barbecue' flavour. A smoke flavour adds to the barbecue flavour.

●

104   A thicker Hollandaise sauce + tarragon, vinegar, white wine and shallots = ... sauce.

Béarnaise

●

105   Demi-glace sauce + Burgundy wine, shallots, thyme, bayleaf and parsley = ... sauce.

Burgundy

●

106   Demi-glace sauce + Bordeaux wine, shallots, thyme, bayleaf and parsley = ... sauce.

Bordelaise

●

107   Velouté sauce + egg yolks and cream or Hollandaise, white wine, shallots and parsley = ... sauce.

Bercy, for fish

●

WELL KNOWN COLD SAUCES

108   Among the well-known basic cold sauces are those using a mayonnaise base or a French dressing base. Of the two, French dressing is simpler to make, being merely a combination of oil, salt, pepper, and

vinegar or lemon juice and French mustard. (two or three parts oil, one part liquid) Mayonnaise uses salad oil, vinegar, plus egg yolks, and the difficulty is holding the oil in a stable emulsion. The eggs are an emulsifier helping to hold the oil in the vinegar. The emulsion can be broken by overheating, by adding salts that precipitate the emulsion, by drying off the surface, by freezing—even jarring will cause a separation. Anything that destroys the film-forming properties of the emulsifying agent and lets the dispersed particles run together, destroys the emulsion. Mayonnaise and French dressing have the same ingredients except that mayonnaise contains . . . .

egg yolks

●

109   We see, then, that hollandaise and mayonnaise are similar in that egg yolks are used as an emulsifier in both. What ingredient is contained in mayonnaise which is not contained in hollandaise?

Salad oil is used in the mayonnaise and melted butter in the hollandaise.

●

110   *Salad dressings* are cold sauces poured over salads. Mayonnaise is often considered a dressing even though it is not poured.

Most dressings used in this country are variations of mayonnaise or basic French dressing. Both are considered basic sauces. There are many variations or secondary sauces made from these two sauces or dressings.

French dressing, we said, is simply vinegar and oil with salt, pepper and French mustard added.

Chiffonade dressing is French dressing plus eggs, onions, pickled beetroots and parsley.

Piquante dressing is the same as chiffonade plus catsup and dry mustard.

Vinaigrette starts as French to which is added chopped parsley, chives, capers, pickles and hard-cooked eggs.

What do these sauces—chiffonade, piquante, vinaigrette—have in common?

They all start as French dressing, oil and vinegar.

111   Mayonnaise is the base for these popular sauces
or dressings:
Tartare: mayonnaise with gherkins, capers and
parsley.
Thousand island: mayonnaise, chili sauce, chives,
ketchup, vinegar, pepper, paprika.
Russian: like thousand island, with chives, pickled
beetroots, parsley, olives, may contain caviar.
Sour cream, blue or Roquefort dressings are mayonnaise mixed with the name ingredient.
We see that with most salad dressings the base in
either mayonnaise or French dressing; the latter is
simply . . . . and . . . .

oil, vinegar,
French mustard

●

112   Of all the sauces which are used in the United
States, the two best known and most widely used are
ketchup and mayonnaise. Ketchup would be classified
as . . . . sauce under the French system but is
usually served cold instead of warm.

tomato

●

113   Another basic sauce is boiled dressing, thickened
with starch and sometimes eggs. It is used with cole
slaw, potato salad and, if sweetened and blended with
whipped cream, for fruit salad. It too is a basic sauce
or dressing, for many variations or secondary dressings
or sauces are derived from it. A cold sauce made from
this sauce for meat might be mustard sauce or horseradish sauce to be used with cold meat or sometimes with
hot meat such as boiled beef or roast cured ham.
    Name the three basic cold dressings.

Mayonnaise
French and boiled

●

114   Based on what you know about sauces in general,
how would you classify each of these in column 1 with
their characteristic listed in column 2:

Applesauce	( )	1). Acid, warm or cold
Fish velouté	( )	2) Warm, smooth
Chili sauce	( )	3) Piquant, warm or cold
Chocolate	( )	4) Sweet, warm or cold
French dressing	( )	5) Piquant, smooth, cold

1, 2, 3, 4, 5

115. Sauces are often *finished* with egg yolks and cream, sour cream, wine or butter. A finish is an ingredient added at the last moment to complete the flavour and texture. To finish a sauce is not the same as brushing the surface with a liquid or melted butter to prevent scum formation.

Would you boil a sauce after it has been finished?

No, the quality of the finish would be lost. The sauce is only brought to serving temperature

●

REVISION

1. Sauces are served with food for the purposes of complementing the food, adding a smoothness to some food, complementing the flavour of some food, providing acid contrast when needed, and also to do what to bland foods?

Provide piquancy or zest

●

2. Fish is often served à la meunière style, which means it is served with a butter sauce containing melted butter plus what other two ingredients?

Lemon juice and chopped parsley

●

3. A popular compounded butter often served with grilled meats is . . . .

maître d'hôtel butter

●

4. As butter continues to be heated, it turns brown (beurre noisette), later turns black or beurre . . . . . .

noir

●

5. What kind of velouté sauce would you expect to use with a fish or seafood item?

fish velouté

●

6. What kind of velouté would you expect to serve with chicken?

chicken velouté (made with chicken stock)

7. What are the ingredients of a roux?

50% fat, 50% flour by weight.

●

8. By adding cream to a chicken velouté, what kind of sauce is developed?

Supreme

●

9. What is the usual purpose of deglazing a cooking pan?

To soften the browned bits of hardened meat and juices for later use in a sauce or gravy.

●

10. What kind of flour should be used in making a sauce which will later be frozen?

Waxy maize which is less likely to break when frozen.

●

11. Would you use bread flour for making a roux?

Preferably not, it contains too much gluten.

●

12. What is a popular warm sauce derived from the mother sauce, hollandaise, which is often served with meat?

Béarnaise

●

13. The basic cream or white sauce is similar to what French sauce?

Béchamel

●

14. A popular meat sauce containing wine, and bone marrow, and which starts from a demi-glace sauce is . . . .

Bordelaise

15. The five warm mother sauces are béchamel, velouté, tomato, espagnole and .... (contains egg yolks).

Hollandaise

●

16. The French name for brown stock and espagnole which has been reduced by one-half or more to a gelatinous mass is ....

demi-glace

●

17. Which of the warm sauces cannot be heated above 82C (180F)?

Those containing egg yolks.

●

18. Give the common name to each of these sauces:

1. Espagnole ....
2. Béchamel ....
3. Tomate ....
4. Velouté ....
5. Hollandaise ....

1. Brown
2. Cream
3. Tomato
4. Velouté
5. Hollandaise

●

19. Why is a larger quantity of brown roux needed for a particular sauce than if white or blond roux is called for?

The browning process reduces the thickening property of the flour.

●

20. Flour or starch are the most widely used thickening agents in warm sauces. What else is used in thickening warm sauces?

Egg yolks.

●

21. Instead of making stocks for sauces, which requires hours of simmering time, what are widely used substitutes?

Prepared meat bases and gravies.

94

22. What is the basic mother sauce used to make Béarnaise sauce and mousseline sauce?

Hollandaise

●

23. What are the five B's in meat sauces?

Bercy, Bordelaise, Burgundy, Béarnaise, Barbecue.

●

24. Curdling of milk is caused by heat or by the addition of salt or . . . .

acid

●

25. What is a quick way of getting a beef stock?

Use a base, bouillon or bouillon cubes in water.

●

26. Velouté means what?

Velvety

●

27. Hollandaise is difficult to make because the butter must be held in . . . .

an emulsion, suspended in lemon juice or vinegar

●

28. Which kind of milk—homogenized or evaporated —gives the thicker, richer sauce?

evaporated

●

29. A fast way to correct a thin, warm sauce is to add . . . .

beurre manié

●

30. Is cornflour widely used in making warm meat sauces?

No

31. Why use waxy maize starch when making sauces which will be frozen?

Such sauces resist 'breaking'.

32. Can we brown butter using absolutely *pure* butter fat?

No, the solids in butter turn brown, not the fat.

33. Bordelaise and Burgundy sauces include red wine, Bercy uses . . . .

white wine

34. Barbecue sauce is fundamentally a . . . . sauce?

tomato

35. Can we hold hollandaise sauce for a few days at room temperature before serving?

No, about $1\frac{1}{2}$ hours is maximum.

36. True or False: Soup and gravy bases are sometimes used as substitutes for glace de viande and demi-glace.

True

37. Is it reasonable to add meat glaze to a sauce such as Burgundy?

Yes, meat glaze can be added to any brown sauce to give it added flavour and strength.

38. Would you serve a sauce made from a lamb or mutton stock with beef items?

No

39. Roux + chicken stock + cream = ... suprême
    sauce.

    ●

40. Cream sauce + cheese = ... sauce. cheese or Mornay

    ●

41. Cream sauce + chopped hard boiled egg =
    . . . . sauce. egg

    ●

42. Cream sauce + chopped or cubed meat, pimentos,
    green peppers, hard cooked egg yolks = ... à la King
    sauce.

    ●

43. Velouté + cream + egg yolks = ... Allemande
    sauce.

    ●

44. Just in case you have forgotten, what is the The velouté uses
    difference between a velouté and a béchamel sauce? chicken or fish stock
    as a liquid. When
    milk is the basic
    liquid used in a
    sauce, call it a
    béchamel or white
    sauce.

    ●

Soups

1 Although soups are not served as frequently as a first course as they used to be they are often a principal part of a light meal or can be a main course. Soups are liquids which can be very thin or quite thick depending upon what they contain and are classified according to their thickness or to the principle liquid or other ingredients they contain.

Here is one system of classification:

Consommés, clear soups prepared from beef, chicken or game stock; good stocks generously garnished with vegetables and rice or barley.

Cream soups, those thickened with a thin velouté, Bechamel or cream.

Bisques, heavy cream soups containing shellfish.

Purées, thickened with cooked vegetables or fish passed through a sieve or puréed by some other device such as a blender.

Chowders, thick soups or stews usually containing seafood, potatoes and milk or cream.

Potages, broths heavy with ingredients, such as chicken noodle or vegetable.

By definition, a cream soup is thickened by a . . . .

velouté, Béchamel or white sauce

●

2 A bisque contains . . . .

shellfish

●

3 Purées are thickened by food materials which have been . . . .

puréed, broken up into small particles

98

4 A chowder may be similar to a bisque but is likely
to contain potatoes and would probably not be thickened
with a . . . .

velouté, Béchamel
or white sauce

●

5 Basic soups are similar to basic or mother sauces
in that dozens of variations can be made from the
fundamental item. A basic brown stock is used in
making bouillons, French onion soup, vegetable beef
soup, or the popular Slavic soup, borsch.

Garnishes added to soups also change their character
and call for a new name. Escoffier lists 91 different
consommés, each slightly different because of a
particular garnish.

Soups are like sauces in that hundreds of variation
can be derived from . . . .

basic soups

●

6 Since cream soups contain milk or cream, there
is always the possibility that the milk will curdle.
Curdling, it is recalled, can be caused by high or extended heat or by the presence of excessive acid or salt.

A stable cream soup is made by cooking vegetables
gently in butter until soft, using a lid on the pan and
not allowing colouring, adding flour to make a roux
and then adding pulped vegetables and stock. This is
then blended into rich milk.

From the previous chapter we know that when we
add unbrowned roux to a white stock we have a
. . . .

velouté sauce

●

7 The hot velouté is added to the hot milk or cream,
not the milk to the velouté. As a matter of logic, why
is this important?

Acids or excessive
heat in the
velouté might
curdle the milk
since the milk
would be
'overwhelmed' by
the larger quantity
of velouté.

8   As a further precaution against curdling, milk can be thickened with starch before velouté is added. Starch acts to prevent separation of the casein in the milk (curdling).

The velouté and milk are blended only when needed for serving. Both the velouté and milk can be kept hot, but separately. They are blended in an amount required for a 20 to 30 minute serving period.

Cream soups are simple to make but safeguards must be taken to prevent . . . .   the milk from curdling

●

9   The finest of cream soups are finished with an egg yolk liaison. This mixture of one part egg yolk to three parts whipping cream is blended with a portion of the hot cream soup and the blend is stirred vigorously into the hot soup mixture. The soup is heated until the egg yolks thicken or coagulate but the soup is never boiled once the liaison has been added.

If soup containing the liaison of egg yolks and cream is boiled, the eggs might . . . .   curdle

●

10   An excellent finish for a cream soup is a liaison made of . . . . part egg yolks to . . . . parts of whipping cream.   one to three

●

11   Cream soups can also be made by making a white sauce and adding purée or other finely divided food, but the best way is to start with the heavy velouté sauce. Then add the main flavouring ingredient such as puréed asparagus or tomato purée. Half a litre of puréed food is the correct amount for $2\frac{1}{2}$ litres of velouté sauce. This is then thinned with 2 litres of milk.

Since soup may curdle if it stands too long in the steam table, we prepare it in batches to cover a 20 to 30 minute serving period.

We also avoid over-salting and to prevent over-heating may double pan the soup in the steam table.

An old batch of soup is not mixed with a new batch; the first is used completely before starting a fresh batch.

To avoid curdling in a cream soup make it as needed; don't mix an old batch with a new one, avoid over-heating, and over-..........

salting

12 A bisque, we have seen, is a cream soup including shellfish. We could serve a lobster bisque—but could we serve a tomato bisque?

Not and remain true to our definition since it contains no shellfish.

13 Purée soups are usually heavy but can be made light and served as a first course. Purées are made by one of two methods depending upon the ingredients used. Some ingredients have a natural thickening power and when items such as split peas, beans, mashed potatoes, or lentils are used in the soup no additional thickening is needed. Other soups, however, like purée of carrot or asparagus soup, must be further thickened by adding such items as cornflour, flour, or mashed potatoes.
    Would rice flour be a suitable thickener?

Yes, it contains starch and is frequently used to thicken soups.

14 We have seen that a chowder is a heavy soup usually including diced onions, potatoes, bacon or salt pork and seasoning. The word chowder means 'cooking kettle'.
    The main seasoning agent in chowders may be clams, lentils, corn, tuna fish, or tomato. The liquid in the chowder is usually thin, but the quantity of ingredients which are added makes the soup thick and heavy.
    What are the distinguishing ingredients of a chowder?

Diced potatoes, onions, bacon, salt pork combined with a principal seasoning agent.

15 The addition of starchy foods such as rice or macaroni contribute to the thickening of the soup. Chicken noodle soup, for example, is classified as thick. A French onion soup can be made heavy with onions and even heavier by the addition of a large crouton covered

with toasted Parmesan cheese. A gumbo soup is made heavy by the addition of shellfish, okra, tomatoes, and rice. Such heavy soups are frequently called potages or peasant soups.

Thickness or heaviness of a soup may depend both upon thickeners used and upon . . . .

the other ingredients added

●

16   Some soups are so heavy as to be more like stews than soups. Bouillabaise (literally 'low boil'), a delightful soup originated in Marseilles, is an example. It is made from six or seven types of fish caught in the Rhone River and in the Mediterranean. If the proper types of fish are not used along with the correct vegetables and seasonings, some authorities state that the bouillabaise is not of the true classic type.

Be that as it may, the soup ends up with so many ingredients that it could be called a stew rather than a soup.

Bouillabaise is a stew/soup.

Take your choice; served with hard bread and red wine, it can be a meal.

●

17   Another heavy soup is a petite marmite, named after the small earthenware casserole in which it is made. It contains a number of vegetables in a rich stock and is served either with a liberal piece of meat or fowl. Service is in the marmite pot. Henry IV of France was very fond of a chicken soup in which parts of the fowl were served. Was this a petite marmite?

Yes, when cooked in a marmite.

●

18   Mulligatawny, originated in India, literally means 'pepper water'. It is chicken broth with different vegetables and diced chicken meat. Raw grated apples and curry give it a distinctive flavour.

A traditional Canadian soup is habitant or pea soup. It contains yellow peas cooked with ham or salt pork until tender and then puréed. It is often served with corn bread.

Cock-a-leekie is a traditional Scotch soup.
Can you guess what is in cock-a-leekie?

Chicken and leeks.

102

19   A Spanish national soup is called olla podrida (literally 'smelly pot'), seasoned with saffron. The Chinese are great soup fans and favour very delicate ones which contain vegetables barely cooked in a light broth. Liver soup made from thinly sliced calves liver and water cress is a delicacy. Boiling hot rich stock, usually chicken stock, is poured over thinly sliced liver to cook it and wilt the water cress. The soup is served immediately and frequently a bit of sesame oil is passed around for seasoning.

True or False: It should not be too difficult to select a 'national' soup when planning a menu for a particular national group.

True

●

20   We usually think of soups as being served hot but there are many cold ones as well. Jellied consommé may contain enough gelatine to gel when cooled or gelatine can be added. Jellied turtle soup served on a bed of ice and accompanied by a slice of lemon is a prestige first course for a simple luncheon.

Vichyssoise is a cream of potato soup which is served cold and garnished with chopped chives. Borsch may be served chilled and Scandinavians love a cold fruit soup which contains a quantity of cooked dried fruits.

The Spanish gazpacho is a refreshing whole tomato soup served chilled.

Does cold consommé need the addition of gelatine to make it gel?

Not always

●

21   Some clear soups may be clarified by chilling. The flocculent materials settle to the bottom and the stock or clear soup may be decanted, leaving the solids on the bottom.

A simple way to clarify soup is to chill and . . . .

decant

●

22   To obtain maximum clarity the process of clarification is more complicated. Egg whites, raw minced lean beef, and a mirepoix, bouquet garni and sometimes

browned onions are put in the stock or broth. As the eggs and meat coagulate, they carry with them the solid materials in the stock.

The mixture can be stirred until it becomes warm but once coagulation has started further stirring disturbs the clarification process.

The eggs and meat coagulate and rise to the top carrying with them the bouquet garni, mirepoix and solid materials in the stock which form a solid mass called a raft.

After several hours of gentle simmering, the clear liquid is strained from the pot through a tap in the bottom of the pot. To further insure clarity, the stock can be strained through layers of muslin.

Clarification of stock by means of coagulated egg whites and raw minced beef takes place when the clarifying ingredients rise to the surface to form a ....

raft

●

23   Because of the progress of the food technology, soup bases are available on the market which can be used for making excellent soups. The bases eliminate much labour, reduce costs and mess in the kitchen. Of course, if meat, fish, and poultry bones and other materials for making stock are on hand, they should be used. A base can be added to heighten the flavour.

Soup bases list their ingredients according to the amount present, from the most to the least. Select bases that list as principle ingredients the essence of the flavour desired. In the United States if the label carries a circled stamp which states that the product was inspected and passed as wholesome by the Federal government, it means that the base contains so much meat or chicken that it is classed as meat or chicken and must undergo Federal inspection before it can be shipped interstate. This is another indication of quality.

A label on a soup base lists the ingredients as follows: 'salt, monosodium glutamate, chicken fat, essence of chicken, colouring, spices'. Is this chicken base of high quality?

Not especially since there is more salt than any other ingredient. Some soup bases contain as much as 25% salt. At $37\frac{1}{2}$p a kilo the salt is expensive.

REVISION

1. What kind of a soup would logically be served with a heavy meal?

   A light one

2. A consommé is a . . . . soup.

   clear

3. A bisque is a heavy cream soup which includes . . . .

   shellfish

4. A liaison which is suitable for finishing a cream soup is made from . . . .

   egg yolks and cream

5. Blending a velouté soup base with hot milk to make a cream soup we add the base to the milk, not the milk to the base, to avoid . . . .

   curdling

6. A potage or peasant soup is a heavy/light soup.

   heavy

7. Purée soups are thickened by their ingredients or by added . . . .

   starch thickeners

8. Is it necessary to add gelatine to consommé to produce a jellied consommé?

   Not if the consommé has enough of its own natural gelatine in it.

9. A wide variety of consommés can be made by merely varying the . . . .

garnish used

●

10. Soups can be clarified by chilling and decanting or with the use of . . . .

egg whites and lean beef minced

●

11. Matching:
   1. chowder
   2. bouillabaise
   3. cock-a-leekie
   4. mulligatawny
   5. olla podrida

   a. contains a purée of black beans
   b. identified by the presence of apples and curry powder
   c. a Scottish soup
   d. a famous French seafood stew or soup
   e. brought to American continent by French fishermen

   Ans: 1. e
        2. d
        3. c
        4. b
        5. a

Egg Cookery

1   Eggs are cooked in a variety of ways: soft, medium and hard cooked in water, pan fried, broiled, baked, poached, scrambled, and made into omelets, custards and soufflés. They are used as a raising agent for cakes, as a principal ingredient of choux paste, as an emulsifying agent to hold oil in emulsion as in mayonnaise and salad dressings and for binding such items as meat loaves and breadcrumbing. They are used to add colour and sheen on baked dough products and as coating material for deep fried foods. Eggs contain all ten of the essential amino acids necessary for the growth and well being of the human child (nine are needed for human adults).

Let's start with the fresh egg, eggs which are under twenty-nine days old. The egg has considerable liquid in it, but the older it gets, the more moisture it loses. As it ages some of the liquids are lost and the air space inside the egg enlarges. It would follow that one way to test an egg's freshness is to place it in water. The old egg will float/sink.

float

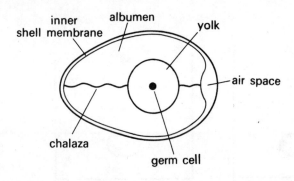

The structure of an egg.

2　As with so many foods, quality standards should be set with a purpose in mind. Fresh eggs are necessary for a satisfactory breakfast egg; however, old eggs which are not spoiled are satisfactory for use in baked items, and stored, dried or frozen eggs develop a greater volume of foam when beaten. Quality standards for foods should be set in accordance with the . . . . to which they will be put.

use

•

3　As an egg ages, it becomes more alkaline. Alkalinity favours the development of sulphides which are dark in colour and strong tasting. The chances for formation of sulphides can be reduced by using fresh eggs or by adding an acid ingredient such as cream of tartar, vinegar, or lemon.

The formation of sulphides, compounds dark in colour and strong tasting, is favoured by an acid/ alkaline condition.

alkaline

•

4　So called hard boiled eggs (cooked in the shell in water) should never be boiled. Rather simmer them in water, between 85 and 91C (185—195F). If boiled or cooked too long the protein toughens and a greenish or purplish ring forms around the yolk.

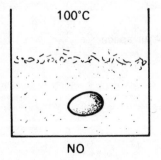

NO

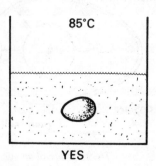

YES

To cook eggs in the shell simmer:

Soft boiled eggs 3 to 5 minutes.
Hard boiled eggs about 10 minutes.

Boiling eggs does what to the protein?

Rubberizes it.

4a   If high or long temperatures are used to cook eggs in the shell or scrambled eggs, iron in the yolk and sulphur compounds in the white are released to form ferrous sulphide. It is seen as the blackish or purple ring around the yolk or as darkened scrambled eggs.
   To avoid the dark ring around the yolk in the 'boiled' egg, simmer rather than boil. When the egg is done plunge it into cold water. Why?

To stop further cooking and release the pressure inside the egg which brings on the colouration.

5   A good practice is to serve eggs as soon as possible after cooking. Extended cooking or high heat also toughen eggs. What two rules then would you observe in cooking eggs?

Short time cooking and low temperature cookery with the exception of omelets.

6   The pan used to fry eggs should have a bottom diameter of about six inches if two eggs are to be fried in it, less if a single egg is to be fried. Condition egg pans by putting about one-eighth of an inch of fat onto the bottom and covering it with salt. Heat the pan until the fat almost smokes, then scour the bottom with a cloth or a wad of paper. Repeat this process until a smooth surface is built up on the bottom of the pan. Once the pan is conditioned, it would consequently follow that such pans should/should not be washed.

Should not. They should be wiped clean with a soft cloth and set aside for use only in egg cooking. Teflon coated frying pans of course are not so conditioned.

7   *Clarified butter*, butter from which the butter fat is removed by skimming or pouring it off when the butter is heated, is often used for egg cooking as it does not burn as quickly as does regular butter. When milk solids and salt have been removed from the butter, it is said to be . . . .

clarified.

8 What is the advantage of using clarified butter for pan frying?

It does not burn or smoke as quickly when the milk solids have been removed. Vegetable oil is often mixed with butter to achieve the same purpose.

●

9 To fry eggs, heat one to two tablespoons of fat in the pan. Break the eggs and put them in a saucer, then slide them into the pan so that they will retain their shape. Use low heat and pan fry for three to four minutes. Whole eggs coagulate (cook to firmness) when they reach 65 to 70C (149—158F). We have learned in previous sections that high protein foods such as cheese, eggs or meat . . . . when high heat is applied to them.

toughen

●

10 During the frying, the eggs can be basted (fat spooned over cooking food), the pan may be covered, or the eggs may be turned over according to the preference. Basting is merely a process of spooning . . . . over cooking food.

hot fat

●

11 A tender fried egg, called country style, is made by frying until about half done at which time about one-half teaspoon of water is added for each egg. The pan is covered. The water changes to steam, cooking the egg, keeping it tender and coating the egg. A tight cover placed over fried eggs can also achieve the same results. When fried eggs are fried in a manner that gives a soft, white coating over the eggs, the eggs are called . . . .

country style

12   Four common faults are encountered in frying eggs:

1. Temperatures are so high that the bottom and the edge of the egg is browned and the egg is tough.
2. Temperatures are so low that the egg white spreads.
3. There is so much fat that the egg is greasy.
4. There is too little fat so that the egg sticks to the pan.

Would you want to see a low, spread-out fried egg on a breakfast plate or an egg in which the yolk stands high and the white is tightly bunched around the yolk?

The latter

●

13   To reduce the tendency of an egg to spread out in the frying pan, heat the pan fairly hot. The hot fat coagulates the whites quickly. Having firmed the white you would then raise/lower the heat.

lower to prevent toughening

●

14   Since eggs are delicate in flavour, it would follow that unless another fat flavour such as had with bacon fat is desired, only what kind of fats should be used in frying them?

Bland or neutral; butter is preferred when cost is not a factor.

●

15   A variation of frying eggs is to broil them. When the fat is just hot enough to sizzle a drop of water, eggs are slipped into an egg dish and cooked on top of the stove until the edges turn white, which requires about a minute. The dish is then placed under a broiler for about 2 to 4 minutes. An egg broiled in this manner may be called *shirred*. The only difference between broiling and frying is that the heat source in the final step of broiling comes from . . . . instead of from below the dish. In European cookery this method is known as oeuf sur le plat (egg dish).

above

16   Scrambled eggs are prepared by thoroughly mixing the eggs, seasoning them with salt and pepper, adding them to a little butter melted in a thick bottomed pan. Then cooking slowly stirring continuously with a wooden spoon until lightly set. They may then be finished with butter or cream.

Scrambled eggs should be cooked quickly/slowly?   slowly

●

17   If scrambled eggs have to be held—for example, on a buffet breakfast table—mix the eggs with water, milk or cream, one tablespoon for each egg (a standard measuring cup for sixteen eggs). They are then cooked to a soft stage and held at between 54 and 60C (130–140F). 54C (130F) is the lowest temperature one can use without encouraging bacteria growth.

The added liquid quite logically keeps eggs from . . . . out.   drying

●

18   To hold scrambled eggs in a steam table, the eggs should be double panned, the pan holding the eggs set into an outer pan partially filled with water. Or, they can be held in a heavy earthenware dish. Both methods keep the eggs warm, minimize further cooking, and reduce the tendency to develop off-flavours and off-colours.

The purpose of the thick-walled utensil or double pan for holding scrambled eggs is to reduce/increase the rapid heat flow into the eggs.   reduce

●

19   To poach eggs fill a deep pan with about $2\frac{1}{2}$ inches of water, add 1 T of salt and 2 T of vinegar per gallon of water. The vinegar, an acid, helps to set the egg white and prevent it from spreading. Acid also makes eggs more tender, whites whiter.

A poached egg must be fresh or it will spread, even though vinegar is used. Vinegar acts to set the . . . . and keep them from running.

Both salt and vinegar help to coagulate the egg as soon as it enters the poaching liquid, so that it retain a better shape.   egg whites or egg protein

112

20   To help eggs hold their shape in poaching, break each egg into a sauce dish and slip it into the water quickly at the surface at the side of the pan, not the centre. Another way to achieve the same result is to stir the water so that it forms a whirlpool, sliding the egg into the whirlpool. Is it possible to poach a number of eggs at one time, since each must be dropped in one at a time?

Yes, they can be poached together even though introduced singly. Poach about 16 eggs to a gallon of water.

●

21   A close relative to the poached egg is the *coddled* egg. Eggs are coddled in the shell. They are cooked by pouring boiling water over the eggs, one pint of boiling water to each egg. The eggs are then covered and held in a warm place until cooked (6 to 10 minutes for firm yolks, pleasantly soft whites.)

Coddled eggs are very tender eggs. As with all eggs cooked in quantity, they should be slightly undercooked since the cooking continues even after the source of heat has been removed.

Coddled eggs are the same as poached eggs except that in poaching, eggs are taken from the shell and placed in water, and the water is brought to a boil, whereas in coddling boiling water is . . . .

Poured over the eggs in their shells

●

22   Cooking eggs *en cocotte* is similar to poaching eggs except that the eggs are poached while in ramekins or other small porcelain or earthenware dishes. The dishes are buttered, the eggs placed in them and both placed in a water bath (bain Marie) for about 2—3 minutes. Eggs *en cocotte* are actually cooked by . . . . . . , but the eggs are not in direct contact with the water.

poaching

●

23   *Baked or shirred* eggs are cooked in shallow baking dishes in an oven at a 163C (325F) temperature. Baking takes about 12 to 18 minutes depending upon the firmness desired in the eggs. Shirred eggs, then, are cooked using what cooking method?

Baking

OMELETS

24   Omelets are similar to scrambled eggs except that they form a solid sheet of coagulated eggs which are folded and often filled with herbs, jams, mushrooms, ham, cheese or other ingredients.

Methods for making omelets vary. Some people like their omelets well done, some just done, still others think they should be runny. Some use high heat in cooking; others comparatively low heat. High heat is usually used.

Omelets made from three eggs are considered a normal portion. A quarter of a teaspoon of salt and a teaspoon of water are added to the eggs and they are well mixed. One to three tablespoons of butter and vegetable oil are heated in an omelet pan until it begins to foam or bubble. The eggs are added and stirred until the bottom layer sets. Then only the top layer is stirred or the coagulated bottom is raised and the pan tilted or shaken to allow the uncooked eggs to reach the surface of the pan and coagulate. Any filling to be used is then added.

The omelet is folded over the filling and allowed to set for a few seconds, then slid or rolled out of the pan after being jarred loose or freed from the pan with a fork or spatula.

If high heat is used the omelet is cooked within a half to one minute.

Omelets are like scrambled eggs except that instead of being an aggregate of pieces of lightly coagulated egg the omelet is made into . . . .

a solid sheet or mass of lightly coagulated eggs, often filled.

●

25   French omelets with sweet fillings may be dusted with icing sugar and burned lightly with a hot metal rod. Marks are left similar to grid marks on a broiled steak.

Is this 'burning' step necessary?

Yes, if the dish is to have its traditional slightly caramelized flavour.

26   When new, omelet pans, like new pans and griddles are seasoned in the manner described for pans, then never washed again.

The seasoning acts to seal the surface and prevent food from sticking to the pan.

Does not washing omelet pans present a health hazard?

No, since the pans are wiped dry and sterilized with high heat before eggs are placed in the pan.

●

27   Eggs continue to cook after removal from the heat. It follows, then, that they should be slightly over/under cooked when taken from the range.

under

●

28   A puffy or soufflé omelet is made by beating the yolks and whites separately to a soft foam in which the tips of the foam fall or bend over when peaked. It is then started in a pan with fat the same way as the usual omelet, but it is finished in an oven at 163C (325F). In baking, the omelet becomes puffy or souffleéd. The omelet is baked until a knife inserted into the centre comes out clean. This usually requires twelve to fifteen minutes.

Puffy omelets are different from the usual omelet in that they acquire the puffed quality because the eggs are beaten to a soft . . . .

foam

●

29   The omelet made from well mixed eggs (not beaten to a foam) is called a French omelet. Another name for the other type or puffy omelet is . . . .

soufflé

115

SOUFFLÉS

30   *Soufflés* are similar to puffy, or foamy, omelets except that they have a starch-thickened sauce base— usually of flour, butter and milk—and other food such as grated cheese, vegetable pulp, or ground meats or fruits added for flavour. The word 'soufflé' means puffed. The proportion of the egg is lower than in an omelet. Soufflés can be baked or steamed. (Turn to the chapter on sauces for more on starch-thickened sauces.) The white sauce and other ingredients are prepared separately.

The casserole in which soufflés are baked is buttered to prevent the soufflé from sticking. If the soufflés are sweetened, they are served as desserts.

To make a soufflé the eggs are separated and added to the white sauce or starch thickened mixture. The whites are beaten to a soft foam before being folded into the rest of the materials. Egg whites whip more quickly and produce more volume if brought to room temperature (removed from refrigerator half an hour before beating). Essentially, a soufflé is the same as a puffy omelet except that a soufflé also contains a . . . . and other ingredients.

sauce.
Another way to think of a soufflé is to define it as a white sauce which is 'lightened' with egg whites. Fairly small pans are used; otherwise the sheer mass of it in a large container would prevent proper rising.

●

31   Soufflés are baked in a 149C (300F) oven and come out dry and stable. At higher temperatures the casserole must be placed in water to slow down heat transfer through the casserole.

After baking, soufflés should be left a few minutes at the oven entrance with the door open to stabilize them and guard against sudden collapse.

What is the recommended oven temperature for soufflés?

149 C (300 F)

32   Soufflés must be served soon for it is only a matter of time before they collapse. What holds them up?

The air in the egg whites, which eventually escapes.

33   Dessert soufflés such as those using strawberries, chocolate and liqueurs can be sprinkled with icing sugar about two minutes before removing from the oven.

The sugar caramelizes and adds to the flavour.

Quite logically dessert soufflés are . . . . than the standard soufflé.

sweeter

●

34   Be sure in making a soufflé or puffy omelet that the egg whites are beaten to a point at which they turn over when peaked. If overbeaten to where the foam is dull and brittle and the foam can be cut into rigid parts, the whites will not extend further when cooked.

The whites are folded into the sauce and egg yolks, that is they are mixed slowly with a spatula or whip using a ferris wheel motion.

Why are not the whites beaten into the sauce and yolks?

The whites would lose their foam which contains the air needed to puff the soufflé.

BEATEN EGG WHITES

35   At this point we should examine the how and why of beating egg whites. Egg whites are beaten or whipped to increase their volume and used for meringue toppings for pies and other desserts in a number of other recipes. The whipped eggs can incorporate several times their weight of flour and sugar and are basic to most cakes.

With the application of heat, the eggs firm and provide volume and 'lightness' to the product. The reason egg whites increases in volume when whipped is that they are so high in the proteins (about 11%, the rest mostly water). The proteins form tiny filaments and stretch on beating, incorporate air in tiny sacs or bubbles, then set to form a fairly stable puffed-up structure expanding to seven times its bulk. When baked the proteins further coagulate and firm, forming soufflé, foams, and meringues and provide volume for a number of items.

What substance in eggs makes it possible for them to stretch, coagulate and multiply in volume?

•

The egg proteins

36   It stands to reason that if the foam formed by stretching the proteins are ruptured or otherwise do not remain stable, the air which is incorporated in the foam will escape and the foam will do what?

Collapse

●

37   Particular conditions favour the maximum development of foam and of its stability. Oddly enough fresh eggs are too viscous and non-homogeneous to foam well. Eggs one to three days old, or good quality eggs that have been frozen or dried, are less viscous and are more homogeneous, therefore produce greater . . . . when beaten.

volume, quantity

●

38   Another condition which favours foam development and stability is a slightly acid condition in the egg white. The acid denatures the egg protein and makes it more extensible so it makes a better and more stable foam. An acid/alkaline added to an egg makes it more extensible which assists in creating a more . . . . and . . . . foam.

acid; stable and better

●

39   Various acids are added, but cream of tartar usually gives the best results. If moisture is desired in addition to acidity, lemon juice or vinegar are used. About $\frac{1}{8}$ teaspoon of cream of tartar added for every three egg whites is about right for obtaining the desired acidity.

The reason cream of tartar is added to egg whites when whipping them is to . . . . the volume of whipped eggs and provide greater . . . . in them.

increase, stability

●

40   When a sweet foam is wanted, sugar is added to the eggs. The sugar strengthens the foam and reduces the possibility of overbeating the eggs. The cream of tartar is added to the liquid eggs, the sugar is added gradually during the beating process. Ordinarily one tablespoon of sugar is added for each white but for meringue toppings, meringues and for baked Alaskas

where a stiffer, more stable foam is needed, two table-spoons of fine or powdered sugar is added for each white. Sugar adds sweetness, strength and . . . . to beaten egg whites.

stability

●

41   The temperature at which the eggs are at the start of beating also affects foam development. Contrary to what might be imagined, the eggs should be at room temperature or above for best results. In fact, one variation of Swiss meringue is beaten over boiling water at the start, later finished at medium or high speed until stiff.

True or False: Fresh eggs at refrigerator temperature produce the highest volume, most stable foam.

False in each case

●

42   Another odd phenomenon that occurs with egg whites is that the presence of even a trace of fat such as is present in milk or egg yolks inhibits foam production. This means that if a piece of yolk is left in the whites it should be removed. Suppose you were making an angel food cake and the egg whites failed to whip, what would you suspect?

An unclean bowl or whisk that has a thin film of grease remaining on it.

●

43   In commercial bakeries stabilizers are added to egg whites to provide added stability. Even with the sugar added to act as a stabilizer in making a foam, it is possible to overbeat so that the filaments of protein are over extended and collapse when baked.

As beating progresses the eggs pass through three stages: (1) soft foam in which the peaks bend; this is used for sponge or angel food cakes, soft meringues, soufflés and foamy omelets; (2) a second stage where the foam becomes stiff but is still moist and glossy and forms peaks which stand once formed. Stiff foam is used for frostings, hard meringues and other bakery items. (3) The last stage is when the foam is overbeaten, is dry, dull and rigid. This foam has no use in cooking.

Egg whites which are very stiff, dry and brittle are . . . .

overbeaten

44   Though it is possible to overbeat eggs, failure also results from underbeating. Sitting the finished foam on top of a pie or other food which is cold is another mistake. Underbeating results in a part of the water separating from the foam and forming a runny substance at the bottom. The same thing is likely to happen when a meringue is placed on a cold food.

Underbeating of egg whites results in a watery/dry product.

watery

●

45   Eggs are likely to contain the Salmonella germ and precautions must be taken to destroy it with heat. Formerly meringues were dried rather than heated— which did not kill Salmonella present. Meringues can be cooked in a 218C (425F) oven in about six minutes or in a 163C (325F) oven in 20 to 25 minutes. If a temperature lower than 163C (325F) is used, meringue is likely to leak fluid, shrink excessively and toughen. Thinking about Salmonella would it be wise to thaw frozen eggs to room temperature and hold them for any length of time?

No, any Salmonella present would multiply.

●

46   We see that to strengthen egg white foam, commercial stabilizers are added and also sugar, and what acid?

Cream of tartar

CUSTARDS

47   True custards consist of only milk, eggs, sugar and flavouring. No starchy agent is added. A baked custard is allowed to coagulate without stirring. It thus forms a firm clabber or firm solid. It must contain enough eggs to produce a firm mass, particularly if it is to be turned out of a mould for serving. Both custards, soft and firm,

should be cooked in a container of water to prevent overheating. For a firm custard heat the milk to about 66C (150F), then add this to a mixture of sugar, eggs, and flavouring.

An oven temperature of about 177C (350F) is used for baking custard, but if the temperature of the custard itself exceeds 85C (185F), the custard is likely to contain holes, be watery, and have a concave top surface.

What is the difference between a custard and a soufflé?

Egg whites are not beaten separately in a custard. Custard contains only milk, eggs, sugar and flavouring; a soufflé has a starch-thickened paste and other ingredients.

●

48   When raw, eggs bind their water in loosely; as heat is applied and coagulation sets in, the water is bound in tightly and the egg becomes firm. Whole eggs coagulate at about 69C (156F). When sugar and milk is added to eggs, as for a custard, the coagulation temperature rises to about 79—85C (175—185F).

Sugar added to a custard mixture raises/lowers the coagulation temperature.

raises

●

48a   Custards made with egg whites thicken at a lower temperature than those made with whole eggs. Egg yolk custards have the highest thickening temperature, are more firm and of superior quality.

True or False: The thickening temperature of an egg custard depends upon the ingredients used.

True

●

48b   Custards cooked rapidly thicken at about 87C (189F) and curdle at about 90C (194F). Custards cooked slowly gel at about 80C (176F) and curdle at about 87C (189F).

If you want a greater margin of error to avoid curdling of eggs in custards, cook them slowly/quickly.

slowly

E

49 Test to see if a custard is cooked by inserting a stainless steel knife at the edge of the custard. If done, the knife will come out clean.

Why not test in the centre of the custard?

The centre continues to cook after removal from heat. Experienced cooks test by shaking the pan and noting the firmness of the custard.

●

49a Once a custard is cooked, stop the cooking process by placing it in a cool spot or setting it in a pan of cold water. If a custard is cooked at a temperature which is too high, syneresis occurs. This is the separation of the liquid from the gel, caused by contraction of the proteins.

Syneresis in a gel product such as custard is seen as . . . .

moisture escaping from the gel, or weeping

●

49b Non-fat dry milk makes a much less expensive custard but the flavour is not usually preferred as compared with the use of whole milk. Why?

The fat of the whole milk adds smoothness and flavour.

●

50 If we want to add flour, cornflour or other starches to a custard, should we first cook the starch before adding it to the custard? (Remember that starches only complete their thickening at over 93C (200F)).

Yes, the starches should be cooked first for about ten minutes. Their final cooking temperature is too high for the eggs.

PUDDINGS AND CREAMS

51 A thickened mixture of cornflour, milk, sugar and flavouring is called a blancmange or cornflour pudding. If eggs are added to this mixture, the pudding is called a cream pudding. Adding eggs to a cornflour pudding makes the pudding a . . . . pudding.

cream

52   When a cream or cornflour pudding is made with a large amount of sugar, withhold part of the sugar until the starch and eggs are cooked. Too much sugar interferes with the thickening of the eggs and starch.

We see then that the coagulation of eggs is affected not only by temperature but can be affected by . . . . and . . . . as well.

sugar, starch

53   Bavarian creams (Bavarois) are cornflour or cream puddings made light by gelatine, whipped cream, beaten eggs, or other ingredients. Various flavours and garnishes are added.

Originally Bavarian creams were desserts bound together with clarified isinglass, the predecessor of gelatine.

What is a Bavarian (Bavarois)?

A light, rich pudding set with gelatine and made tight by eggs or whipping cream.

54   In making a Bavarian, gelatine may be added to the cornflour or cream pudding and beaten egg whites are then folded in.

The egg whites are beaten at moderate speed until they foam. Then $\frac{1}{4}$ teaspoon of cream of tartar is added for each 5 whites. The cream of tartar denatures the whites and gives a better foam. One tablespoon of sugar is also added to give stability and to add sweetening. The rough edges of the sugar carry small particles of air into the foam.

To give beaten egg whites a more stable foam two ingredients are added: . . . . and . . . .

sugar, cream of tartar

55   Cream of tartar tenderizes the . . . . of the egg; sugar carries additional . . . . into the foam.

protein, air

56 Adding the sugar to egg whites also acts to buffer them from overbeating.

Overbeating is less/more of a problem when beating egg whites if sugar is added.

less

●

57 Whipped cream may also be folded into Bavarian creams. Use non-homogenized cream with a butterfat content of at least 30%. To speed the whipping process, have the cream at 4C (40F), chill the whip and the bowl in which the cream is to be whipped. If the kitchen is hot set the whipping bowl on ice.

Whipping cream can be whipped quicker if the cream, the whip and the whipping bowl are all . . . .

pre-chilled

●

58 We see then that Bavarian creams are cold desserts, a mixture of a starch-thickened pudding, gelatine, beaten egg whites and . . . .

whipped cream

●

59 A Spanish cream is a stirred custard set firm with gelatine. To make, add hot milk and sugar to egg yolks slowly. If high heat is used or too much of any ingredient is added at one time—or if the yolks are overbeaten—they become granular or curdled. Stir until the product is like thick rich cream. Remove from the heat and add gelatine. Chill to firm.

To prevent curdling of stirred custards, use low heat, and add other ingredients gradually/quickly, stirring them as added.

gradually

●

60 The custard for Spanish creams is ready when it thickens on the stirring spoon, a temperature of about 77—85C (170—185F). To avoid higher temperatures the cooking pan is moved on and off the heat source as necessary.

Gelatine is stirred in until dissolved. To speed the setting of the gel put the preparation pan on ice.

The cooking of custards should be stopped when they reach 77—85C (170—185F), or when the custard does what?

Coats the stirring spoon.

●

61 *Zabaglione* or *Sabayon* (its French name) is a dessert of Italian origin made with egg yolks, sugar and wine (usually marsala).

Knowing the ingredients of this dessert what do you know about how it will have to be cooked?

The egg yolks and wine must be cooked over water and stirred constantly.

●

62 *Quiches* are custards baked in a pastry case. Quiche Lorraine, originated in the Lorraine region of France, is the best known of the quiches and contains eggs, milk, Swiss cheese, bacon and onion. Variations of quiche contain ham, spinach and other ingredients.

Quiche is made in either a pie dough or tart shell but sometimes a puff paste lining is used. Quiches are used either as an appetizer or an entrée.

Would it be reasonable to add such foods as lobster, crab meat or clams to a basic quiche mixture?

Yes, lobster quiche, crab quiche and other similar quiches are made.

●

62a Pastry shells for quiches can be baked separately. If not, bake for 3 to 4 minutes in a hot oven, or until the pastry is lightly set. Why?

So that it will not soak up the custard mixture and make the pastry soggy.

OTHER EGG ITEMS

63 *Crêpes* are thin pancakes made from flour, sugar, milk, various other ingredients and a high quantity of eggs. No baking powder is added to them as in American style pancakes. Crêpes are popular both as desserts and

as entrées. For extra light crêpes, the eggs are separated and yolks mixed with the dry ingredients. Sometimes a little water is added to thin the batter and make the crêpes even thinner. The egg whites are beaten until stiff, then added after the melted butter.

One of the better known crêpes is Crêpes Suzette, usually made at the table using a rechaud or chafing dish. The sauce used on them contains orange rind and juice, Grand Marnier (an orange liqueur) and cognac. The cognac is flamed just before serving the crêpes.

What is the difference between crêpes and American pancakes?

American pancakes contain a raising agent; therefore are thicker than crêpes.

●

64   After mixing, crêpe batter should be allowed to stand in the refrigerator for a half hour. This helps bind it, making the finished crêpes less likely to fall apart. It is then cooked in a well-seasoned pan which has been greased with a few drops of salad oil. A small quantity of batter is poured in the pan and the pan tilted so that the bottom is covered. When the crêpe is brown on the bottom, slide it out and over. Would adding butter to the batter reduce the likelihood of the crêpe sticking to the bottom of the pan?

Yes, but the pan must be absolutely free of bits of already cooked crêpes. Teflon coated pans make crêpe cooking easier.

●

65   Many *fondues* contain eggs, especially that of Geneva which is made of egg yolks and cheese. Some fondues are baked custards containing parts of bread and closely resemble the soufflé.

The cheese fondue probably originated in Switzerland. In its basic form, it is aged Swiss cheese melted in white wine. The wooden or earthenware bowl in which it is served is rubbed with garlic and kirsch (a cherry brandy) added just before the fondue is served. It is then picked up on chunks of bread for eating. Dry white wine is an accompaniment.

Cheese, like eggs, is high in protein. If a cheese fondue separates (become stringy and oily) what is likely to have happened?

The protein coagulated. You cooked the fondue too long or used an excessive temperature in cooking it.

66   Eggs are basic to many baked desserts including all those using sweet dough, puff paste, sponge or Genoise cake (Genoise is a rich sponge cake). They are also used in mousses (frozen ice cream and whipped cream mixtures) and in biscuit glacé, similar to mousses.

Angel food cake is baked egg whites, sugar and cake flour.

Pastry cream is nothing but egg yolks, milk, sugar, flour and cornflour. A rich vanilla custard used as a base for sweet soufflés and pastries.

When we think of baked desserts we usually think of flour, sugar, shortening, and . . . .

eggs

●

REVISION

1. Why does an egg toughen when exposed to high heat?

Because of its high protein content.

●

2. Why does an old egg float in water?

Gas replaces evaporated liquid within the eggs.

●

3. Is *hard boiling* of eggs recommended?

No, simmering is desirable.

●

4. Why do a few drops of water added to frying eggs that have been covered make for a tender fried egg?

The water changes to steam, keeps the egg moist and tender.

●

5. A soufflé omelet is cooked differently from a regular omelet in that a soufflé omelet is finished by . . . . . .

baking

6. Clarified butter is prepared by heating butter, then pouring off the butterfat while . . . . settle on the bottom.

solids

●

7. Soufflé means . . . .

puffed

●

8. Are eggs ever prepared by broiling?

Yes

●

9. Is a baked egg the same as a shirred egg?

Yes

●

10. True or False: Eggs are beaten for use in a soufflé, but not beaten for use in a custard or a fondue.

True

●

11. A custard should not be heated above what temperature?

85C (185F)

●

12. What does acid such as vinegar do to egg whites?

Makes them whiter, denatures the protein.

●

13. Are old eggs (not spoiled) satisfactory for making egg foams?

Yes

●

14. What effect does cream of tartar have on whipped egg whites?

Adds stability, delays foaming action.

15. What else is added to egg whites to produce a more stable foam?

Sugar

16. What is done to prevent a green ring caused by iron sulphide forming in hard cooked eggs?

The carry-over cooking is stopped by placing the eggs in cold water.

17. Pans for frying and omelet making are conditioned by heating fat and salt in them and wiping them out. Are these pans washed thereafter whenever used?

No, only wiped dry.

18. Is anything added to eggs to prepare them for scrambling

Yes, milk or cream and sometimes water.

19. True or False: Coddling of eggs is the same as poaching them except that for coddled eggs boiling water is poured over them in the shell; in poaching, the eggs are placed in water which is then heated.

True

20. How does fat added to egg whites affect their ability to foam?

It inhibits the foam development.

21. What is wrong with placing a meringue topping over ice-cold food?

The coldness causes some of the meringue to liquify and become runny.

22. Why should we **not** dry foams in a very low oven as is sometimes recommended?

At least 163C (325F), is needed to destroy any Salmonella present.

●

23. As we add flour or other ingredients to eggs the coagulation temperature of the eggs lowers/rises.

rises

●

24. Why add vinegar to the water in which eggs are to be poached?

Vinegar, an acid, denatures, whitens, and sets the egg whites.

●

25. Omelets require higher/lower heat than scrambled eggs.

Higher to set a solid mass of coagulated eggs quickly.

●

26. Eggs beat to greater volume if warm/cold.

warm

●

27. Egg whites that have been overbeaten are of little value in cookery because they have lost their . . . . . .

elasticity

●

28. A Bavarois or Bavarian cream is a rich, light pudding set by . . . .

gelatine

●

29. Sugar adds sweetness to beaten egg whites but also has what effect as regards to the likelihood of their being overbeaten?

Sugar buffers the eggs from overbeating.

30. Crêpes might well be called thick/thin pancakes rich in eggs.

thin

●

31. Pastry cream (créme pâtissiére) is nothing but a rich vanilla . . . .

custard.

Fish and Shellfish Cookery

1 We decide how to cook meat and birds largely on the basis of the tenderness of the flesh, which is closely related to age. With fish, *the fat content dictates the cooking method*. Shellfish are low in fat and must be cooked accordingly.

Lean fish are poached, deep fried, or baked in a sauce.

Fat fish are baked, grilled or pan fried.

Both types can be steamed or baked.

In cooking fish, the . . . . content is the important factor in deciding which method to use in cooking it.

fat

●

2 The fat content of the flesh, much of which is in the form of oil, varies widely according to the specie. (Though over 300 species of fish are commercially valuable, only nine species make up over 60% of those sold.)

By weight, cod has only ·4% of fat, raw scallops only ·1%. Compare this to salmon which has over 16% fat and oil.

Here are the fat contents by weight of a few of the more commonly eaten fish:

raw plaice	·5%
raw haddock	5·2%
canned tuna	8·2%
canned mackerel	11·1%
raw herring	12·5%
salmon	16·5%

Shellfish are all low in fat:

raw scallops	1·4%
shrimp	1·4%
raw lobster	1·9%
oysters	2·1%
cooked crabs	2·8%

Judging from its fat content which method of cooking is best for plaice?

It is a lean fish: fry, poach or bake it with a sauce.

●

3   Some of the commonly eaten fresh or frozen fish which are lean are cod, haddock, plaice, sole, whiting and halibut. The flesh is low in fat. The liver, however, may be high in fat and be a source of cod liver oil used for therapeutic purposes. Fat fish such as mackerel, salmon and tuna have oil or fat throughout their flesh. Which type of fish—fat or lean—will have the drier flesh?

the lean

●

4   Which type of fish—fat or lean—would be deep fried?

The lean, e.g. cod, haddock. Some people deep fry fat fish such as mackerel. The result is an excessively greasy product not to be recommended.

●

5   Which of the fish mentioned shallow or pan fry well?

Any of the lean type: flounder, sole, small cod or haddock.

6　Fish and shellfish are high in protein, yielding all the essential amino acids necessary for tissue growth. Most fish are cheaper per kilo of protein than meat. Like other protein foods, fish and shellfish should be cooked only long enough to develop maximum flavour and tenderness, but should be cooked through. Only a few shellfish such as clams and oysters are eaten raw. Americans and the British unlike some other national peoples, like their fish cooked thoroughly.

The connective tissue in fish is softer and in less quantity than in animal meat.

If it is overcooked, the fish flesh is likely to do what?

Break into pieces, loose flavour and become tough as is true of all flesh foods.

●

7　For moist cooking, fish should be steamed, simmered or poached, never boiled, never overcooked. Most fish are delicately flavoured, and must be handled carefully if the flavour is to come through in the cooking.

Some fish, however, are strong flavoured. Would these be cooked differently than those with mild flavours?

Yes, moist heat cooking methods may be used to modify or reduce such flavours.

●

FACTORS IN QUALITY LOSS

8　Seafood deteriorates much more quickly than most meats. Bacterial growth is faster and flavour falls off quickly when it is not fresh or when the frozen item is not kept below zero until ready for use. A 'fishy', sharp ammonia odour means deterioration.

About five days is the maximum holding time for the top quality fresh fish, even though it has been cooled quickly after being caught and is held in ice at 0 to 3C (32—35F). Well-iced fish remains edible from 5 to 10 days after catching. Sometimes fish caught at sea are already ten or more days old upon arrival at port so that the fish has lost 'freshness' before it gets to market.

Whiting, for example, begins losing acceptability after four days of being caught.

Oysters in the shell have a possible storage life of 20 days because they are alive.

Shrimp stored in ice lose their delicate flavour and sweetness within 6 to 8 days. Live scallops, crab and lobster will hold for one to two weeks. The meat will hold refrigerated three days and if kept very cold longer.

A rule to follow in purchasing fish is to get it as fresh as possible.

Fresh fish begins to fall off in quality at what time?   As soon as caught.

●

9   Fish giving off a strong odour are . . . .   not fresh and have lost their top quality.

●

10   The flesh of really fresh fish is sweet in flavour. In light of this fact would you say that much of the fish eaten in this country is really fresh?   No, most fish is processed and shipped and has lost its sweetness.

●

11   The fat contained in fish is highly unsaturated. and takes up oxygen readily. This is a major cause of rancidity.

True or false: The oil in fish can turn rancid quite easily.   true

●

12   Should frozen fish be held at a low temperature?   Yes, indeed. A temperature of zero or lower is needed to hold fish and shellfish satisfactorily. In one study cod held quality for 24 months when held at $-28 \cdot 5C$ ($-33F$), but lost quality in only two months held at $-6 \cdot 5C$ ($-21F$).

135

13 Experiments show that cobalt irradiation of fish and shellfish destroys about 99% of the bacteria present. This doubles the storage life of these foods. The irradiation by gamma rays is really a pasteurization process, the gamma rays themselves being active only a fraction of a second.

Even though 99% of the bacteria is destroyed would it be necessary to hold the fish and shellfish by refrigeration or freezing?

Yes, without the usual care, bacteria will soon multiply again.

14 To store fresh fish and other seafood, pack in ice or cover with a damp cloth, then place ice upon the cloth so that a high humidity is maintained and the fish do not dry out. The ideal storage temperature for fish is − ·5C (31F) which will keep fish twice as long as at 3C (37F). Most good seafood restaurants maintain separate storage cabinets for their fish and seafoods. This prevents the odour of the fish or seafood from mingling with other foods. All fish and seafood begin losing quality as soon as they die. One cause of quality loss is from drying out. Why pack fish and seafood in ice for storage?

To maintain their moisture.

15 One reason sport fishermen are so fond of the fish they catch is that it is usually eaten while fresh. The typical way to prepare a freshly caught lean fish is to dip it in milk and then into seasoned flour, pan fry or deep fry it. Some just flour it and fry it.

Would freshly caught fish have maximum flavour if prepared by griddling or grilling?

Yes, indeed especially if the fish is fat. If grilled, do not flour, but leave it as is.

FRYING FISH

16 Because of the delicacy of flavour of many fresh fish, experts recommend the use of butter for griddling, broiling, or pan frying. The butter imparts a sweetness to the seafood not found in other fats or oils.

When shallow or pan frying fish would you use clarified butter, butter from which the solids have been removed?

Yes, from a previous section we learned that clarified butter will not burn as readily as unclarified butter.

136

17 For a delicate crisp surface texture and appetizing appearance in shallow-fried and deep-fried fish and shellfish, use a triple ground cracker meal as bread crumb. The meal is ground fine to a powdery form and can be used for breadcrumbing all deep-fried and shallow-fried items. Dip first into seasoned flour, then milk (or evaporated milk, or milk and well mixed eggs, or just well mixed eggs) and then into the crumbs. Dry on a rack 15 minutes before using. Monosodium glutamate, a crystalline salt which accentuates flavours present, may be added to the flour. Paprika also aids in giving a nice brown colour.

Would you expect when deep frying with a breadcrumbed item that some of the breadcrumbs will fall into the deep fat?

Yes, this invariably happens and is a major reason for filtering the fat frequently.

●

18 *In pan or shallow-frying* fish, the fat should be hot before the fish is placed into the pan so that the heat will sear the surface making a crisp coating and give a good appearance. The common way of shallow-frying is to use the à la meunière method. The fish is floured and fried in the usual manner with a small amount of very hot butter. The butter used must be clarified to prevent burning. When the fish is cooked and nicely browned with a crisp outer surface, it is removed from the pan, the pan is cleared, more butter is added and browned lightly to make the meunière butter or brown butter. A few drops of lemon juice and chopped parsley are sprinkled over the fish and the hot butter is poured over the fish. The lemon juice and butter coming together causes them to froth. To make fish fried à la Amandine, add a few slivered or sliced almonds when making the meunière butter.

The à la meunière is accomplished merely by adding browned butter, chopped parsley and . . . . over the fish.

lemon juice

●

19 The side of the fish to be first placed down in the pan depends upon the firmness of the flesh of the fish. If not firm, the skin side should go down. If firm, the flesh side goes down. Whichever side goes down first

gets the highest heat for the longest time. The preference is for placing the flesh side down first because the muscle of the skin side tighten up, toughen and become unappetizing in appearance with long cooking. The presentation side should always be fried first as after a piece of food being fried is turned—particles of burnt flow will spoil the second side.

In shallow-frying less firm fish place which side down first in the pan?

Skin side

●

20   Many cooks brown a fish in a pan and finish in a 162·5C (325F) oven. Why?

To assure a brown surface in the browning and then slow heat to complete cooking inside the fish.

●

POACHING

21   In poaching, fish is simmered at 88 to 95C (190F–205F) for 10 to 15 minutes per $\frac{1}{2}$ kg of fish. Longer simmering produces a more gelatinous fish, one especially tasty when served cold. A court bouillon is used by the experts as a liquid in which to do the poaching. This adds flavour to the fish. It usually consists of celery, carrots, water, vinegar or lemon juice or wine, and a bouquet garni which has been simmered about a half hour and strained. Fish bones and trimmings may be used to enrich the stock. The fish is simmered, not boiled, in the stock.

Why is it that we do not boil but poach seafood?

High heat produces toughness; low heat gives a more tender and delicately flavoured product. Boiling also breaks up the flesh.

●

22   Why use a fish stock as a liquid in which to poach a fish?

The fish stock adds flavour rather than taking away flavour as would plain water.

23 A bouquet garni or sachet garni is a bunch of aromatic herbs such as parsley, chervil, bay leaves, and thyme, tied into a bundle and placed into the poaching liquid to season it. Do you think it would be possible to over-season a court bouillon?

Yes, this would mask the flavour of the seafood.

●

24 When simmering or poaching a large fish, it should be started in a cold liquid. Small or portion-sized pieces of fish should be started in hot liquid. The reason for such precautions is that, like vegetables, fish should cook only until tender, never overcooked. To prevent fish from flaking or breaking into pieces, it is sometimes wrapped in a cheese cloth or tied to thin boards. It is also placed on a greased trivet which is used to raise the fish from the water without breaking after it is cooked. Fish that is to be served cold should be slightly under/over cooked.

under

●

25 When a poached or simmered fish is to be served cold, allow it to cool in the court bouillon and then remove. Why?

The fish firms in cooling and there is less danger of breaking up.

●

FISH SAUCES

26 The French often poach fillets or whole fish in liquid containing white wine in an oven (sometimes referred to as shallow poaching), then serve it in a wine sauce. The rich fish sauce which is made with roux (half fat, half flour) and fish stock, is known as *fish velouté*, and if white wine is added, *Sauce Vin Blanc*. If a fish velouté is enriched with egg yolks and cream the sauce is a *Normandy Sauce*. (See Sauces.)

The fish stock can be the court bouillon in which the fish was poached. The stock further reduced by boiling to a sticky consistency is known as glace de poisson (fish glaze).

A fish velouté is made with what kind of stock?

The liquid from the court bouillon or fish stock.

27 Roux + fish stock = ...   fish velouté

●

28 Fish velouté + white wine = ...   Sauce Vin Blanc

●

29 Fish velouté + egg yolks and cream = ...   Normandy Sauce

●

30 Reduced fish stock is also known as . . . .   Glace de poisson

●

31 Probably the best known sauce other than fish velouté or Sauce Vin Blanc, a rich, velvety sauce, which is served with fish is *Mornay sauce*, made by adding cheese to Béchamel (white) sauce.

Another well known sauce which goes well with fish is Bonne Femme which is made as a non-elaborate sauce of wine, herbs, shallots, and sliced mushrooms. Using a glazed white wine sauce and a garnish of grapes the dish is known as Véronique.

Fish Marguery includes white wine, mushrooms, mussels, and shrimp.

Bercy Sauce, served with poached or baked fish, is a fish velouté plus white wine, chopped shallots, lemon juice, and parsley.

Fish Florentine is fish on a bed of leaf spinach masked with mornay sauce.

Let's see now if you can identify the following fish dishes or sauces

1. Well known cheese sauce . . . .
2. Rich, velvety fish sauce . . . .
3. Contains whole grapes . . . .
4. Contains leaf spinach . . . .
5. A wine and mushroom sauce containing mussels and shrimp . . . .

1. Mornay
2. Fish velouté or Sauce Vin Blanc
3. Veronique
4. Florentine
5. Marguery

32   Fish is often glazed just before serving. It is covered with a mousseline sauce (see the chapter on sauces) and placed under a salamander for just long enough to create a lightly browned surface. Another sauce used is made of $\frac{1}{3}$ Hollandaise or mayonnaise, $\frac{1}{3}$ Mornay and $\frac{1}{3}$ whipped cream.

Could a very hot oven be used for glazing?

Yes, the moisture in the glaze prevents burning. The high heat is needed to firm the glaze.

●

BAKING

33   Rapid baking helps to keep lean fish moist. Baked fish are usually accompanied with a sauce such as Sauce Vin Blanc, Hollandaise, lemon butter (Maître d'hôtel), Bercy, Mornay, Normandy, or one of the derivatives of Normandy or Hollandaise Sauce.

Why sauce for a baked fish?

The fish has lost some of its moisture and needs the liquid. The added flavour helps too to complement the flavour of the fish.

●

34   When baking fish, the skin side is placed down in the pan. A fish being baked is not turned at all.

What happens if the flesh side is placed down in baking?

It sticks to the pan and is likely to break when being removed.

●

35   For baking fish most chefs use a 162·5 to 175C (325F—350F) oven. The higher temperatures are used with large, fat fish. The fish is done when the flesh flakes away when pulled with a fork.

Some chefs bake fillets of fish at 233·5C (450F) for 10 to 12 minutes after adding milk to the pan for moisture.

What is the test for doneness of a baked fish?

Pull with a fork. The fish is cooked if it flakes away.

36   A high oven 260C (500F) is needed only when fish is 'oven fried'. Since the fish is dipped in oil the high heat is needed to do what to the surface of the fish?

crisp it

●

37   Baking is often combined with poaching or steaming to produce creamed or au gratin dishes. *Au gratin* refers to bread crumbs or cheese, or both, usually placed on top of food and browned.

How would you brown an au gratin dish?

In an oven or under a salamander.

●

38   Fish are sometimes cooked in a greased paper bag or wrapped in buttered brown or parchment paper, called 'en papillote' (in paper). Of what value is such a practice?

The bag or paper serves to hold in moisture of the fish and its accompaniments.

●

GRILLING

39   In grilling fish, grease the grill rack and place the fish skin down. Brush or dip the fish in clarified butter or oil and place it about five inches away from the heat source. When the flesh side is slightly brown, turn the fish over, brush the skin with clarified butter and grill for 5 to 8 minutes, depending upon the thickness of the fish. To avoid breaking the fish in the process, place the fish in a double grid so it can be easily turned in the grilling process. A maître d'hôtel butter can be added to the fish just before serving. It is a soft or melted compounded butter which is spread onto grilled meat, fish or poultry just before serving. Some experts grill a fillet for eight minutes, add bread crumbs and 'finish' it for additional 4 minutes.

40   Which fish would be placed closer to the grill element, a thick or a thin fish?

The thin one for fast grilling. The surface of the thick one would be burned before the inside were cooked if it were placed close to the heat element.

●

FISH STEWS

41   Several fish stews or chowders have gained prominence around the world. In classical cookery the best known fish stew is bouillabaise made using a variety of ocean fish, shrimp, lobster, and wine. Dozens of versions of bouillabaise are made. Variations exist between regions in France and between individuals. Purists say that to be bouillabaise the dish must contain tomatoes, olive oil, saffron and rascasse, a bay fish. Some persons insist that lobster be a part of the dish; others, that it be excluded. Marseilles has the greatest bouillabaise reputation.

A matelot is also a fish stew and usually contains eel, perch, carp, cray fish, bass and other fish; usually fresh water fish are used. Either red or white wine is used as part of the stock.

Turtle soup served with Madeira or sherry wine is a gourmet item.

A French fish dish of world-wide reputation is . . . .

bouillabaise

●

POUNDED FISH ITEMS

42   Sometimes fish is pounded or crushed into a forcemeat and shaped into little balls, or dumplings with the aid of an egg binding and poached. The French call these quenelles. Fish is also pounded or chopped

finely, folded into whipped cream and eggs and baked to form a mousse or mousseline, which means light and fluffy. Sometimes a mousse is not baked but gelatine is added to the mixture of fish and whipped cream and this mixture is set by chilling. (Quenelles and mousselines can also be made of meat.) Fish is also poached, flaked or pounded and mixed with Hollandaise sauce; then, shaped into various forms for service on a buffet table. A whole fish, poached, chilled and then decorated can be one of the more interesting items on a buffet table. It is usually presented complete with head and tail.

A fishball would be called a . . . . by the French.

quenelle

●

43   A light mixture of chopped fish and whipped cream and eggs might be called a . . . .

mousse

●

SHELLFISH COOKERY

44   Shrimp are often overcooked. To cook, place $1\frac{1}{2}$ kilo of shrimp in a litre of rapidly boiling water, salted with 3 tablespoons of salt.

Cover and return to the boil—then simmer for 5 minutes, or until the flesh has lost its glossy appearance.

Once shrimp are cooked they should be plunged into cold water. Why?

To stop the cooking process.

●

45   Shrimp are cleaned either before or after cooking but the most economical way of cleaning them is to only slit the back of the shrimp where the black vein is located, then simmer them in salted water until cooked. During the simmering process most of the vein will fall out, avoiding the necessity of hand cleaning. If shrimp are cleaned after cooking the yield is reduced by as much as 10 to 20 per cent. To achieve the greatest yield when cooking shrimp, slit the shrimp down the black vein before/after cooking.

before

46   Scallops are extremely tender, bay scallops even more tender and sweet than sea scallops. Only three to four minutes are required to cook them in simmering water. Would you stop their cooking by dousing them in cold water?

Yes

●

47   Generally speaking, the yield—the percentage of edible food—is greater in the larger of a specie than in the smaller size. A large haddock or turkey has a higher proportion of edible flesh than smaller sizes, but in fish, the larger the fish, the coarser the flesh and while some large fish may give an excellent yield, the quality of the flesh obtained is not as high.

Small lobsters give an 18—20% yield; very large ones about 25% yield. However, lobster connoisseurs believe the smaller lobsters to be more sweet.

For yield, which lobster would you buy, a $\frac{1}{2}$ to $3\frac{1}{2}$ kilo lobster?

The $3\frac{1}{2}$ kilo

●

48   Live lobsters keep best when covered with seaweed or heavy wet paper. Lobsters that do not close their claws tightly or move when handled are dead and unfit for service. Most lobster experts feel that the lobster must be alive when dropped into boiling water for cooking. To see if a lobster is alive before it is cooked, straighten out the tail. The tail will spring back if the lobster is alive. A lack of spring in the tail of a lobster means that it is probably . . . .

dead

●

49   Customarily lobsters, like shrimp, are overcooked. A chicken lobster ($\frac{1}{2}$ to $\frac{3}{4}$ kilo) should never be boiled but simmered at 96C (205F) for only 10 to 15 minutes; a $\frac{3}{4}$ kg lobster is best cooked for only 15 to 20 minutes, while a 1 kilo lobster requires about 20 minutes. When lobster, crab or shrimp are cooked they turn a reddish colour or turn a bright red. Cook lobsters and shrimp in a 5% salt brine ($\frac{2}{3}$ c. salt to 4 litres of water). Shorter cooking time and lower than boiling temperatures can be expected to result in more/less tender meat.

more

50   Would it be reasonable to cook a lobster in a high pressure steamer rather than boiling it?

Yes, one such cooker steams lobster in three minutes and produces a tasty product.

●

51   Whole lobsters are 'boiled' (simmered) and served split, split and grilled (which may dry them out excessively) or split, stuffed and grilled. Lobster meat is served with various sauces. One of the best known lobster sauce is Newburg. Newburg sauce is made from lobster or lobster butter, egg yolks, cream and sherry (or brandy or Madeira), but often either a rich Bechamel Sauce or Allemande Sauce is seasoned with sherry and used instead. One of the best known lobster sauces is . . . .

Newburg

●

52   May we 'roast' lobster in a very hot oven instead if placing them under a grill?

Yes, this is done. Some restaurants have ovens which go as high as 371C (700F). This heat is still low compared to 649C (1200F) and up of the grill.

●

53   To avoid drying out a lobster by grilling, would it be wise to roast in an oven for 15 minutes, add butter and slip it under the grill for about three minutes?
      Alternatively is it wise to boil a live lobster that is required for grilling 5−7 minutes in order to counteract any drying out that may occur during grilling?

Yes, this is preferable to complete grilling.

●

54   Another well known way of serving lobster is lobster thermidor, which is made by removing the lobster meat, mixing it with Mornay or white wine sauce plus a reduc-

146

tion of shallot cooked in butter, parsley and mustard and placing it back into the lobster shell. The whole is sprinkled with Parmesan or dried Swiss cheese and the whole browned under a grill or placed in a very hot oven at 282C (540F).

Name four ways of serving lobster.

1. Boiled
2. Grilled
3. Lobster à la Newburg
4. Lobster Thermidor

●

55 Flaked fish is sometimes used to 'stretch' crab meat without indicating to the guest that such a mixture is being served. Are such practices ethical?

No

●

56 Scallops and sometimes other seafood items are served 'En coquille' which means that they are served in a shell. Coquilles Saint-Jacques are scallops which have been removed from their shells, grilled and served in the shell.

Coquille means . . . .

shell

●

57 A recent addition to the seafood menu is the South African lobster tail which is usually grilled, sautéed in butter, or boiled. They are crayfish rather than lobster since they have no claws. For best results first poach them from the frozen state about five minutes and then split and complete cooking by slow grilling.

Would serving in a butter sauce be appropriate?

Yes, since they tend to be dry and like all shellfish low in fat.

●

COOKING FROZEN FISH AND SHELLFISH

58 Most seafood served away from the coasts is frozen. The best way to thaw frozen seafood, or any other food for that matter, is to place in a refrigerator for eight to fifteen hours, depending upon the thickness of the item. It can be thawed faster if necessary by placing it under cold running water. If this is done for seafood or fish, neither should be unwrapped until after thawing.

Would it be possible to thaw seafood in a microwave oven?

Yes, since the energy penetrates the food, this is a fast way, but it would also partially cook it and is not as satisfactory as thawing in the refrigerator.

147

59 In grilling steaks and chops it was recommended that those 3 cm or less thick be grilled from the frozen state. This is not true for fish. Better results are obtained by thawing fish before grilling. Once thawed, seafood is grilled following the same principles used for other food materials.

Would you expect a greater drip loss with frozen fish than with other flesh?

Yes, sometimes the amount of moisture which is lost when fish is thawed is surprisingly large.

●

REVISION

1. What temperatures should be used for holding frozen fish?

Below zero

●

2. What is a court bouillon?

A seasoned liquid in which fish is poached.

●

3. What is a bouquet garni?

A bunch of aromatic herbs or spices such as parsley, thyme, chervil and bay leaves.

●

4. How would you prevent a whole fish from breaking into pieces during the cooking process?

Tie it to a board, wrap it in cheese cloth, or place it on a greased trivet.

5. How do you know when shrimp are cooked sufficiently when simmering them?

When they lose their glassy appearance and turn a reddish colour.

●

6. What is Mornay sauce?

Béchamel plus cheese.

●

7. What is a fish velouté sauce? A Sauce Vin Blanc?

A fish velouté is a sauce made from fish stock or glace de Poisson and roux. A Sauce Vin Blanc is a fish velouté that contains white wine.

●

8. Matching:

a. Sauce Marguery	1. Fish stock thickened with roux	
b. Fish Veronique	2. Béchamel plus cheese	
c. Sauce Mornay	3. Contains whole grapes	
d. Sauce Bonne-Femme	4. Contains white wine mushrooms and shallots	a. 6. b. 3.
e. Fish Velouté	5. Contains spinach	c. 2. d. 4.
f. Fish Florentine	6. Contains shrimp, wine, mussels and mushrooms	e. 1. f. 5.

9. What is the difference between butter served à la meuniére and maître d'hôtel?

Maître d'hôtel is served as a cold butter sauce compounded (seasoned) butter; meuniére sauce is the same butter browned.

●

10. What is the difference between a bouillabaise and a matelote fish stew?

The types of fish are different. A true bouillabaise uses ocean fish; the matelote is usually made from fresh water fish, and eel is one of them.

●

11. What is a beurre noisette?

Nut-brown butter, browned by heating.

●

12. When shallow-frying a firm fish fillet, which side (skin or skinned) should be placed down in the pan first?

skinned

●

13. Should you clean shrimp before/after cooking?

partially before

●

14. What is the last step in glazing fish?

Finish it under a grill, or in a very hot oven.

15. Chopped fish added to whipped cream and set by combining with eggs and baking or set by combining with gelatine and refrigerating results in a . . . .

mousse or mousseline

●

16. What is one of the most popular sauces served with lobster?

Newburg

●

17. What is the principal ingredient of Coquilles Saint-Jacques?

scallops

●

18. Once the cooking water is brought to 96C (205F) how many minutes should these items be simmered?
    Shrimp   . . . .
    Chicken lobster   . . . .
    Medium lobster   . . . .
    1 kilo lobster   . . . .
    Scallops   . . . .

Shrimp 6, Chicken lobster 10 to 15, Medium lobster 15 to 20, 1 kilo lobster 20, Scallops 4.

●

19. What is the best way to thaw frozen seafood?

By putting it in the refrigerator.

●

20. What is the principal factor in determining the way in which a fish should be cooked?

Its fat content

●

21. Fish belonging to the cod and flounder family are fat/lean.

lean

●

22. All shellfish are fat/lean.

lean

23. Why does fish break into pieces more easily than does meat?

It has less connective tissue.

●

24. The fat recommended for use in pan frying or grilling fish and shellfish is . . . .

clarified butter

●

25. When a fish smells 'unpleasant' it is . . . .

not fresh

●

26. Shallow-frying fish and finishing with nut-brown butter, lemon-juice and parsley is called.

à la meuniére

●

27. What is the well-flavoured liquid in which fish is sometimes poached?

A court bouillon

●

28. What usually accompanies or is served with a baked fish?

A sauce to compensate for the dryness

●

29. Which wine ordinarily is added to turtle soup?

Sherry or Madeira

●

30. In international cookery the best known seafood stew is . . . .

bouillabaise

The Frying Process

1 People have fried food since cooking utensils were first used. Food is fried when it is placed or immersed in oil or fat and a sufficiently high temperature used to brown the surface and at least partially cook the interior of the food

    What is the essential factor in frying food?

Cooking in fat;
fat acts as a
conductor of heat
to the food and some
fat is absorbed by
the food.

●

2 There are two types of frying, deep-frying and shallow-frying or sautéing. Deep frying is cooking food by immersing it in fat while shallow-frying is cooking it in shallow fat

    Deep frying is cooking in . . . . fat while shallow-frying or sautéing is cooking in . . . . fat

deep, shallow

●

3 Relatively tender foods, those lacking fat of their own, are often fried. Young chicken, fish, shrimp and veal are examples of such foods.

    Since the fat must be hot to quickly cook the food and prevent excessive fat soakage, would you think that thick pieces of food should be fried?

Not the really thick
ones because the
outside will be
overdone before the
interior is cooked.

●

4 Recommended frying temperatures are between 149C (300F) and 196C (385F) depending upon the equipment used, the food fried, the amount of fat absorption desired, the degree to which food is required to be cooked, and the method used.

    Is it reasonable to expect that food can be fried without some fat absorption?

No, fat absorption
varies from about
5% to 40% of the
weight of the food
being fried.

F

5   Food that is fried absorbs varying amounts of fat, depending upon the type and proportion of the food surface which is exposed to the fat, the temperature of the fat and food, and the frying time. At higher temperatures the fat to some extent seals the outside of the food, keeping additional fat out.

Most frying has the principal purpose of adding flavour to otherwise bland and tender foods such as chicken, fish, and veal, and to create a crisp, crunchy texture such as in French fried potatoes and onions.

Cold food will absorb more fat in deep fat frying. Will putting food into cold fat also increase absorption?

Yes, the product will be grease soaked and poor in flavour. It will also lack a crisp surface.

●

6   Shallow-frying or sautéing, is frying food in shallow fat in a frying pan. Deep-frying, or frying items immersed in fat, can also be done in a deep-frying pan. The latter can be dangerous because the fat or oil may catch on fire. More kitchen fires are caused by burning fat than by any other single cause. Use a deep, straight-sided pan when deep-fat frying on a stove because this type of pan reduces the danger of boiling over. In pan frying and deep fat frying on the top of the stove the temperature is controlled by the judgement of the cook, and the tendency is to use too high a temperature to get the job done in a hurry.

Shallow and deep fat frying present a fire hazard because cooks are likely to allow the fat to . . . .

catch fire

●

7   Sautéing comes from the French word 'sautoir' which means 'to jump'. The French sauté meat, fish, game or vegetables by cutting them first into small pieces of about equal size and placing these in a heavy pan in which vegetable oil or vegetable oil and clarified butter has been placed. The pan is shaken using both hands, thumbs upon the handle, shaking and flipping the foods being sautéed. Thus, the food is literally jumped to keep it from remaining in the fat too long and burning. The high temperature seals the food and frying is done quickly.

Sautéing is similar to the . . . . method of frying foods and terms are often used interchangeably.

shallow-frying

154

8. Only tender cuts of meat are sautéed because the cooking is done rapidly and at relatively high/low temperatures.

high

9 When sautéing meat, the cook knows when it is time to turn over the meat as soon as he sees the blood or juices appearing on the top of the meat. When this happens he . . . . it over.

turns

10 The smaller and thinner the meat is cut the more rapidly it should be seared and fried to prevent . . . .

burning and drying

11 Food to be sautéed should be as dry as possible and uncrowded in the pan to avoid the development of a layer of steam around the food while cooking. A steam layer prevents browning and searing the food. Crowding also prevents good browning at the edges.
    Food to be sautéed should be dried and not too crowded in the pan, otherwise the food is . . . . instead of fried.

steamed or braised

12 Before sautéing food having a high water content such as egg plant, the food is salted and allowed to drain for 30 minutes. The salt draws much of the moisture out. It is then dried on paper towels or other absorbent material and sautéed.
    Salt is sometimes used to draw out moisture from moist foods. After this the item is . . . . and then sautéed.

dried

13 The sauté pan or 'sautoir' has a thick bottom, low sides, and is usually made of aluminum, stainless steel, or copper with a tin lining inside. In the light of what has been said above, is a cover used on the sauté pan when frying?

Not usually

14 Pan frying is similar to sautéing except that large pieces of meat, fowl, and fish are pan fried as well as small ones. More fat may be used.

When larger pieces of food are being fried it follows that higher/lower temperature must be used than in sautéing to avoid burning the surface before the interior is done.

lower

15 For maximum flavour, meats and vegetables are browned in a mixture of clarified butter and vegetable oil. The vegetable oil is added to increase the smoke point of the butter and prevent it from burning at comparatively low temperatures. This mixture is heated until it foams; the meat or vegetables are added just as the foaming subsides, before the fat itself browns.

Would fat for browning be needed if the meat to be browned has a good covering and enough heat is present to melt the fat?

No

16 When frying sausage, the sausage often bursts. To avoid this, partially fry, then pour two to three tablespoons of water in the pan, cover it and evaporate the water by low heat. Next, remove the cover and brown the sausages with higher heat. The water turns to steam, and some of it is absorbed in the skin making it more flexible and soft.

To avoid bursting the skins of sausages when frying, add . . . .

a few drops of water and cover with a lid.

FRYING FATS AND FAT BREAKDOWN

17 The fat used for frying partly determines the quality of the fried food. Delicately flavoured foods such as fish and bland vegetables are often shallow-fried or sautéed in butter—or part butter, part vegetable oil—because butter adds a sweet, delicate flavour to them.

Special frying fats are used for deep-frying because they do not smoke at temperatures required for frying and also resist breaking down chemically in the presence of heat and moisture. Such fats are treated so that their original smoke point is 232C (450F) or higher.

What would be wrong with filling a deep fry kettle with butter?

The butter burns at the required frying temperature and would soon break down chemically. It is also expensive.

●

18   Fats are composed of glycerine and fatty acids, the fatty acids constituting about 95% of the weight. Most of the fats we eat are called triglycerides because they contain one glycerol molecule to which 3 long chain fatty acids (made of 16 or 18 carbon atoms) are attached.

A triglyceride is a fat made up of one glycerol molecule and 3 molecules of . . . .

And here is the formula for stearic acid, one of several fatty acids, this one obtained from beef suet:

$$C_{17}H_{35}COOH$$

Combining three stearic acids with a glycerine we get a fat which chemically would be written:

tristearin

fatty acids

●

18a   We see that fats and oils are combination of glycerine (also calley glycerol) and . . . .

fatty acids

19   Depending on the number of double bond carbon linkages, fats are known as saturated, unsaturated or polyunsaturated. Saturated fats contain only single bond carbon linkages and are the least active chemically.

$$\begin{array}{ccc} H & & H \\ | & & | \\ -C & - & C- \\ | & & | \\ H & & H \end{array}$$

Palmitic acid is an example of a saturated acid and is found in most animal and vegetable fat.

Which fats are most stable, the saturated or unsaturated?

The saturated ones

●

19a   Unsaturated fats contain one or more double bonds.

$$\begin{array}{ccc} H & & H \\ | & & | \\ -C & = & C- \end{array}$$

Polyunsaturated fats contain more than one such double bond. Oleic acid is an example of an unsaturated fatty acid found in most fats. Because of the double bonds, the unsaturated fatty acids are more active chemically than the saturated acids.

True or False: Saturated fats are more likely to become rancid than unsaturated ones.

False, the more double bonds present the less stable the fat.

●

19b   Some fats are naturally saturated which means that they have their full complement of hydrogen atoms. At room temperatures such fats are likely to be plastic; oils are usually less saturated and are liquid at room temperature.

Unsaturated fats are less stable at the double bond linkages and more readily combine with hydrogen and oxygen. They smoke at relatively low temperatures and turn rancid easily. They break down more quickly and form decomposition products which are responsible for off flavours, dark colour, and unpleasant odours in foods.

For deep frying at high temperatures, what kind of fat would be most suitable, a saturated or an unsaturated one?

saturated

●

20   Fats and oils are similar chemically; both are esters of glycerine and fatty acids. By definition a glyceride (glycerine and fatty acids) is a fat if solid at 20C (68F) and an oil if liquid at this temperature.

On the average, fats contain a high percentage of saturated fatty acids attached to the glycerine while oils contain more unsaturated acids.

Fats are different from oils in that at usual room temperatures fats are solids and oils are liquid. Fats have more .... fatty acids than oils.

saturated

●

21   Saturated fats have several advantages for frying over the unsaturated fats. The saturated fats have a higher smoke point, are more stable and are less likely to foam.

A saturated fat is one in which the carbon chain has a single/double bond.

single

●

22   Most fats for frying have only ·05 per cent of free fatty acids in them and have a smoke point greater than 227C (440F). If the free fatty acids are increased to ·10 per cent the smoke point is lowered to 204C (400F). At one half of a per cent of free fatty acids, the smoke point is 177C (350F).

As the free fatty acids increase in fats the smoke point increases/drops.

drops

23 Most animal fats have comparatively low smoke points. Suet smokes at 107—118C (225—245F), butter at 160—165C (320—330F), lard at 171—177C (340—350F), and cottonseed oil at 210—221C (410—430F). All purpose fully hydrogenated shortenings have smoke points at 238C (460F) and special deep-frying shortenings 260C (500F). Under kitchen conditions these smoke points are much lower.

They smoke at low temperatures and break down chemically, imparting off flavours to food being fried.

Why not use left over suet and fat scraps for deep-frying?

●

24 From a practical cookery viewpoint, we want a fat which is especially suited for the temperatures used in frying and we want to use this fat in such a way that we will be able to fry in it for the longest possible time. Anti-oxidants may be added to frying fats to reduce their tendency to grow rancid and stabilizers, such as silicon compounds, may be added to give them frying life. These give frying fats longer frying life.

What compounds are added to frying fats to give them longer frying life?

Anti-oxidants and stabilizers

●

25 We should use frying temperatures which will produce a fine product, but select a temperature which is as low as possible to get the result wanted. *High frying temperatures* hasten fat breakdown. Particles that break off from the fats during fat breakdown combine to form large molecules called polymers. No longer fats they change to resins, waxes and gums which are highly insoluble and tend to collect as yellow gummy substances on the sides of the fry kettle.

Resins, gums, and waxes are formed by . . . . of fats.

polymerisation

●

26 When a frying fat breaks down, the smoking temperature is lowered. Acrolein, the result, produces a whitish smoke, which causes irritation of the eyes, nose, and throat.

The whitish smoke seen when fat is heated to a point where it breaks down indicates the presence of . . . .

acrolein

27 Free fatty acids develop when fat breaks down. A fat high in free fatty acids will have a low smoking temperature. Animal and fish fats are high in free fatty acids.

Would you use these fats for deep frying?

No

28 If you fried mackerel, a fish high in oil in deep fat what do you think would happen to the frying fat?

It would absorb free fatty acids from the mackerel and the smoke point would lower.

29 Water in fat at high temperatures causes *hydrolysis*. *Hydrolysis* frees the fatty acids from the fat so that part of the mixture separates into acrolein and free fatty acids.

Drying foods to be fried helps some in preventing *hydrolysis* and the consequent build up of free fatty acids.

Water added to the fat in the presence of heat results in . . . . (technical term).

hydrolysis

30 Water will boil giving off its excess heat in the form of steam. Fat will not do this. Instead, it will break down and smoke. Evidence of the breakdown is seen in the fact that the fat . . . . at frying temperatures.

smokes

31 A broken down fat forms a heavy, yellow foam. Foaming is not the same as bubbling which occurs with the rapid evaporation of water in frying foods. The bubbles are fairly large and soon stop foaming, but the foam consists of small bubbles which creep slowly up the sides of the deep fat kettle. It is also yellowish in colour unless the fat has turned brown or black. When foaming takes place, the fat is beyond redemption and should be discarded.

If a hydrogenated frying fat smokes at a frying temperature it has broken down. What is another good indicator of fat breakdown?

The fat foams

32   In addition to high temperatures, rapid fat break-down can be caused by food particles in the fat, increased area exposed to air, metals, salts or other contaminating products. Copper or iron encourage fat breakdown; stainless steel, an inert metal, does not. Curing salts, ordinary table salt and other chemical compounds used in cooking also cause breakdown.

If common salt breaks down frying fat, should you salt foods over a deep fat fryer?

You should not

●

33   Small bits of food and crumbs in deep fat burn when left in the fat too long. These break down fat. To eliminate these particles, the fat should be filtered through several layers of muslin or special filter. This should be done each day, or oftener when in heavy use. The cheese cloth can be placed inside a chinois (cone-shaped strainer) or sieve, or in one of the fry baskets as a lining.

What foods would you say leave the most crumbs in the frying fat to burn?

bread-crumbed foods

●

DEEP FRYING PROCEDURES

34   When solid fat is first loaded into a commercial kettle, pack it solidly around the heating elements or melt it first on a range top or in a steam kettle. This prevents chunks of fat from being overheated and burned. When melting such fat in the fry kettle, keep the temperature down to 93C (200F). Because of this problem most of the newer types of frying fats are liquid or semi-liquid.

What temperature do you set the deep-fat fryer at when melting solid fat?

93C (200F)

162

35　Because copper is a good conductor, thermostats may be made of nickel-plated copper.

Would you use an abrasive on this thermostat in a deep-fat fryer in cleaning it?

No, if you did you would wear off the nickel exposing the copper and cause a breakdown of the frying fat.

●

36　Some fat processors state that if frying volume is enough so that 20% of the fat in a kettle is absorbed by the food fried each day, no fat need be discarded. This is called fat turnover. New fat should be added daily to replace that used. The new fat mixes with the old and the mixture is satisfactory for frying.

A . . . . turnover per day is desirable in deep frying.

20%

●

37　At times, however, this system does not work. Fats may then be used first for one purpose such as deep frying of potatoes and then used for meats and fish, which leave in the fats contaminating products which cause rapid fat breakdown.

Why would meats or fish be fried last?

The fats of meats and fish are high in free fatty acids and fat is quickly broken down when meat and fish are fried in it.

●

38　The use of deep fat fryers for frying grew in popularity before World War I and during that war thermostats were developed to automatically control fat temperatures.

Thermostats are located in the fryers so that the fat surrounds them. They control temperature in a range of from 93C (200F) to about 204C (400F) and are accurate to within ($\pm$5·5C) (10F) degrees of the setting.

The use of what instruments has helped to popularize deep frying and has reduced the number of kitchen fires?

The thermostat; however, the thermostat should be checked at least weekly by using a thermometer to check the thermostat setting.

39   What is the correct frying temperature for deep frying food? At least eight factors influence the answer:

a. *Size and shape of the food item:* More time is required for heat to be conducted into thick pieces of food than is the case with thin pieces.

b. *Quantity of frying fat as compared with the amount of food fried:* The greater the ratio of fat to food, the more heat energy available per unit of food and the less drop in fat temperature when food is introduced into it. (Of course there is a limit beyond which more fat is of no advantage.)

c. *Presence or absence of breading on the food:* Breaded foods require a little longer to fry since the mass is greater and the breading itself must be fried. The breading acts as a partial insulator, slowing heat transfer.

d. *Amount of fat desired in the food consumer:* Young people usually prefer more fat than older adults. More fat will be absorbed the longer the food is fried and the lower the temperature—within limits.

e. *Recovery time of the kettle:* The more heat energy available for input into the kettle, the quicker the cooking fat recovers its temperature when food is introduced into it. Somewhat lower thermostat settings can be used with fast recovery kettles.

f. *Degree of crust desired on the food item:* Higher frying temperatures give more crust to most food items.

g. *Pressure at which the fat is frying:* Cooking food under pressure utilizes steam as well as heat from the fat for cooking and food cooks more rapidly.

h. *The amount of water in the food:* More heat is required to raise the temperature of water than any other food material. Commonly fried foods have high water content: potatoes about 78%, chicken 75%, and veal 68%. Food with less water content requires less frying time for a given size and quantity of food.

39a   Would you expect a chicken leg to require longer frying time than a thin chipped potato?   **Yes**

39b   As food fries, steam is formed from the water on and near the surface of the food. The steam is seen in the form of small bubbles popping on the surface of the fat in the kettle.

Would you expect this steam to act as a barrier in keeping the fat from soaking into the food?

Yes, as long as you see the bubbles fat absorption is minimal. When there is no more steam fat rushes into the surface of the food.

●

40   Which would fry faster: a kilogramme of food in eight kilos of fat or a kilogramme of food in four kilos of fat?

Within limits, the more fat, the more heat available for transfer and less drop in temperature. In the older frying kettles, an 8 to 1 fat food ratio is recommended, and 6 to 1 in the newer high-heat input kettles.

●

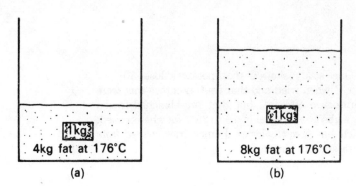

(a)   (b)

kettle (a) contains twice as many
Btu's as kettle (b) though both are
at the same temperature

41   About one half as much fat clings to the surface of potatoes cut to a 1 cm cross section as to those cut 0·5 cm section cut. A successful restaurant chain obtains a fat

content of about 17% by cutting their potatoes into 1 cm strips.

If a French fried potato rich in fat is desired how should the potatoes be cut?

Thin (or cooked longer in the fat).

●

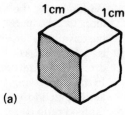

(a)

Surface area = 6cm²

Volume   „   = 1cm³

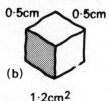

(b)

1·2cm²

0·125cm³

A potato chip like (b) has a larger surface area per volume of potato than one like (a)

41a   One study showed that potatoes lose 50% of vitamin C when fried and that fresh potatoes that were fried absorbed 9% fat, but that pre-blanched frozen potatoes absorbed a total of 19 to 28% fat when cooked.

Which has fewer calories, French fries cooked from the fresh state or the frozen?

Fresh

●

42   Because of rapid recovery times through higher heat energy input, the newer deep frying kettles should use lower frying temperatures than the older relatively low heat input kettles.

True or False?

True. The average frying temperature is higher since the new kettles recover frying temperature faster.

43 Is it reasonable to expect that a higher frying temperature will result in more/less frying time and more/less fat absorption.

less, less. Frying time of potatoes in one study was $6\frac{1}{2}$ minutes at 199C (390F). Fat absorption based on raw weight was 6·85%.

●

43a Would it be wise to thaw potatoes that have been blanched and frozen, then fry them?

No, not unless you want about twice as much fat absorption.

●

44 Because of the factors which apply to pan and deep fat frying, charts listing time and temperature for foods cannot be made. Even so, such charts are widely used.

Such charts specify frying temperatures of between 149C (300F) and 196C (385F). The frying temperature for chicken is usually given as 163C (325F). For French fried potatoes from the raw state, 177C (350F) to 196C (385F), 177C (350F) from the frozen state. 163C (325F) for frozen breaded chicken.

Frying is often done to lower temperatures. For example, a successful chain of restaurants featuring fried chicken follows this procedure in frying chicken:

Breaded chicken is dropped piece by piece into a fry kettle at 135C (275F). At the end of 8 minutes the temperature control is moved up to 163C (325F) and a tight cover is placed over the fry kettle creating some pressure within the kettle. Frying continues an additional 4 minutes, for a total of 12 minutes. The chicken is drained by hanging the fry basket over the kettle. The product is tasty and popular.

Do you think that this chicken was fried at 163C (325F) during the last 4 minutes of frying?

No. Even though the temperature control was set at 163C (325F) the fat in the kettle does not reach 163C (325F) until the end of the 4 minutes. Average frying temperature is about 149C (300F).

45 Frying temperatures used for chicken vary considerably. The frying procedure of another leading franchise plan uses a home-style pressure cooker. Temperature of the fat is brought to 204C (400F); then the breaded chicken is dropped to about 177C (350F); the lid is then secured into place and the chicken is fried at about 103·4 kN/m² (15 lb/in²) pressure for eight minutes; it is then removed and drained well.

Under this plan, the fat used in the pressure cooker is poured back into a larger kettle where it is mechanically filtered Freshly cleaned fat is used for each batch of chicken fried in the smaller pressure cooker

The product is extremely popular, quite moist and can be held for several hours and reheated with little quality loss.

True or False: Differences in taste allow for chicken to be fried at temperatures which vary as much as 55·5C (100F).

True

●

46 Many foods are prepared in two stages, 'pre-cooking' and 'finish' cooking. Chicken or potatoes are often fried in two stages. One restaurant operator pre-fries breaded chicken at 143C (290F) for ten minutes, refrigerates it and finishes it when needed. Or he blanches it in a conventional steamer for about ten minutes and refrigerates it. When needed the chicken is breaded and fried for one or two minutes. When ordered the chicken is finished fried at 163C (325F) for 3 to 5 minutes. Potatoes also can be pre-blanched in 177C (350F) fat for 3 to 4 minutes, held for quick processing at 177C (350F) for 3 minutes.

Would it be reasonable to blanch chicken a few minutes in a high pressure steamer?

Yes, the higher pressure and heat blanches the chicken in about half the time required by the conventional steamer which operates at 34·5 kN/M²(5lb/in²) pressure.

●

47 Temperature for frying potatoes varies with the variety, growing conditions, and maturity of the potato. One of the largest potato chip manufacturers uses a constant frying temperature of 180C (356F). Mature potatoes with less than a 3% sugar content and low moisture content (over 1·08 specific gravity) should be used for deep frying.

Would you guess that a new potato would have more water in it than an old potato?

Yes, and because of this, new potatoes are seldom used for deep frying. Sugar content is also too high.

168

48   Sometimes French fried potatoes show layers of brown and white. This means that the potato has excessive sugars in it, the sugars reacting with amino acids present, or that they are sticking together because of excessive starch on the surface. Most of such potatoes can be conditioned before frying, allowed to remain at room temperature for two to three weeks, until the sugars had had time to turn to starch. Sugar content of the potatoes ranges from almost none up to 10% of the solids present. A potato under 3% sugar is desirable

Potatoes build up glucose in the leaves from CO_2 H_2O using chlorophyll and sunlight. As the potato grows this glucose is transferred from the leaves to the tuber where it is stored as starch (starch simply consists of many thousands of glucose molecules linked together). The older the potato, the smaller its sugar content. One exception to this is that if potatoes are stored in a refrigerator the starch is converted back into glucose molecules. This glucose (or sugar) if present to the extent of more than 30% would be responsible for extensive darkening of colour on frying.

To avoid sticking because of excessive surface starch wash and rinse.

Would you expect sugars on the surface to caramelize and become bitter at frying temperatures?

Yes, this does occur and the potatoes show dark streaks where this occurs.

●

49   Keeping in mind that potatoes are about 80% water, would you think that deep-frying them is possible without a considerable amount of water passing as steam into the fat?

In frying the water content drops from about 80% to 47%.

●

50   In frying potatoes fat is absorbed and a large percentage of the . . . . is lost.

water

●

51   When preparation time is limited, fried items can be blanched (partially cooked) and fried off (finished) near the serving time. As previously noted, French fried potatoes can be blanched in deep fat for three to four minutes, depending upon the maturity

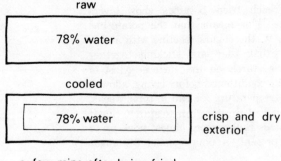

raw

78% water

cooled

78% water

crisp and dry
exterior

a few mins. after being fried

78% water

water from inner zone
moves to exterior

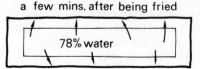

How a potato chip loses crispness.

and variety of the potato. (More on this in the Chapter 'Vegetable Cooking'!)

They are drained, held at room temperature or refrigerated until needed, then finished at between 163C (325F) and 196C (385F).

What type of potato is best for deep frying?

A mature potato low in moisture, high in starch.

●

52   As noted fat frying is also done under pressure. In 1956 a deep fat pressure fryer was introduced to the commercial market. Since then several other manufacturers have produced deep fat pressure cookers.

These cookers are deep fat fry kettles which are sealed. Pressure from steam generated in the food or from added water after the food is introduced builds up within the kettle. Cooking time is reduced about half. Chicken which normally takes about 15 minutes to fry in a deep fat kettle can be fried in a pressure deep fat fryer in about 7 to 8½ minutes, depending on the pressure used.

The higher the pressure used the faster/slower the frying time.

faster

53 In deep frying, foods must be immersed in the fat. Some foods float while frying and so must logically be turned over about . . . . in the frying cycle.

half-way

●

54 By placing a securely sealed lid on a fat fryer pressure is built up and cooking time is increased/reduced. (This should only be carried out when using a special fryer with a lid fitted.)

reduced

●

55 Thawing frozen foods before frying them reduces frying time. Bringing foods to room temperature before frying reduces the frying . . . . by 25%, thereby increasing the production of the fryer.

time

●

56 Another way to increase production of a deep fryer is to insert a moveable wire-frame shelf in the fry basket. The shelf divides the basket so that two layers of food can be fried at the same time without touching each other, providing the ratio of 1 of a food to 6 of fat is not violated.

In using such a shelf the cook should be careful not to exceed the food to . . . . ratio.

fat

●

57 The capacity of the fryer is also increased by keeping the fry basket immersed in the fat even when not in use. Use a standby temperature of 93C—121C (200—250F). This reduces the . . . . necessary to bring the food to frying temperature.

recovery time

58 Some foods are both fried and baked. Veal cutlets, for example, can be breaded and fried at about 171C (340F) for 4 to 6 minutes, then drained and baked for 30 minutes.

The breading serves to reduce moisture loss and the baking finishes the cooking process without further fat absorption and results in a tender cutlet.

Can you see any other advantage in using this two stage, two method type of cooking?

Such foods will hold better when in an oven than on a steam table. Fried foods lose quality after about 15 minutes on a steam table. The oven can be turned down low and the food held a little longer if necessary.

●

SOME DO'S IN DEEP FRYING

59 Use a hydrogenated, stabilized fat.

When it smokes at about 177C (350F), foams or tastes bad, it should be discarded.

Use the frying temperatures which produce the taste and quality of fried food preferred by your guests.

Filter the fat at least once a day when in use, oftener when used heavily.

Salt food away from the fryer; keep metals (other than those in the fryer) away from the fat.

Keep the fryer and basket clean; rinse out any alkali used in cleaning.

Dry the foods to be fried as much as is practicable before frying.

Drain the foods once fried.

Keep food separated while frying and don't overload the basket.

Use standby temperatures of 93—121C (200—250F) when fryer is not in use.

Keep oxidation to a minimum by using lower frying temperatures and covering fat when not in use.

Check the accuracy of the thermostat weekly.

Remember that frozen foods require about 25% longer frying time than foods at room temperature.

172

REVISION

1. What temperature should not be exceeded in deep frying to avoid fat breakdown?

196C (385F)

2. Most fat used in deep frying has been . . . ., a process which makes the fat more saturated, gives it greater stability and a higher smoke point.

hydrogenated

3. A major reason why fat develops off-flavours is the combination in the air of which gas with the fat?

Oxygen

4. By using high heat input fry kettles which permit fast recovery of temperature when cold food is introduced, higher/lower thermostat settings can be used in deep frying?

lower

5. To produce a high fat content in fried foods use a higher/lower frying temperature and cut the food into thinner pieces.

lower

6. Thicker pieces of food require higher/lower frying temperatures.

lower

7. Some materials act as catalytic agents in the breakdown of frying fat. Among these are metals, salts and particles of . . . .

burned food

8. In two-stage cooking using blanching as a first step, food is first blanched, or partially cooked, then held until ready for final frying. Is blanching really a partial cooking process?

Yes, it usually is done when time is not at a premium so that final cooking requires less time.

9. When pressure is applied to fat in a deep fat kettle the time for food to be fried is reduced by about . . . .

one-half

●

10. If French fried potatoes show brown streaks, they probably have too much of what substance in them?

Sugar

●

11. Smoking fat indicates that animal or poor type frying fats are being used or that what has happened to the fat?

It has broken down and contains excessive free fatty acids.

●

12. Frying foods under pressure reduces frying time. Is fat absorption increased?

No, the shorter frying time offsets greater fat absorption.

●

13. Would you fry tough, large pieces of meat?

No, only tender, relatively small pieces.

●

14. What is the reason we should not deep-fry bacon?

It would be too greasy and would render some of its own low quality fat into the cooking fat.

●

15. Should we deep-fry mackerel, a fat fish?

No, for the same reasons as for not deep-frying bacon.

16. Why not use butter alone when sautéing?

It breaks down under high heat.

●

17. Polymers are large molecules seen in deep-frying in what form?

Fat foaming and as gum on the sides of the kettle.

●

18. When foaming occurs in fat what should be done with it?

Discard it

●

19. Thermostats in deep fry kettles should be checked about how often?

Weekly

●

20. Temperature charts for frying are useful as broad guides. They should not/should be followed precisely.

Should not— because of the variables involved in frying.

●

21. A higher/lower temperature is appropriate for a food that is battered as compared with the same food not battered.

lower

●

22. Using a fast-recovery kettle the fat to food ratio should be about . . . .

6 to 1

●

23. Frozen foods require about . . . . longer to fry than those at room temperature when started to fry.

25%

●

24. When a fry kettle is in standby condition the fat temperature should be about . . . . ,

93—121C (200—250F)

25. Fat used in deep-frying should be filtered how often?

Daily or more frequently depending upon amount of use.

●

26. If a food floats while deep-frying, it will be necessary to do what about half way through the frying process?

Turn it over.

●

27. Salt in fat does what to the fat?

Causes it to break down.

●

28. Would you use a lower temperature to fry frozen chicken than for unfrozen?

Yes, the frozen takes longer to cook. Proctor and Gamble recommends 163C (325F) for frozen chicken, 177C (350F) for unfrozen.

●

29. Would you expect potatoes that are deep-fried, cooked and then reheated in fat to absorb much additional fat during the reheating?

Yes, during the second heating little steam is formed to keep out the fat and the fat rushes in.

●

30. If French fried potatoes fried at 177C (350F) are done in $9\frac{1}{2}$ minutes, how long is needed to cook them at 299C (390F)?

$6\frac{1}{2}$ minutes

Meat Cookery

1 A few years ago meat cooking was indeed artistry. Thermometers were seldom used and cooking information based on research was scarce. Although we still need much more information, we are today cooking meats more precisely and according to research-based knowledge than in the past.

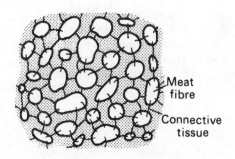

Meat
fibre

Connective
tissue

To understand how to achieve maximum acceptability and yield in meat, we must know something about its composition and structure and what happens in the cooking process.

Muscle is composed of about 60—70% moisture by weight, the amount varies inversely with the amount of fat present. One of the problems in meat cookery is to achieve at least 60C (140F) internal temperature in meat, an attractive, brown surface, high palatability, low shrinkage, and retain as much nutrients as possible. Some loss of moisture is inevitable through *shrinkage* caused by evaporation and denaturation. Because of denaturation, meat will shrink even though cooked completely immersed in liquid. A freeze-dry or dehydrated meat will absorb some moisture in cooking. The term of loss of weight experienced in cooking is known as *shrinkage*.

In cooking all but dehydrated and freeze-dried meat, some . . . . is inevitable.

shrinkage

●

2   Meat begins to cook at about 60C (140F), a process in which the flavour of the meat changes. Meat proteins coagulate at from 74—79C (165—175F), denaturation occurring before this. Normally, then, we would think that meat cookery begins at . . C . . . (F) and ends at . . C . . . (F).

60C (140F), 79C (175F)

●

3   In the cooking process, the protein fibres pull away from the bones and shrink when heat strikes them. Moisture is forced out, denaturation occurs, and the juices flow from the meat as meat drippings. Therefore, if meat is to be cooked, some . . . . (technical term) is to be expected.

shrinkage

●

4   Of the solids in meat, about 80% are protein and 20% fat, although pork may have a slightly higher fat ratio to proteins. It would be expected as a part of shrinkage that in cooking some of the . . . . would be melted and lost from the meat.

fat

●

5   Evaporation takes place when meat is browned; browning occurs when some of the carbohydrates in meat and other compounds are caramelized. Evaporation also occurs as juices come to the surface in cooking. Some . . . . of weight by evaporation occurs in browning.

loss (shrinkage)

178

MEAT QUALITY

6   The presence of fat is usually associated with meat quality and carries much of the flavour. Fat in animals is present inside the carcass in the thoracic and pelvic areas and around the outside muscles as '*covering*' or '*finish*', between the muscle fibres themselves as *marbling*, and as emulsified fatty substances in the meat juices held within the meat fibres. The amount of *marbling*, or fat interspersed between the muscle fibres, and seen as flecks of fat within the muscle, is a clue to the flavour of the meat.

The fat in meat contains about 15% moisture; thus, fat also contributes moistness to meat.

Fat in the form of marbling is related to what qualities of eating of the meat?

Flavour and
juiciness

●

7   Research has shown that marbling is not completely correlated with tenderness but is an important factor in establishing flavour and juiciness.

To introduce fat into meat which is excessively lean for our taste, strips of fat are laid in between pieces of meat or threaded in between the muscles. This is called *larding*. Or, strips of fat are laid on top of the meat or wrapped around it, a process called *barding*. The strips of fat introduced into the meat are called *lardons* and the needle used to thread the fat strips through the meat are called larding needles. Liquid fat can also be introduced into meat under pressure.

Larding or barding is done to add flavour/tenderness to lean meat.

flavour

●

8   Strips of bacon are often used to bard liver and strips of bacon or fat meat are often wrapped around fillet or beef· because it characteristically is not well marbled. Would you think that game or poultry, being fairly lean, would be improved by larding or barding?

Usually yes

9   Another indication of quality is the colour of the muscle and the fat. Older animals tend to have darker coloured meat and a yellowish fat. Younger animals usually have a lighter coloured meat with a firm, dry, creamy white fat. Veal flesh is a light pinkish tan colour while old cow is a dark red. Very young animals such as veal lack a fat cover. This is important as will be seen later in selecting procedures for cooking it.

Not all yellow colour in fat is a result of age. Grass and hay fed animals incorporate yellow carotenes from these feeds into their fat and some dairy breeds of cattle tend to have a more yellowish fat regardless of their feed or age.

A dark red meat with yellowish fat is more/less likely to be tender than bright cherry red meat with white, firm fat.

less

●

10   Tenderness is meat is related to the character of the muscle. Muscles are made up of fibres with a diameter of about 0·1mm and may be as long as 50mm. Each fibre contains a cell which is multi-nucleated. The fibre itself itself is like a tube containing liquids, most of which is protein, emulsified fat, minerals, vitamins and other compounds. When bunched together in bundles, the fibres form a muscle held together by a network of connective tissue. It would be reasonable that the finer the size of the muscle fibre, the finer the grain of the meat. To the eater of meat, the finer the grain, the more . . . . the meat.

tender

●

11   Quality in meat is related to age and the amount of marbling present. Look for a soft, velvety texture and marbling. As an animal ages or exercises, the connective tissues increase, which makes for tougher meat. Therefore a meat buyer should look for a smooth textured meat from an animal of what age?

Younger animals

180

MAKING MEAT MORE TENDER

12   The *collagen*, white connective tissue, can be changed into a gelatine by subjecting it to moist heat. Acids from foods such as tomatoes or acids in a marinade will speed this change. The yellow connective tissue called *elastin* is not materially changed by cooking or marination and must be broken down mechanically or removed.

The two types of connective tissue in meat are collagen and . . . .

elastin

●

13   Another way of breaking down or tenderizing meat is to expose it to proteolytic enzymes. These are tenderizers which digest or breakdown both of the connective tissues, making meat more tender. Commercial tenderizers, usually containing the enzyme, papain, must be controlled, otherwise, the meat is over-tenderized and becomes soft and mushy. Papain also breaks down the muscle fibres in addition to the connective tissue. Some meat is on the market today that comes from animals which receive an injection of tenderizer just before slaughter. This tenderizer is spread throughout the body via the capillary system.

The use of enzymes softens the collagen, elastin and muscle fibres while moist cooking softens mainly the . . . .

collagen

●

14   The ageing of meat, also called 'hanging' or 'ripening', tenderizes it. Beef is a meat suitable for ageing; lamb and mutton are seldom aged. Veal and pork are not. Actually, however, all meat receives some ageing because there is about a seven-day period between slaughter and receipt of the meat by the consumer. Tenderness, flavour and moisture improve rapidly in ageing up to two weeks at 1–2C (34–36F). Relative humidity is best if held to 85% in ageing. After two weeks, improvement slows down a great deal, but some meats may be aged six weeks or more.

True or False: Would you guess that the amount of ageing desired varies widely among people?

True, connoisseurs of food tend to favour more age in their meat than the average person.

15 To age well, meat must be well covered with an outside and inside layer of fat. The lower grades with poor fat finish are seldom aged. During hanging, mould growth, called whiskers, and some discolouration occur on the fat surfaces and this must be trimmed away before use. Trimming loss (9%) and evaporative loss (8%) may total 17% of the original weight at the start of ageing. Some game is aged almost to the point of putrefaction by hanging it in a refrigerator or outdoors in cold weather, a process called 'hanging until high'. Venison is best hung eight to ten days at 4C (40F).

Would you expect aged meat to be more expensive?

Considerably more so because of the weight loss, cost of ageing and the time a costly piece of meat must be withheld from sale.

●

16 Would you expect aged beef to require slightly less time to reach the desired degree of cooking than comparable unaged meat?

Yes, because of the acidity of the meat, the colour pigments change to a 'done' colour at a lower temperature.

●

17 Tough meats can be marinated (soaked) in a marinade (acid solution) of wine, vinegar and spices for several days to tenderize it and add flavour. If the meat has a strong flavour, such as game may have, discard the marinade; otherwise, use it as a part of the cooking liquid. Usually meats that are tough and have to be cooked by moist cookery are marinated. A joint of beef for braising is an example.

Soaking a cut of meat in a marinade will give . . . . and . . . .

tenderness, flavour

●

18 Mechanical pounding and cutting is also done to break down the connective tissue (collagen and elastin).

We see then that there are four common ways, other than cooking, of making meat more tender: mechanical breakdown of connective tissue, ageing, marination in an acid liquid, and the use of . . . .

Commercial tenderizers containing proteolytic enzymes.

SELECTING A COOKING METHOD

19   The method of cooking which is most suitable for a particular piece of meat will be decided by the kind of animal from which it comes, its condition and age (quality), its fat content, the part of the animal from which it comes and the size of the cut and its tenderness.

The effect desired and the preference of the person who is to eat the meat are also considerations in the selection of the cooking method.

Meat is cooked using either dry heat or moist heat. It is recognized that heat is neither dry nor moist, but a degree of molecular activity. We use the terms dry and moist heat cooking to differentiate between cooking with and without moisture, moisture surrounding the meat as liquid or steam as a principal heat transfer medium. Usually, tender meat is cooked by dry heat methods and tough cuts by moist heat methods. The methods of cookery using dry and moist heat are:

Cooking by Dry Heat:
> Roasting (baking)
> Griddling
> Grilling

Cooking by Moist Heat:
> Braising (pot roasting)
> Steaming
> Stewing
> Boiling
> Poaching

Cooking with Fat:
> Deep-frying
> Shallow-frying
> Sautéeing

If the meat were being cooked by microwave and the meat were in a liquid, the method of cooking would be related to braising or stewing and would be considered a dry/moist heat method.

moist

●

20   Suppose meat were being grilled by infra-red heat. What method would be in use, dry/or moist?

dry

21 What type of heat would be recommended for cooking chuck steak, a less tender cut of meat from the forequarter of the animal?

A method using moist heat: steaming, braising or stewing.

●

22 Would you expect less or more shrinkage using moist heat methods?

While cooking in water reduces evaporative loss, the fact that the meat is cooked longer and to a greater degree (about 85C (185F)) by this method usually means that the shrinkage is greater.

●

23 When proteins coagulate they become firm and this firmness given by heat may actually toughen meat. Thus, a piece of meat subjected to excessive heat becomes dry and toughened. Since this is undesirable, we should use . . . . temperatures in cooking it.

Low, except when we want to quickly form a tasty, brown crust on the surface or to avoid a high evaporative loss on a thin piece of meat.

●

ROASTING MEAT

24 The term roasting was originally applied to the cooking of large pieces of meat over an open fire, a practice which would be reasonably called grilling or perhaps barbecueing today.

The term grilling is restricted to meat being cooked largely by radiant heat, the meat being in individual portions or a few portions.

The terms roasting and baking refer to cooking foods uncovered in an oven with no liquid added. Roasting and baking are the same process except that meat and birds are said to be roasted while other items are baked. If there is a difference, it is that sometimes in baking a meat item may be covered. In roasting, covering never occurs. Would it be proper to refer to a ham as being baked?

Yes, since this is a matter of practice and ham may be covered; but it does not fall into the logical pattern of cookery terms.

●

25   If meat cooking in an oven is basted by pouring oil or a basting liquid over it during the cooking process but is not sitting in liquid, would this method still properly be called roasting?

Yes

●

26   All tender cuts of meat roast well. With beef these are the less-used muscles or those attached to the back-bone. In veal, pork, and lamb almost any cut may be roasted. Pork, loin veal chops and steaks can be roasted but are better grilled because the liquid present keeps them from drying out.
    Can less tender cuts of meat be roasted?

Not in their whole form, but they roast well after being minced and formed into meat loaf.

●

27   Roasting of meat is usually done by putting meat in a pan uncovered and cooking it by dry heat. The heat comes usually from the oven floor by convection but there may be some heat conducted into the roast through the pan itself although it is desirable to avoid this. Select a pan suited to the size of the roast so that drippings do not burn and char. Do not have too small a roasting pan so that drippings run over the edge outside. Select the proper temperature. If the meat is to be browned before roasting, set the oven at 232 to 246C (450—475F) and brown for about 15 minutes and then drop the oven temperature to around 149C (300F) and complete the roasting. Do not add moisture.
    Roasting is a method of cooking by moist/dry heat.

dry

28   A 'mirepoix'—a combination of roughly cut carrots, onions and celery—may be added either at the beginning or during the roasting period, depending upon the length of the roasting period. This adds to the flavour of the roast and especially the drippings. For long periods of roasting, the mirepoix is added near the end of the period so that the vegetables will not be burned. The name mirepoix come from a Marshal who lived during the time of Louis XV.

The French like to season roasts with herbs and seasoning. They also often slit a roast and insert buds of garlic. This flavours the meat but has the disadvantage of permitting some of the juices to escape.

The purpose of a mirepoix is to add . . . . to a roast.

flavour

●

29   Roasts should be salted after the surface has been browned or cooked. Studies have shown that the penetration of the salt is only about 6 millimetres deep into the surface and since it attracts juices on the surface it acts to delay browning of the meat.

Would it be wise to salt a roast immediately after browning or delay until the roast is cooked?

Normally, salting is done immediately after browning since some people like to taste the excessive salt that is carried down into the browned surface in roasting.

●

30   Rib joints roasted on the bone require as much as ten to twenty minutes per kg less time to cook than if the same roasts are boned and rolled. This is probably due to the fact that after boning and rolling the roll is much thicker and more time is required for the heat to reach the centre.

Boning and rolling meat increases/decreases the time to cook?

increases

31   When boned meat is roasted it is necessary to turn the meat at least once during roasting so that the meat is cooked evenly. Why is this turning not so important when a bone is present?

Heat tends to flow up the areas where the meat is firmly attached to the bone; this speeds cooking.

●

32   If three pieces of meat, each of a different size, are roasted together, in which of the three pieces would you first place the meat thermometer?

In the smallest. When it has reached the desired internal temperature, remove that roast and place the thermometer in the centre of the largest muscle of the next smallest size and continue roasting until it is done, and so on.

●

33   Place most meat for roasting on a rack whenever possible. Ribs of beef on the bone may not need to be on a rack since the chine and the rib ends on the roast may hold the meat up from touching the bottom of the pan. Temperatures at the bottom of the pan may be 260C (500F), even though the oven temperature is only 149C (300F). This happens because the heat is applied continually through the floor of the oven. Placing a leg of lamb or roast directly on the bottom of the pan exposes the meat to this high heat. Fats accumulate in the bottom of the pan, and the meat is fried rather than roasted. Also, the high heat denatures the meat on the bottom and the meat is turned into an inedible over-browned crust which must be discarded.

    How is it possible that the floor of an oven is hotter than the oven itself?

The heat is applied to the floor below; the heat is then circulated by convection through-out the oven.

34   There are many variations in the roasting procedure. For example, an old English method of roasting of beef in a roasting pan is to place the ribs in the pan, bone down, and cover the meat entirely with rock salt. During the roasting the rock salt becomes a solid mass, forming a shield through which vapour cannot pass.

Wrapping meat in aluminum foil achieves somewhat the same effect. In both cases, the meat is not browned in the same way as when roasted without a cover and the meat is partially steamed rather than roasted in the usual sense. The use of aluminum foil increases shrinkage. It does not reduce the cooking time nor noticeably increase the flavour of the meat.

What advantage is there, then, in wrapping meat in aluminum foil and roasting it?

No advantage, except that the pan is kept clean and the aluminum foil can be discarded after the juices have been drained from it.

●

35   Pot-roasting is cooking on a bed of root vegetables in a covered pan using butter for basting. Only good quality meats, game and poultry are cooked in this way. After the joint is cooked the vegetables and juices are used with a good stock to form the base of the accompanying sauce or gravy.

36   To facilitate slicing roasts and other large cuts of cooked meat, the piece should be allowed to remain at room temperature after removal from the heat for 15 to 30 minutes. This 'sets' the juices allowing them to soak back into the muscle. It also makes the meat easier to slice because the meat firms up. The result is a more succulent roast.

Will some cooking occur during this resting of the meat?

Yes, some carry-over cooking continues.

●

37   Most cooking charts recommend browning beef, veal and lamb for roasting, finishing it at 150C (300F). However, factors that must be considered in setting the temperature are the type of meat, its size and shape, the amount of time available for roasting.

Generally speaking, beef, lamb and veal are roasted what temperature?

149C (300F)

●

3 Temperatures recommended for roasting meat ave been coming down. Ohio State University studies ' cooking choice grade top rounds found the best results hen roasted at 107C (225F) to

60C (140F) (rare)
70C (158F) (medium)
82—85C (180—185) (well done)

As might be expected yield was greatest for the re stage, lowest for the well done stage. In fact, the amber of 75 gramme portions was reduced from 40 to 2 between these two stages.

Within limits, lower roasting temperatures for beef ve more/less yield.

more

●

9 The thicker the meat, the lower the cooking temperature. An example of the rule 'heavy beef, slow ooking temperature' is the cooking of a baron of beef, a excellent display item for a buffet, which weighs out 32 kilogrammes unboned. After boning and trimming the weight is about 28 kilogrammes.

Such a large joint of meat requires long roasting at low eat. Eight hours at 107C (225F) or until the internal mperature reaches 43C (110F) is recommended.

Such a low finish temperature is too low for serving. ow will the internal temperature rise to the 52 to 54C 25—130F) needed for serving.

Carry-over cooking continues after the roast is removed from the oven. The meat is 'full' of heat which continues to move into the centre of the meat by means of conduction.

●

Low cooking temperatures for meat offer nutrional as well as economical advantages. Fewer B itamins are leached out into the drippings or estroyed by heat.

If high heat is used, the fat present produces substances irritating to the digestive tract and the proteins re toughened and made less easily digested.

True or False: High heat unfavourably affects fats, roteins and the B vitamins.

True

189

41 Searing meat increases shrinkage rather than reducing it as formerly believed. Even so, meat is often browned to develop the aroma and flavour of the surfaces. Constant oven temperature—instead of browning at high temperature—results in less shrinkage, requires less fuel and less watching by the cook. Also there is less spattering and burning of fat on ovens, pans, and racks with a constant low temperature.

Is it necessary to brown meat to develop surface flavour and aroma?

No, longer cooking gives the same effect and aside from the longer time required, offers several advantages.

●

42 True or False: Roasting at high temperature consumes less heat than if a lower temperature were used.

False, usually the total fuel consumed is more, even though the lower temperature takes longer.

●

43 When meat is subjected to heat, the change from raw to completely cooked proceeds by stages. As was noted, cooking begins at about 60C (140F) and coagulation does not occur at a set point but over a space of ten degrees, 74 to 79C (165—175F). People vary in their taste with regard to the degree they like meat cooked and therefore meat is cooked to various internal . . . . to satisfy different tastes.

temperatures

●

44 Meat is considered rare when it reaches a temperature of 60C (140F). This is an internal temperature at the coolest spot and therefore the meat is cooked to a higher degree in other areas around this. For medium cooked meat, the final internal temperature of fresh

beef should reach 71C (160F), and for well done, 82—85C (180—185F). Medium cooked for lamb is 71C (160F) and 82—85C (180—185F) for well done. Well-done veal is 74C (165F). For lean pork we want at least 82C (180F). All pork is cooked well done.

Meat cooked to a specific stage is at a higher/lower temperature in areas other than the centre of the meat.

higher

●

45 *Carry-over cooking* must always be considered when cooking meat. Preferences for different degrees to which meat is cooked are especially noticeable with beef. Some people prefer rare beef, done to 60C (140F) internally. We learned earlier that most heat is transferred internally within food by conduction, and that even though the source of heat has been removed, cooking still continues as the heat flows into the product—known as *carry-over cooking*.

To achieve a rare piece of roast beef when using a 149C (300F) oven, it must be removed from the oven when the thermometer, placed within the big muscle of the meat, reaches 46 to 52C (115—125F). If the meat is allowed time to set, it will continue to cook until the meat reaches 60C (140F). For medium done, remove at from 57 to 63C (135—145F), and for well done, 68 to 74C (155—165F).

The amount of temperature rise is conditioned by the size of the roast, the roasting temperature, surface area and other factors; consequently, it is not possible to use set temperatures for all roasts. Aged meat loses its colour more rapidly than unaged meat and so it will appear more done than it actually is. This should be remembered in grilling meat where the change between degrees of cooking can occur rapidly. In other words, remove a roast you want at a desired temperature when the roast is . . . . to . . . . degrees C below that desired temperature.

15, 25

46   Determining the degrees of cooking of roasted
meats can be done in four ways:

   a. by following charts which specify the number of
      minutes per kilogramme of meat
   b. the insertion of needles, an old practice by which
      the needle is inserted in the meat, withdrawn, and
      the temperature determined by passing the needle
      over the cheek or some other sensitive skin area
   c. determining the degree of firmness of the flesh by
      pushing it with a finger, knife or fork
   d. by using a thermometer placed in the middle of the
      thickest muscle.

Professional cooks usually use the pressure method,
the more flabby or yielding the meat, the less done it is;
conversely, the less yielding or firmer the flesh, the
greater the degree of cooking.

Of the four methods which is the most accurate?

The use of a
thermometer, since
it avoids the
necessity of making
subjective temper-
ature judgements.
(The thermometer
must not touch a
bone, for the bone
temperature is not
necessarily the same
as that of the
muscle.)

●

47   Cooking meat according to minutes per kilogramme
is not always a safe guide. A flat piece of meat with a
large surface area will cook in less time than a thick
roast of equal weight. Meat containing bone will cook in
a shorter period of time than boned meat since the heat
can flow up around the bone faster than it can through
the flesh. Other things being equal, a roast with bone
in/out will tend to cook more quickly.

in

●

48   The popularity of beef cooked rare is growing.
Some people even like raw meat; e.g. Tartar steak,
which is raw ground beef on which is served a raw egg.
To satisfy several persons who prefer different degrees
of cooking in roast beef, how would you cook a large rib
roast?

Roast it so that it is
rare in the middle,
well done towards
the outside. This
way everyone can
have it as he likes it.

GRILLING MEAT

49   Grilling is cooking largely by radiant heat although some cooking occurs by means of convection. Grilling is recommended for tender cuts of meat, such as cutlets and chops, beef steaks, ham steaks and bacon. The heat may come from coke, charcoal, gas or electric elements. Charcoal and coke are used less in cooking because of the labour and unhygienic conditions which may result.

Could an alcohol lamp flame or a kerosene lamp flame be used to grill?

Yes, but the flavour imparted to the meat by these fuels is not palatable.

●

50   While the temperature of a grill at the heat source is apt to be very high, the temperature at the meat itself should normally be from 177 to 204C (350—400F). Some experimental work shows that moderately low grilling temperatures—149—177C (300—350F)—produce more tender, more uniformly cooked and juicier steaks and chops than do higher temperatures. Temperatures of grills at the heat source vary from 288 to 982C (500—1800F). This variation is usually no problem for temperatures can be adjusted by varying the distance of the grid on which the meat is cooked. Some grills are fired from below and the distance to the grid is often fixed. With such equipment the amount of heat on the meat cannot be controlled by moving the grid closer or away from the heat source but the temperature of the heat source must be changed. With gas or electricity this requires lowering of the heat by regulator, and with charcoal, spreading out of the hot coals so that less heat is produced. A grill should be brought to the proper temperature before being used.

The quantity of heat brought to bear on a piece of meat on a grill can/cannot be controlled.

can

●

51   Several factors determine the temperature desired and the time required to grill meat to a desired stage of cooking. These are: the kind of meat, tenderness, the

initial temperature of the meat, the thickness and size of the piece of meat, the heat intensity, the amount of fat in the meat, and the quantity of ageing it has had. Aged meat appears to be cooked to a specific degree more quickly than non-aged meat. Therefore, it is not practical to follow time charts exactly in grilling meat. Thermometers can be used with thick pieces of meat, but cooking is usually tested visually and by pressure. A piece of meat that yields more to pressure is less/more cooked than a firm one.

less

●

52   Testing steaks and chops for the degree to which they are cooked in grilling is almost always accomplished by visual inspection and by feel. By pressing the meat with tongs or other blunt utensil the firmness of the meat can be tested; furthermore, this pressure brings juices to the surface and their colour is a guide to doneness.

The meat is often too thin and most cooks are not willing to take the time.

Why not use a meat thermometer for testing the degree of cooking in chops and steaks?

●

53   A piece of meat to be grilled is dipped into or brushed with vegetable oil. Seasonings such as salt, pepper, garlic and paprika can be added to the oil. The oil coats the meat preventing it from sticking when it touches the hot grid. Furthermore, the oil aids in cooking and browning the meat by acting as a conductor for the heat on the surface of the meat and probably permits a higher surface temperature than is normally possible. It also helps appearance by giving a sheen to the surface. Salting is not done until the meat is browned, for, as noted previously, salt delays browning. The number of turns given a piece of meat on a grill varies. Thin pieces will be grilled on one side until nearly half cooked and then turned and finished. Thicker pieces will require more turns. Grid marks indicate the number of turns, two turns on one side showing as x's across the surface.

Although the flavour of butter is superior to oil, its smoke point is too low for the heat of the grill. For flavour, butter is added after grilling, often as a maître d'hôtel butter. (This is described in the chapter on sauces.)

Why not dip steak or chops into melted butter before grilling?

54 Before placing steaks or chops on a grill the outside fat covering is scored (slit) with a knife about every 2 cm. Why is this done?

The scoring prevents the fat from shrinking as a whole and twisting the steak away from a flat plane.

●

55 Providing it has a fairly high fat content, the thinner the piece of meat the closer it can be placed to the heat source. Thick pieces of meat should be kept farther away from the heat, even though they are very fat. High heat close to a thick steak overbrowns a thick steak forming a hard, crusty dry portion before the interior is cooked. This hard portion seems to act as a nonconductor of heat into the interior and a poor product is obtained. More gentle heat produces a much better product.

Will shrinkage of the meat be affected by the closeness with which it is cooked to a flame?

Yes; however, it is possible to get a thin piece of meat too far from the flame so that it dries out too much in the delay of its cookery.

●

56 Steaks and chops $2\frac{1}{2}$ to 4 cm thick should be cooked with moderate heat. Those between $1\frac{1}{2}$ cm and 2 cm thick should be exposed to higher heat. As noted, fatter cuts can be grilled at higher temperatures than leaner cuts. Extremely lean meat such as veal cannot be grilled because it lacks the required fat content to give a moist product. Grilled veal is very dry and unpalatable. Some chefs start meats at high heat and then use lower heat to complete the grilling.

It is reasonable to think that steaks to be cooked to the rare stage would be grilled faster than those cooked medium or well-done?

Yes, less time is needed to reach the rare stage and higher heat is needed to brown the surface in the time available. Therefore, the stage of cooking desired is also a factor in deciding the degree of heat to use.

●

57 Very thin steaks can be cooked rare more successfully from a frozen state than from the unfrozen state. Why is this possible?

The surface can be browned nicely while the interior is delayed in cooking because it is frozen.

195

58   Frozen steaks cut into $2\frac{1}{2}$ cm thicknesses can be placed directly on the grill but steaks over this thickness should be almost completely defrosted before they are grilled. Frozen steaks will require a lower temperature initially when they are placed upon the grid. The heat can be increased when they are almost defrosted. (A thick **frozen** steak can be grilled while still frozen, if low heat is used initially—too high a heat forms a hard crust on the outside while the steak remains cold inside.)

To preserve juice do not puncture the meat with a fork. Use tongs or a spatula to turn it or stick the fork in the fat covering only.

Should frozen steaks 5cm thick be cooked directly on the grill?

Not usually. Nothing over $2\frac{1}{2}$ cm thick.

●

59   When frozen meat is cooked, it must be remembered that considerable heat will be required merely to thaw the meat. About 344 kilojoules of heat energy are required to change a kilogramme of ice at 0C (32F) to water *at the same temperature*. In other words, 344 kilojoules of heat energy are used to change the ice to water—*with no temperature change*.

Allow about $2\frac{1}{2}$ times as long to roast frozen meat as with meat at refrigerator temperature. Allow about 2 times as long to grill frozen meat.

Is it going to be more and more important to know how to cook frozen meat?

Yes, the trend on the market today is towards more frozen cuts and more frozen meat.

●

60   In grilling steak or chops, cook them to a degree slightly less than that desired for serving. Serve on a hot plate or dish soon after removing from the grill.

If an item on the grill must be delayed, it can be pulled to the front where the heat is less, or if other items are not on the grid, the grid can be moved farther from the heat.

It is possible/not possible to control cooking time once an item is placed on a grill.

possible

61   True or False: When the steak is removed from the heat source, cooking continues for a short time.

True, which explains why steaks should be cooked slightly less done than what is requested.

●

62   The tender beef steaks are sirloin, porter-house, T-bone, and Fillet. These are all excellent for grilling providing they come from good quality beef. Lamb chops and steaks can be grilled. Minced meats with about 15 to 25% fat content broil well. Bacon and some other fat meats grill well. Ham can be grilled. Pork chops if grilled must be well done. If a loin veal chop is fat, it may be grilled.

Is barbecueing, grilling?

Barbecueing may be grilling with basting of the product with a barbecue sauce while it grills; again it may be roasting with basting with a barbecue sauce while it roasts; strictly speaking, barbecueing is roasting in a pit. Roasting on a spit near an open fire is often called barbecueing—it is, if the sauce is used.

●

63   Some steak fanciers insist that their steaks be grilled over charcoal or even *on* charcoal. Is the heat produced by charcoal any different than that produced by electricity or gas?

No, except that the temperature is apt to be different. Consequently, the wave length of the radiant heat is different.

64　The temperature of charcoal varies according to the amount of charcoal and its stage of burning. Is there any real advantage in using charcoal for grilling steaks?

Little if any. It is more costly and messy. Some charcoal such as hickory or apple-wood impart a flavour to the meat grilled over it and some people prefer this.

●

65　In cooking over charcoal some cooks do not place the meat directly over the charcoal but to one side. When this is done less convected heat reaches the meat. More/ less of the energy used to cook the meat will then be in infra-red wave lengths.

more

●

66　One of the most expensive dishes served in restaurants is the Chateaubriand steak, cut from the middle of fillet of beef, and usually large enough for two persons. It is grilled and often garnished with potatoes cooked in butter and accompanied with a Béarnaise sauce. The dish was named by a French chef who originated it for his employer, Chateaubriand.

A Chateaubriand, then, is a large fillet steak cooked using what method?

Grilling

●

67　Some unusual methods of cooking meat have been used. To get one juicy piece of meat, the chef of Louis XVIII placed three pieces together, one sandwiched between the other two. The combination was grilled. The middle piece, being protected from the heat source by the other two pieces, did not brown but warmed through and, it was thought, absorbed juices from the two outside pieces as the juices moved from the heat source. When cooked, the two outside pieces were thrown away and the king ate the middle piece!

What do you think of such a practice?

Expensive, isn't it?

198

GRIDDLING MEAT

68   Griddling takes place on a flat hot surface called a griddle, hence the term. Restaurants sometimes list on their menus 'Items from the grill' when they are often referring to griddled foods. The terms broiling, grilling and griddling are usually interchangeable. The term broiling is more acceptable when food is placed a short distance away from radiant heat and cooked. Cooking by grilling is commonly accepted as cooking on top of a griddle but because the term was once used to indicate broiling, it is best not used at all and the term griddling used instead.

Normally, items classed on a menu as coming from the grill are cooked on a . . . .

griddle

●

69   Two methods of griddle cooking are used. The griddle is left dry with no fat and, the item is placed on the hot surface (again salt *can* be used to prevent sticking). It is then cooked on the hot surface, turning as needed. The fat will flow free on its own but it is best to move any accumulated fat away from the cooking item.

The second method of griddling is much the same as shallow frying. A small quantity of fat is placed on the griddle—about 3 millimetres deep—and the item is fried in this fat, the fat conducting the heat rapidly from the surface of the griddle into the item. As fat is required it may be added by dropping it from an oil mop, dipped into a can of oil. The product is not seasoned until completely cooked and removed from the griddle.

One method of griddle cooking resembles . . . . while another resembles . . . .

grilling, shallow-frying

●

70   High griddle heat speeds the cooking but the searing that results does not hold in juices as is sometimes believed. Griddle at moderate temperatures—if the fat smokes, the temperatures is too high for both the meat and the drippings.

True or False: In griddling searing the meat is recommended.

False; nothing is gained by searing except burned food and a little time.

199

70a Griddle manufacturers recommend a temperature of about 163C (325F) for griddling eggs, about 177C (350F) for French toast and about 204C (400F) for pancakes, potatoes, fish and meat.

Why the lower temperature for eggs?

Eggs coagulate at a temperature of about 71C (160F) and can easily toughen if higher temperatures are applied to them.

●

71 The principle of using comparatively low heat applies to the process of griddling of meat as it does to roasting and other methods for cooking meat, but the recovery rate of the griddle is a large factor in determining the setting of the temperature control, especially when cold or frozen items are to be griddled. One large sandwich operation uses a 204C (400F) setting on one griddle and 163C (325F) on another. Some of the new griddles can be controlled in various parts independently and this allows different temperatures to be obtained on the same griddle. It is often desirable to cook items first at a high heat and then move to a slower heat. Fat foods such as bacon should be cooked at a higher temperature than leaner types of meat.

At what temperature would you say griddling occurs?

From 163 to 205C (325—400F) normally.

●

72 In griddling hamburgers, keep the griddles at from 163 to 204C (325—400F). Never press hamburgers while they are griddling. This is a common practice of novices and leaves the meat less juicy and tender. For a medium rare hamburger, the hamburger is griddled on one side until the blood oozes out the top. It is then turned and cooked until the blood rises again to the top. For a well done hamburger, the meat is turned a third time and cooked until the juices rise once more.

It is possible to griddle hamburgers and items on top of a layer of vegetables such as chopped onions. The onions are placed on the griddle with some oil on them, the patties placed on top of the onions and cooked. When handled in this manner, the onions give a moist product and a good flavoured product if one likes onions.

If temperatures exceed 204C (400F) in griddling, what is likely to happen to products?

The surface will be over browned or burned and excess shrinkage will occur.

73   If a 60 gramme hamburger is griddled at 177C (350F) and turns out well, what temperature would probably be most appropriate for a 120 gramme hamburger on the same griddle: 163C or 191C (325F or 375F)?

163C (325F); following the principle that thicker pieces of meat require lower heat to keep the surface from burning.

●

74   Electric fired griddles are usually operated at 177 to 205C (350—400F) for griddling such items as steaks. Should fat which renders out of the steak be removed from the griddle as it accumulates?

Yes; otherwise, the steak will have a more fried or sautéed appearance.

●

75   In griddling, sautéing and grilling frozen, chopped or minced meats, it is preferable *not* to thaw them but to cook them frozen. They hold together better when cooked in this manner. Allowing them to thaw and handle them makes it possible for them to break, for in freezing the ground meat seems to lose its adhering qualities common with non-frozen patties of meat. Cooking meat from the frozen state also saves time and in some cases is necessary. Studies have shown that meat cooked from the frozen state has more flavour and is more nutritious than meat cooked from the thawed state.
    Cook frozen minced meat patties from the thawed/frozen state.

frozen

●

FRYING MEAT

(See Chapter: *The Frying Process*)
76   Deep-fat frying is a method of cooking meat submerged in fat. It is usually reserved for items which are coated with flour, a batter or breading.
    Would frying meat in a sauté pan be called deep-fat frying?

Yes, as long as the meat was cooked submerged in fat.

77 Pan frying and sautéing are similar procedures. The meat is cooked in a small quantity of fat on the pan bottom, the fat being about 3 mm deep. In either case, the pan made of thick iron, aluminum or copper is heated, using a thick iron, aluminum or copper skillet suited in size to the quantity to be sautéed the item is slid into the fat and fried. Breadcrumbed items are especially suited to this type of preparation. The heat should be dropped after the item is added to the hot fat, especially breadcrumbed or floured items for these burn more easily because of their coatings. Sometimes, items will be sautéed for a time and then covered so that steam developed can finish the cooking and tenderize the product. Usually, the cover is removed at the end of the cooking period and the product recrisped. Sometimes, the item sautéed is removed and the pan is deglazed, the sauce then being poured over the item when it is placed on to a hot plate for service.

What is deglazing?

Deglazing is a process of removing the dried drippings from the bottom of a frying pan, wine, stock, milk, water or other liquid being added, the pan warmed and the dried contents scraped up with a fork or spoon and incorporated into the liquid.

●

COOKING WITH MOIST HEAT

78 With the tougher cuts of meat, moist heat is desirable. Moist heat is applied through a liquid either by steaming, simmering, stewing, boiling or poaching. Heat conduction is faster using moist heat than in roasting in the oven. Although the cooking temperature in moist heat methods is low (not exceeding 100C (212F) unless pressure is applied) heat penetration is fast because steam and water conduct heat rapidly. Moist cooked meats are cooked until an internal temperature of 85–91C (185–195F) is reached. In roasting, the temperature of the meat containing moisture cannot exceed that of boiling water because of the cooling effect of evaporation of moisture from the surface of the meat. This evaporation has a cooling effect. Of course when meat surfaces are dried, then temperatures can rise, and browning occurs.

Contrary to what appears logical, the temperature of

the surface meat roasting in the usual oven at 149C (300F) is about the same/higher/lower than meat simmering in water at 100C (212F).

about the same

●

79   Some confusion exists in the use of the terms associated with cooking by moist heat and the exact processes each represents. Terms are often used loosely. The following section explains some of the distinctions between the terms and is an attempt to define them precisely.

True or False: Terminology related to moist heat cookery of meat is not well standardized.

True

●

80   *Braising*——cooking in a small amount of liquid—— is perhaps the most common method of cooking meats by moist heat. Certain joints e.g. venison and beef are sometimes marinaded in red wine, vegetables and herbs for a few hours before braising. Often, the meat is rolled in seasoned flour, then browned in a small quantity of fat. The meat is then put into a pot or container that can be tightly covered and it is allowed to cook in the moisture created from its own juices. Thus, some steam is used in the cooking. If sufficient moisture is not found in the juices, wine, demi-glace, stock, vegetables and herbs, or other liquid can be added. About $\frac{1}{3}$ of the meat is covered with the liquid. Cooking during the period the meat is in contact with the moisture is very slow.

If the meat is browned, the braised product is called a browned or brun dish. If lightly browned, it is called a blond braised dish and if no browning occurs the item is called a white braised dish.

The French use braising in much of their cookery. Variations, too, are used. *L'etuver* is a method of braising in butter instead of liquid, the heat kept low during the process, e.g. vegetables (peas, cabbage, chicory).

Could braising be termed a combination of roasting and stewing?

Yes, because large joints are sometimes roasted first to brown and are then cooked in liquid.

81 Would you expect that braising could be accomplished using a steam-jacketed kettle?

Yes, although the temperature in a steam-jacketed kettle will usually not exceed 104C (220F) if the pressure is $5lb/in^2$ this is sufficient to brown the meat as is necessary in braising.

82 *Stewing* is gentle simmering in the smallest quantity of water, stock or sauce. The food is always cut up, and both the liquid and food are served together. This method has economical and nutritional advantages as it will render tender and palatable the coarsed, older and cheaper types of poultry or meat which would be unsuitable for grilling or roasting. There are many others. Stews can be simmered meats and vegetables or other foods such as oysters and milk. The liquid in meat stews is usually thickened and served with the meat and vegetables. Browned, blond and white stews are characteristic as in braised items.

In a stew, would you add the vegetables required as a garnish at the start of cooking?

Usually no, since it is for tough meat, the cooking time will be extended until tenderness is obtained and in this time vegetables would be overcooked. Add the vegetables 30 minutes before the meat is done, or, cook the vegetables in stock and add them as the thickened meat and sauce are dished up.

83 What is the difference between a fricassée and a stew?

a fricassée is a white stew usually of poultry or veal. The meat is simmered in the sauce.

84   What is the difference between braising and stewing?

Very little in the cooking process. Braised meats and poultry are usually cooked in large joints, stewed meats are always cut up.

●

85   To simmer meat, keep the temperature below boiling, somewhere around 85—91C (185—195F), so that the protein in the meat is not toughened. Since most people like the caramelized flavour of browned meat, cooking meat by simmering is not done unless it is something to be cooked for other entrées such as a hash, or is a piece of meat typically 'boiled' such as cornbeef, brisket of beef, tongue, pork or sauerkraut. While the term 'boiling' is used as a moist method of meat cookery, actually in cooking procedures, meat is seldom, if ever boiled. Boiled meat is simmered, for boiling toughens the meat and increases shrinkage. Gentle heat gives a much more palatable product in flavour and tenderness.

Is it wrong then to use the term 'boiled' on a menu?

No, it is a term understood by the public and refers more to a type of item rather than a procedure of cooking. On a menu it is 'boiled' but in the kitchen it is 'simmered'.

●

86   With steaming, the least amount of moisture in moist heat cooking is applied to the food. Steam is applied directly to the food, condensing, and giving up its latent heat to the surface of the food where it travels into the food by conduction. Steam cooks quickly and it is an efficient means of transferring heat. Although steam is one of the most efficient means we have of changing the connective tissue, collagen, to gelatine and water, because of the high amount of heat contained in steam, meats cook quickly in it and there is danger of overcooking.

At what pressure is steam best used in the kitchen for cooking meat?

Five to seven pounds pressure is considered standard.

205

87   Poaching is cooking slowly in a minimum amount of liquid which should never be allowed to boil, but which should reach a degree of heat as near as possible to boiling point.

COOKING SPECIFIC MEATS

88   Beef is cooked by all the methods mentioned in this chapter. It is a multi-use meat and one of the most popular. Pork is a poor second in popularity while veal, lamb and mutton vary in popularity in different countries. Veal is much prized in Europe. Mutton and lamb (which are also popular in Britain) along with kid and goat are favoured in the Near East, and in certain parts of Asia, pork is a prized meat. Religion can be an important factor in dictating meat preferences. Let us first consider veal.

Veal is meat from a young beef, lacking fat and is usually thought to have little connective tissue. The best quality is found in calves not yet weaned and not over 12 weeks old and coming from heavy beef type animals, not dairy type. Since veal has almost no fat and is delicately flavoured it is frequently served with a sauce, deep-fat fried or sautéed. It can, of course, be roasted, braised or stewed. Minced veal patties, loaf, balls, and so forth are also possibilities.

Only loin chops are grilled and then only if they are fat. Meat that comes from older veal, called 'grassers', or older and called 'baby beef', may be fatter and respond better to grilling.

Sautéed veal cutlets served in many ways are featured in many continental dining rooms. Examples are veal scallopine (served with a brown sauce to which wine and mushrooms are added), veal cordon bleu slices of ham and cheese between sautéed veal cutlets), saltimbocca (literally 'jump in the mouth', prosciutto ham rolled between veal cutlets and braised), and veal Parmigiana (veal cutlet with Parmesan and Mozzerella cheese). The cutlets for these dishes are sliced from the leg and should be about three-eighths inch thick and should be well pounded. This is the same product called 'escalopes' by the French. After drying, they are sautéed for four or five minutes on each side in butter, vegetable oil or olive oil, depending upon the recipe. The meat when fried in butter should not be put into the pan until the butter has foamed and the foam is subsiding.

For roasting, veal is first barded. It is roasted until an internal temperature of about 77 to 79C (170—175F) is reached.

Remember the meaning for the term 'bard'?

Fat, usually bacon, is either laid across or around lean meat to aid in cooking and to add flavour.

●

89   What method of cooking is recommended for veal cutlets?

Sautéing, braising, deep-frying.

●

90   Why is young veal not grilled?

It is too lean.

●

91   Leg of veal is often cut into small, thin cutlets and sautéed, braised or deep-fried. Which method of cooking would develop the most flavour?

Braising

●

92   Pork must always be well cooked. This is necessary because trichinae (parasitic worms) may be present and must be destroyed by heat. Furthermore, it is necessary for good palatability to cook pork so that the fat exterior is crisp on the surface. Trichinae are present in many animals, especially hogs. Trichinae must be thermally destroyed in cooking or they will find their way into the voluntary muscles of those who eat the pork, where they will continue to live. They are killed by a temperature 55C (132F) held for at least 15 minutes, but to be safe we cook to higher temperatures.

For some years it has been recommended that fresh pork be roasted at 177C (350F) until an internal temperature of 85C (185F) is reached. This comparatively high oven temperature crisps the surface of the roast and the 85C (185F) internal temperature provides a wide margin for the destruction of any trichinae present. The comparatively high temperatures were needed for the fat pork produced then. Now, however, far more tenderness and greater yield is found in pork on the market, especially in the pork loin roast, and it need only be cooked at 163C (325F) to an internal temperature of 74C (165F). This provides plenty of safety against trichinae and is satisfactory for the leaner type of pork now on the market.

There is also an additional rise in temperature after cooking to this temperature unless the meat item is very small such as might be the case in a chop or cutlet.

If the pork is very fat, a higher internal temperature should be reached. Why is pork cooked at higher temperatures and to higher internal temperatures than beef?

To be certain of killing trichinae and to crisp the outer surface; cooking to a higher temperature aids also in reducing the fattiness of the meat.

●

92a   Meat loaf should be cooked to an internal temperature of 85C (185F) so that any harmful bacteria present will be destroyed.

Why is meat loaf more subject to bacterial contamination than solid pieces of meat?

Chopping or grinding exposes the meat to contamination. Greater surface area is exposed to possible contamination.

●

93   Grilling is not often used to cook pork chops, because grilling to the well-done stage dries out the chops. Braising is the usual method of cooking. Ham steaks, if at least 1 cm thick, grill satisfactory.

Canned or precooked boneless ham requires heating. An oven temperature of 149C (300F) is satisfactory, and the ham is ready when it reaches an internal temperature of 63C (145F). By federal regulation, all smoked meat that might contain trichinae must reach an internal temperature of 71C (160F) in processing. It is recommended that cooking smoked hams that have not been canned reach an internal temperature of around 71 to 77C (160–170F) in a 163C (325F) oven. This gives good palatability to such a ham.

Is ham ever eaten in the raw stage?

Yes, specially prepared raw hams are obtained from Bayonne, Ardenne in France and Parma in Italy— thinly sliced and usually offered as hors d'oeuvre.

94   Lamb is the meat of young sheep, from six to twelve months old. That under six months of age is called spring lamb. Leg or shoulder of lamb is usually roasted to an internal temperature of 76C (170F) or higher. However, there are some who prefer it pink or at a 68 to 70C (155—160F) temperature. The French stop the roasting when an internal temperature of 60 to 65C (140—150F) is reached, which leaves the centre pink, making the roast more flavourful and juicy.

Is there any reason why lamb should be roasted to the higher temperature?

None that is presently known; the lower temperature produces more tasty meat and a better yield.

●

94a   The term scallop means thin slice. Some recipes call for escalope (French usage), others for scallopine (Italian).

Veal scallopine would include . . . . of veal.

thin slices

●

95   Lamb and mutton require little treatment other than to see that this type of meat is served either very hot or very cold. The fat of this meat congeals or sets at a higher temperature because it has a higher melting point than that of pork or beef. For this reason, if served only slightly warm, it will cool on eating, and the fat will congeal in the mouth giving a 'pasty' taste or a coating of fat in the mouth. Game meat reacts similarly. If served very cold, the fat is brittle enough to crumble and not give this effect in the mouth. Fatty foods such as lamb and mutton, pork and other meats are best served with tart or piquant sauces or fruits. This is the reason applesauce is served with pork and currant jelly or mint jelly goes so well with lamb or mutton.

What other meats must be cooked like lamb?

Game meat is much like lamb in that the fat congeals at high temperature. For this reason, game too must be served either very hot or cold and piquant, tart or spicy foods go well with this type of meat.

●

REVISION

1. What is it about the composition of meat which makes the possibility of shrinkage so great during cooking?

It is about 60% to 70% liquid.

2. The major advantage in using moist heat for meat cookery is that it . . . .

changes the connective tissue, collagen, to gelatine.

●

3. Two indications of tenderness of meat are the amount of good marbling present and a bright . . . . colour on the surface of the meat.

red

●

4. In grilling or roasting lean meat, fat is added by brushing it in or by . . . .

larding or barding

●

5. Cooking with dry heat breaks down the collagen/ elastin of the meat less than cooking with . . . . . . heat.

collagen, moist

●

6. Delayed cookery for beef uses a finishing temperature of . . . .

60C (140F)

●

7. Which of the following meat cookery methods use dry heat: roasting, pan-frying, steaming, griddling, grilling?

Roasting, pan-frying, griddling, grilling.

●

8. The French often add a mixture of carrots, celery, onions to roasting and braising meat. What is the mixture called?

Mirepoix

●

9. Should a 5 cm steak be defrosted before being placed under a grill?

Yes, anything over 4 cm

10. What is the best way to determine the degree of cooking of a roast?

A meat thermometer

●

11. In roasting or otherwise cooking large pieces of meat, does the cooking process continue after the meat has been removed from the oven or other heat source?

Yes, such carry-over cooking must be considered when deciding when to remove the meat from the heat source.

●

12. Tenderization of meat is done by mechanically cutting the connective tissue, marination, the use of commercial tenderizers, and by cooking with . . . .

moist heat

●

13. Beef served rare is finally brought to an internal temperature of about 60C (140F). Medium cooked means an internal temperature of about . . . . , and well done means an internal temperature of at least 82C (180F).

71C (160F)

●

14. Whereas fresh pork was formerly roasted at 177C (350F) to an internal temperature of 85C (185F), today with leaner pork a final internal temperature of . . . . can be used.

74—77C (165—170F)

●

15. Tartar steak is cooked to what temperature?

It is not cooked at all, but served raw.

●

16. Trichinae are parasitic worms found in fresh pork. A temperature of at least . . . . is needed to destroy them.

55C (132F) for at least 15 minutes

17. Is it necessary to roast lamb to a well done stage of 77C (170F)?

No, but it is customary. Flavour and juiciness are greater if roasting is stopped at 66C (150F).

●

18. True or False: All griddles should be operated by setting the controls at 204C (400F).

False; correct griddling temperature depends upon the rate of recovery of the griddle, the temperature of the food when placed on the griddle, its fat content and thickness.

●

19. Why is it important to place meat on a grid or rack while roasting in a pan?

To keep the meat off the bottom which is excessively hot, and carries the accumulated fat.

●

20. Wrapping meat in aluminum foil and placing it in an oven results in partial . . . . rather than roasting.

steaming

●

21. It is unwise to salt meat before roasting or grilling for the reason that the salt acts to . . . .

draw juices out of the meat and retard browning

22. Pot roasting includes roasting on.......... using.......... as the fat.

a bed of root vegetables, butter

●

23. A brown stew can be called a..........

Ragoût

●

24. True or False: Meats which are cooked in water show no shrinkage.

False, unless the meat has been dehydrated, dried beef for example.

●

25. Veal lacking fat and distinctive flavour is usually cooked by what method?

Sautéing, braising, or stewing

●

26. In testing steaks and chops to see if they are cooked by using pressure, firmness in the meat indicates what degree of cooking?

Well done

●

27. When grilling steaks, the thinner ones that contain fat receive higher/lower heat and are placed closer/farther from the heat source.

higher, closer

●

28. Chateaubriand steak is a large piece of fillet usually served with what sauce?

Béarnaise

●

29. When should hamburgers be turned while being griddled?

When the juices rise to the top of the meat.

30. Will pressing a hamburger down against a griddle speed its cooking?

Yes, but it also squeezes out the flavourful juices and makes the meat dry.

●

31. True or False: To cook a steak, cook it less than the ultimate degree required.

True

●

32. True or False: Remove roast beef when its internal temperature is 15 to 25 degrees lower than the final desired degree of cooking required.

True, again carry-over cookery brings it up the last 15—25 degrees.

●

33. Why is it necessary to serve lamb and mutton well heated or cold?

The fat must be kept soft; at lower temperatures it becomes pasty and congeals in the mouth. If cold it is brittle and breaks.

●

34. Which takes longer to roast, a boned and rolled roast or a bone-in roast (provided they both weigh the same)?

The boned and rolled roast, probably because it is thicker as a roll.

●

35. When using steam for cooking is there any danger of overcooking?

Yes, steam is hotter than water and a few minutes too long results in excessive shrinkage and toughness.

36. Vegetables as garnish are added to stew at what time?

According to the type of vegetable, about 30 minutes before the meat is done. If added earlier, the vegetables will be overcooked.

●

37. When griddling frozen hamburger patties defrost/ do not defrost before placing on the griddle.

do not

●

38. When cooking on a griddle, salt can be placed on the griddle to . . . .

prevent the meat from sticking

●

39. Cooking of meat begins at about . . . . temperature and coagulation of the protein takes place at about . . . .

60C (140F); 79C (175F)

●

40. Whenever you see a blade bone in a cut of beef, you can be almost sure that moist/dry heat will be needed to cook it.

moist

●

41. Aged meat cooks faster/slower than unaged meat.

faster

●

42. Meat thermometer reads when roast comes from oven:

	Colour inside of roast	Degree of Doneness
63 to 65C (145—150F)	Bright pink	. . . .
65 to 71C (150—160F)	Pinkish brown	. . . .
82 to 85C (180—185F)	Greyish or light brown	. . . .

Rare
Medium
Well done

43. In the above table do the degrees of cooking represent the final internal temperature?

No, they allow for carry-over cooking which takes place after the roasts are removed from the oven.

●

44. Salting meat before cooking attracts juices to the surface and consequently delays . . . .

browning

●

45. Low temperature meat cooking usually requires more/less fuel.

less

●

46. Dipping a steak in oil probably allows a higher/lower surface temperature during cooking.

higher

●

47. The surface of meat which contains moisture does not exceed . . . . . C . . . . .(F) during the cooking.

100C (212F)

●

48. If a hamburger patty is frozen, it should be/should not be defrosted before griddling.

should not

●

49. Cooking pans are deglazed for the purpose of acquiring the . . . . for use in sauces and gravies.

meat juices

●

50. A temperature of 104C (220F) as in a steam jacketed kettle is/is not sufficient to brown meat.

is

51. Braised meat ends up at a higher/lower temperature than most roasted meat.

higher 85—91C
(185—195F)

●

52. Because veal has much/little fat, it requires special treatment in cooking.

little

●

53. Lamb chops can/cannot be grilled because they lack/have enough fat.

can, have enough

H

Poultry and Game Bird Cookery

SELECTING A METHOD OF COOKING

1   The age of a bird largely determines its method of cookery. Young birds are usually tender but lack fat and for this reason may need basting while cooking. Older birds are tougher, having more connective tissue in the muscle. Moist heat is needed to break down this tissue in cooking. With chicken, for example, the cooking method is related to age as follows:

(1) 8 to 12 weeks old—broiler or fryer: broiled, sautéed, poached, deep fried, roasted or grilled.
(2) 3 to 5 months old—roaster: broiled, roasted, sautéed, grilled.
(3) More than 10 months old —fowl (hen or stewing chicken): simmered, stewed, fricasséed, steamed, soup stock.
(4) More than 10 months old—rooster (old cock): simmered, stewed, braised, soup stock.

Geese and ducks, as one writer puts it, are 'gastronomically uninteresting' if they are over six months old. Ducklings are usually slaughtered at about 8 weeks of age.

Meat from older birds cooked using moist, long-time cooking methods is picked from the bone and made into such dishes as à la King, curries, stews, chicken pot pie and croquettes.

Would a rooster be suitable for frying?

No, the flesh is too tough.

●

2   Young tender birds can be used for sautées fried, broiled, poached, or roasted; older birds are cooked by use of what kind of heat?

Moist heat: simmered, stewed, steamed, or braised.

3   One way of learning the age of a bird is to bend the keel end of the breast bone. The more flexible and cartilaginous, the younger it is. As animals, including birds (people too) age the bones harden and become brittle.

Birds with flexible breastbones could be cooked by . . . .

poaching, frying, broiling, grilling, or roasting.

●

4   The young, tender birds usually are low in fat. Frying them is a quick way of cooking and of adding fat and flavour. Frying also prevents the flesh from becoming dry when cooked. The flesh and skin of a frying chicken have only about 5 per cent fat in them while that of a roaster is about 13 per cent fat. Birds with a minimum of fat can be roasted or broiled if fat is added by rubbing it in, larding or basting them while cooking.

A simple, quick way to cook such birds low in fat is to . . . . them.

fry

●

5   When frying-broiler types of chicken are low in price as compared with that of fowl, one might be tempted to simmer the younger birds, pick off the meat and use it for creamed dishes like chicken à la King. This can be done but the younger birds contain a greater percentage of water, less fat and offer less flavour than the more mature birds.

True or False: There is some advantage in being older, even if you are a chicken.

True!

●

6   Even so, the lean meat obtained from a broiler is about the same—41 per cent—as from a roaster and if a sauce is to be added to the meat the flavour advantage of the roaster is discounted. Old laying hens are tough and stringy and should be avoided.

True or False: Age in itself is not always an indication of 'character'.

True

7 Poultry are those birds which have been domesticated for egg and meat production. Game birds are those that forage for themselves and consequently get considerable exercise. Game birds usually lack fat but they are likely to be fatter in the autumn, having stored the fat for the winter. A wild duck carries about half the fat of a domesticated duck. Game birds are often 'hung' in preparation for roasting to allow the enzymes to soften the muscles and add flavour. Hanging is done at about 4·5C (40F). The number of days of hanging given a bird is a matter of personal preference. Here is a guide:

duck	at least a week
partridge	two days
pheasant	several days
grouse	several days

Hanging game birds is done for the purpose of . . . . . . the muscles.

softening or tenderizing

●

8 Game birds that lack fat are often cooked by sautéing followed by braising.

The braising liquid may include wine, or other seasonings which adds flavour and is thought to aid in tenderizing the flesh.

Fat may be added and the birds roasted quickly at 233·5C (450F).

Cooking methods for game birds reflect the fact that they are usually more/less fat than domesticated birds.

less

●

9 To some extent the size of the bird also determines its method of cookery. Large birds cannot be conveniently cut into portion size before cooking. They are usually cooked whole by roasting, steaming or simmering, then portioned. Small birds are divided into halves, quarters or sectioned into parts and cooked by grilling, sautéing, poaching or deep frying.

As a fricassee is a white stew, would chicken for a fricassee be cut in pieces or left whole?

Cut in pieces

10   Apart from the cooking method used, bigger birds of a particular breed give a greater percentage of flesh and fat than do small ones. For example, a three-pound good breed male bird yields almost 36 per cent flesh and fat of total carcass weight. A seven-pound bird of the same breed, however, yields 46 per cent flesh and fat.

True or False: A larger bird is likely to give a greater yield of cooked meat than a smaller bird of the same type.

True

11   In hens (mature females), the breed of chicken is related to tenderness and taste of the flesh. The meat of a leghorn, for example, has less flavour and is more stringy than that of a white Plymouth Rock. (The one may be raised for egg production; the other for broilers and broiler breeding.) The quality of hen available on the market may therefore vary considerably depending upon whether they are selected from egg laying flocks or from meat producing stock.

The cooking method used cannot/can overcome lack of quality in the bird itself.

cannot

12 Broilers bought on the market are all about the same since most are produced from about the same breed, a hybrid representing several strains. Breeds of chicken grown commercially are limited since only those breeds giving high yield in eggs or meat are produced.

Capons (desexed males) and the meat breeds offer high quality but are costly to produce.

True or False: Unlike hens, broilers purchased on the market today are likely to be of a similar breed and to have about the same eating quality.

True

13   Poultry flesh is a protein easily toughened by high temperature and long heating. Low temperature cookery is recommended for maximum yield and a moist, tender product. However, high roasting heat can be used for a small bird, and when a bird, such as wild duck, is to be cooked rare. The high heat reduces time and consequently moisture loss.

Generally speaking, poultry should be cooked by low/ high temperature cooking.

Low, except for the smaller birds.

●

14   For older birds use moist cooking methods such as boiling, stewing, steaming, or braising. Tender birds can be cooked in a shorter time by grilling, sautéing, deep frying, poaching or roasting.

In cooking birds select the method of cooking according to the size, amount of fat, and . . . . of the bird.

tenderness or age

●

15   When are birds considered cooked?

Poultry flesh is considered cooked when it reaches a temperature of 85C (185F). This temperature must be reached in the deepest flesh area or all the way to the bone. Since bones contain a large quantity of air, they act as buffers against the flow of heat, and heat to the bone must be carried to it by the flesh.

Since leg and thigh bones are in the centre of the flesh, the heat generated in cooking reaches them earlier/later?

later

●

16   Birds are judged to be cooked by pressure or by use of a thermometer. Using the pressure test, a drumstick is squeezed between thumb and fore-finger. If cooked, the flesh yields easily. If not done the meat is more firm and unyielding.

The bird can be held on a fork placed between the leg joints and held vent down over a plate. If any blood is shown in the liquid issuing from the bird it will require further cooking.

In using a meat thermometer it is placed in the deepest part of the thigh or breast. If done, the thermometer reads 85C (185F). If a bird is stuffed, the thermometer should read 74C (165F) when placed in the centre of the stuffing.

Logically, which method of testing for doneness is more precise, the pressure test or use of a thermometer?

Use of a
thermometer

●

17   Domesticated duck and other poultry are usually roasted until no blood can be seen near the bone or in deep fleshy parts.

While we readily accept rare beef and the connoisseur who fancies wild birds such as grouse, duck, pheasant and goose may cook them to a bloody rare stage, the average customer rebels at the sight of rare poultry. The gourmet thinks otherwise. The pressed duck, is partially roasted, then the juices and blood squeezed out to make a sauce which is flamed and poured over the rare meat.

Ordinarily, poultry is cooked more/less than game birds—those with all dark meat.

more

●

18   Would it seem logical that older birds must be cooked to a greater degree than young birds?

Yes, because longer
cooking time is
required for the
old birds to
become tender.

●

FRYING CHICKEN

19   Fried chicken is as authentically American as the hot dog and hamburger. Young chickens weighing from $\frac{3}{4}$ to $1\frac{1}{2}$ kilogrammes ready-to-cook are usually selected for frying. They can be cut into eight or nine pieces of uniform size, floured, breadcrumbed or battered before frying.

Flouring is rolling in seasoned flour containing some paprika. Some of the coating adheres on the moist flesh which adds colour, aids in giving a crisp surface and tends to seal in the juices.

Breadcrumbing is dipping into seasoned flour, then into a moistening agent such as evaporated milk, eggs or plain milk, and then rolling the chicken into crumbs. It is best to allow the chicken to rest on a rack for about 15 minutes after flouring or breadcrumbing so the coatings tighten up and adhere better to the bird.

In **batter-dipping**, the bird or parts are floured (the flour prevents liquid from the food from leaking through and steaming off the batter). Then dipped into a batter and then, after holding a moment over the batter to drain off the excess, the parts are slid into hot fat. A coating that is over 15% of the weight of the cooked bird is undesirable.

When flouring or breadcrumbling, allow the coating to tighten up for about . . . . minutes before the food is fried.

15 minutes

●

19a   True or false: The gluten in flour that is used for coating foods to be fried literally 'glues' the coating to the item.

True

●

20   Is it wise to stack the coated chicken in piles while letting it stand for the purpose of tightening the coating?

No, the pieces may stick together and pieces of the coating come off.

●

21   When breadcrumbing chicken the sequence is to flour the chicken, then . . . . , then roll it in the bread crumbs.

dip it into a milk or milk and egg mixture

●

22   Some commercial coatings are superior to those assembled on the premises because the commercial coating can be designed to turn brown on the chicken at about the same time the meat is cooked through.

Is it reasonable to mix seasonings into the coating material?

Yes, it is an effective way of distributing the seasoning over the bird.

23   Sometimes poultry is marinated before coating and frying. The marinade usually includes oil and an acid such as vinegar or wine. The marinade adds fat and the acid acts to tenderize the flesh.

Marination is done to increase flavour and . . . .

tenderness

●

24   Two methods of frying chicken are sautéing and deep-frying. Sautéing is done in shallow fat, browning and cooking it well by turning. This method takes about 20 minutes. A 10-minute finish in a moderate 177—191C (350—375F) oven improves the product. Deep frying is usually done at 177C (350F) for 15 minutes. Other temperatures are also used as discussed in the chapter on frying. We learned that some deep-fat fryers have been pressurized. In such a fryer cooking temperatures can be reduced and cooking time shortened by about . . . .

half

●

25   Can precooking treatments such as partially cooking them by steam, fat or in water speed finish cooking time?

Yes, but frequently the quality of the product is not as high as when cooked from the raw to cooked stage in one process.

●

26   Which way of frying requires the longest, deep-frying or sautéing?

Sautéing

●

27   When small quantities of chicken are fried, use a heavy pan of aluminum. Either method, sautéing or deep-frying, may be used. Heat the pan and the fat, and slide the chicken into the pan. In shallow-frying the cover may be left on during the first 15 minutes of frying, but during the last 5 minutes the cover is removed. With the cover on, the chicken is partially steamed; when the cover is removed the surface is crisped.

Why use an aluminum skillet?

Aluminum, unlike copper or iron, does not assist in the breakdown of fats. Furthermore aluminum is light, inexpensive and an excellent heat conductor.

28 There are many ways to deep-fry poultry. Perhaps the best known in America is Southern Fried Chicken. It is lightly coated with seasoned flour and deep-fried until tender. If served with a cream gravy and corn fritter, it becomes Maryland Fried Chicken.

An elegant dish is Chicken à la Kiev. Tender chicken breasts are opened out into thin slices, pounded with a cleaver and rolled around a piece of butter and, if desired, Parmesan cheese. They are then bread crumbed and deep-fried at 177C (350F) for about 5 minutes.

They are finished in a 177C (350F) oven for about 15 minutes. When served and punctured by a knife or fork, the butter spurts out.

Chicken à la Kiev is both deep fat fried and . . . .

roasted

●

29 *Southern Fried Chicken* is fried chicken lightly coated with . . . .

seasoned flour

●

30 *Maryland Fried Chicken* is Southern Fried Chicken served with a corn fritter and . . . . (The European style of this dish includes banana fritter, bacon and horseradish sauce.)

cream gravy

●

31 *Chicken à la Kiev* is cooked in two stages: frying and then roasting. Many other dishes of meat, fish and birds are similarly cooked so that the texture of a crisp fried surface is obtained without the necessity of complete frying. The sequence can be reversed with the item first being baked or roasted and then finished by frying. Grilling is similarly often combined with roasting.

Why not cook all foods using just one method of cookery?

Using two methods often provides the taste advantages of both.

32   *Chicken Suprême* is boned chicken breasts rolled
in seasoned flour and sautéed until tender and golden
brown. It is served with a suprême sauce: chicken stock
(broth), flour, cream, egg yolks and sherry.

A Chicken Suprême dish is identified by two items:
. . . . and . . . .

chicken breasts,
a suprême sauce

●

33   Large quantities of fried chicken can be oven-
fried by a process called ovenizing, oven broiling, or
banquet style cooking. Floured and breaded chicken is
placed loosely on greased baking sheets or pans. Oil
is sprinkled liberally over the single layer of chicken
and the pans are placed into a 177—191C (350—375F)
oven. Use higher temperatures for smaller pieces.
(Breaded veal cutlets and other items that are normally
sautéed or grilled may also be cooked by this method.)
Items normally grilled can be cooked by this method
by first dipping them in oil.

Ovenizing is really a form of . . . . at high
temperature with the food material coated with oil.

roasting

●

33a   *Chicken Sauté.* A popular method of cooking
young ($1-1\frac{1}{2}$ kg) chicken. The birds are cut into 8 pieces—
2 drumsticks, 2 thighs, 2 wings and 2 breasts. They
are cooked in a sauté pan in oil and butter coloured brown
or cooked gently without colour according to the recipe
required. The leg pieces require longer cooking than the
breast pieces and in large scale cookery are cooked separately. When cooked, the chicken pieces are removed,
the fat poured off, the sauté pan is then deglazed
with wine, spirit, stock, gravy or sauce and the sauce
and garnish required to mask the chicken pieces is prepared. This is the classical way to cook a Chicken Sauté
and the chicken pieces should not be allowed to simmer
in the sauce. In certain cases however if the chicken is
slightly tough then having made the sauce, the chicken
pieces are returned to it and the dish is allowed to gently

simmer under a lid until the chicken is tender. Strictly speaking this then becomes a braise, e.g. a fricassée.

There are over a 100 classical recipes for Chicken Sauté. Among the most popular are:

Chicken sauté Chasseur—white wine, shellots, demi-glace, mushrooms, tomatoes, parsley, tarragon

Chicken sauté Bonne-Femme—white wine, thickened gravy, dice of bacon, small onions and potatoes

Chicken sauté Bourguignonne—red wine, demi-glace, garlic, small onions, dice of bacon and mushrooms, parsley

Chicken sauté Stanley—white onion sauce, cream, julienne of tongue, mushrooms and truffle, croûtons.

A chicken for a sauté should be cut in . . . . 8 pieces

●

33b   Chicken sautés may be prepared white or brown. True or False.

True

●

33c   Chicken pieces for sauté should be cooked altogether. Yes or no.

No, the leg pieces require longer cooking.

●

ROASTING FOWL AND OTHER BIRDS

34   To roast all poultry except very fat birds place them on their breast on a rack in a roasting pan. The back is placed up for a good reason: the layer of fat on the back melts during roasting and runs down over the breast and thighs, basting them. Roasting chickens breast down also offers some protection against the breast drying out.

All birds should be roasted on a rack so the downside parts do not burn on the bottom of the pan. (For display or buffet presentation, pick a plump, broad-breasted bird.)

Except for very fat birds use a 163C (325F) oven throughout the roasting period. For the last 30 minutes of roasting turn the poultry, breast side up, to brown it.

Most poultry should be placed in what position for roasting?

In a roasting pan, on a rack, on its breast.

35   Goose and duck require higher roasting temperatures to get rid of excessive fat. Goose is the fattest of the commonly eaten birds, containing about 33 per cent fat by weight, and gives the lowest yield of edible flesh. For roasting select one which weighs about 4 kilogrammes; larger birds are likely to be very fat. The goose should be first browned at 232C (450F) for 20 minutes to give flavour, crisp the skin and render out some of the fat. To allow the fat to escape, use a fork to prick the skin covering the fatty sections which are the thighs, back and lower breast. Do this also in roasting a duck or duckling.

A two-kilo duck should be browned at 218C (425F) for 15 minutes on one side. Then, it is roasted on the other side at this temperature for 20 minutes, and finally finished in an upright position for 15 minutes. This permits the fat to drain off the bird. It may be desirable to lower the temperature during the last period of cooking. Higher temperatures are used in roasting duck and geese for the purpose of . . . .

getting rid of excess fat and crisping the skin

36   Goose and duck, the latter having an average of 28 per cent fat, have a characteristic in common which affects their method of roasting. What is it?

Both are very fat birds.

37   Would you baste a goose or duck while roasting? Why or why not?

A master chef would in order to achieve perfection, but they already have plenty of fat for self-basting.

38 Excess fat can be removed from the bottom of a pan or liquid by using a bulb baster or by spooning if off. Sauces, gravies and stocks often have accumulated grease on the top which must be removed. If time permits, one of the best ways to do this is by chilling the item so that the fat forms a hard cake which can easily be removed. Judging from the name of the item, a bulb baster is used for what purpose?

To collect the fat and juices which gather in the bottom of a cooking utensil and to eject them over the meat or flesh for basting. It is also used for degreasing a pan.

●

39 A rich brown surface colour can be achieved on duck and other birds by brushing the skin with a mixture of three parts honey to one part soy sauce.

For broiled duck, the mixture is brushed on about ten minutes before the end of the cooking time. For roast duck the sauce is brushed on about 15 minutes before the cooking is completed.

Why apply the sauce 15 minutes before the end of cooking for a roasting bird?

The roasting temperature is low enough so that in 15 minutes the sauce does not burn but does soak into the skin and partially browns.

●

40 Will birds be roasted if cooked in a covered roasting pan?

No, steaming will take place, or if liquid is added, braising. The flavour and appearance are different.

●

41 Recognizing that cooking continues in large pieces of food once they are completely heated, would you roast a large bird to a lower internal temperature when it is not to be served immediately?

Yes, when the bird is to be held for an hour before serving, the internal temperature should be 74C (165F) at the deepest part of the thigh or breast (instead of the finished temperature of 85C (185F).

42   Like large pieces of roasted meats, roasted birds, especially big ones, should be allowed to stand out of the oven for 20 to 30 minutes before carving. Why?

To allow the juices to 'set' and be reabsorbed by the muscles; this setting firms up the meat, making it easier to carve and more tasty.

●

43   To carve a large roasted bird, remove the legs and thighs from the carcass and slice them—they may be boned after removal from the carcass and then sliced. The wish bone should be removed from large birds before cooking in order to facilitate carving. The wings are removed and the breast is sliced down across either side against the grain, or, the large breast muscles may be removed from the breast and sliced across the grain. Thin, long slices are desirable.

Is it sensible to portion small birds in this manner?

No; chicken, ducks and other small birds are usually sectioned into portions, bone-in, and served. This gives a better appearance and larger portion.

●

44   Traditionally home cooked birds are stuffed with a stuffing made of bread or similar food material. To assure destruction of bacteria in the stuffing it should reach a temperature of 74C (165F). Would such a stuffing tend to soak up the juices and add to the cooking time?

Yes. To add moisture and seasoning, stuff birds with a well seasoned stuffing.

●

45   Where a large number of servings of roast turkey are required, the birds are roasted to 74C (165F) unstuffed. Then, they are cooled and put under refrigeration for thorough chilling. Drippings are saved for gravy.

After chilling, the turkey is sliced. Mounds of dressing—about 90—120 grammes or a No. 10 or No. 12 ice cream scoop full—are spaced on greased baking sheets or pans. Dark sliced meat is placed on these mounds first, then smaller pieces of light, and the mound is topped finally with a big slice of white meat. From 60 to 90 grammes of meat is used per portion. The pans are refrigerated until needed.

To serve, heat the pans covered in an oven heated to above 60C (140F), or in a steam chest. Lift the portions onto warm plates covering with about two ounces of *hot* turkey gravy.

Why the birds prepared in this manner roasted only to 74C (165F) rather than usual 85C (185F)?

The reheating process completes the cooking.

●

46   In quantity food preparation birds are not stuffed. Instead, the stuffing is baked in pans separately about 4 cm deep. If it is not used at once, it must be chilled immediately. Pan baking of stuffing requires less time and is more satisfactory for quantity work. From 60—120 grammes of stuffing is enough for a portion. Thus, a 15 kg turkey requires about 6 kg of stuffing if 90 grammes portions each of turkey and stuffing are served. Many variety stuffings are popular. To make a sausage, oyster, apple and nut, chestnut, or other type of variety of stuffing use $\frac{1}{2}$ kg of these for every 6 kg of stuffing prepared.

Why must care be taken in handling stuffings?

Food poisoning organisms find stuffing a very favourable medium for growth. Always bring stuffings quickly to a cooking temperature, never leave them out for long periods at room temperature and keep under refrigeration in thin layers for not too long a time.

●

47   Roast chicken or turkey are favourites, but chickens of broiler size and small birds can be 'roast broiled'. Instead of being roasted at low temperatures, high temperatures can be used to prevent these small birds from drying out.

These small birds are rubbed outside with soft butter and then sprinkled with seasonings and flour. Several tablespoons of a mixture of freshly chopped chives and butter are placed into the body cavity, the birds are trussed and roasted at 260C (500F) for 15 minutes, after which temperatures are reduced to 204C (400F) until the birds are tender (about 30 minutes). During the roasting period the birds should be basted frequently with a butter and chicken stock mixture. Is it reasonable to roast other small birds using such high heat?

Small birds such as grouse, doves, squab, pigeons and small poultry parts are usually best roasted at high rather than low heat.

48   Why do we call this process 'roast broiling' rather than roasting?

The temperatures used are higher than the usual roasting temperatures.

●

49   Birds 'cooked to a turn' are roasted on a spit or turned about every five minutes during the roasting to permit more even browning and heat distribution. A squab—a young pigeon—can be roasted in about 30 minutes in a 205C (400F) oven and would be turned about . . . . times.

six

●

50   Since most game birds tend to be lean, would it be well to rub their flesh with butter or oil before roasting?

Yes, this adds fat and flavour.

●

51   When using low heat would it be wise to bard a lean bird with strips of bacon?

Yes, the bacon can be simmered first if you want to rid it of its smoked flavour.

●

52   Strips of plain fat are good for barding and can be tied around birds. How can we brown the bird and develop a nice surface crispness if the bird is barded?

Remove the barding fat the last five minutes of roasting.

233

53 Fat which accumulates from roasting poultry can be skimmed and used in sauce making, especially chicken fat which is a fine substitute for butter or margarine in making white sauce or veloutés. A velouté, as we have seen in chapter 2, is a rich sauce which would logically be served with what kind of meat?

Poultry

•

54 Deglazing is another process which may be required in the preparing of poultry. When poultry is cooked in a pan, drippings collect. Many adhere to the surface and become firmly attached there. This accumulated mass of drippings is called a sediment and it can be removed by a process called deglazing. To do this, add stock, water, wine or other liquid and heat the pan, working with a fork or spoon to loosen the sediment. When the sediment is removed (the pan deglazed) the liquid is used to make a sauce or gravy.

Deglazing a pan is the removal of sediment (cooked drippings) from a cooking pan for use in making a ....

sauce or gravy

•

GRILLING BIRDS

55 Few foods are better than broiled, tender chicken and few things simpler to prepare. The chicken is dipped into oil to which salt, white pepper and paprika have been added. The chicken is then put onto a pre-heated grid under or over the source of heat of a broiler and allowed to broil. The chicken is placed from 10 to 15 cm from the heat source depending upon the intensity of the heat and the size of the chicken.

True or False: The larger the bird being broiled the farther away it must be placed from the heat source.

True—otherwise the surface will burn before the interior is cooked.

234

56 Why is it not wise to broil a bird larger than a broiler?

The increased size requires longer cooking which excessively dries the flesh.

●

57 A broiler size chicken can be finished on a broiler or when almost finished, it can be placed in a pan and finished in a hot 204C (400F) oven. The heat of the oven permits heat conduction into the flesh with less overcooking on the surface.

If finished on a broiler the chicken should be placed about 15 cm from the heat source so that the surface will not burn before the interior is cooked. Basting every four or five minutes with clarified butter or a combination of oil and butter may be advised.

If basting is to be done, would you season the chicken before broiling?

There is a difference of opinion. Some experts urge that salting be delayed until half way through the broiling when the bird can be turned, then salted on the side already cooked. This way the salt does not draw out the juices and expose them to the high heat. Salt also delays browning.

●

58 If the bird is neither dipped in oil nor basted while broiling what may happen to the skin?

If it is not fat the skin will crack and burn.

●

59 To speed broiling and facilitate portioning of the bird after cooking, the backbone can be cut out before broiling. The ball joints of the legs and wings can also be partially cut and the bird pressed flat.

What advantages are there in flattening a bird before broiling?

The various parts of the bird are then about equal distance from the heat source.

60 Two delicious variations of broiled chicken are barbecued chicken and broiled chicken, Japanese style. Barbecued chicken is made by basting broiled chicken with a barbecue sauce. Japanese style broiled chicken is marinated for eight hours or longer in a sauce made of soy sauce, port wine, brown sugar and crushed garlic. It is removed from the sauce, dipped into oil and broiled; while broiling the chicken is basted with the marinade. Care must be taken in broiling this dish, so that the brown sugar in the sauce does not burn.

Barbecued chicken is nothing but broiled chicken basted with . . . .

barbecue sauce

●

61 A double grid which holds meat or fish can be used for broiling birds. It clamps around the bird enclosing it in a grid so that the bird does not fall between the openings in the broiler grid.

Would you expect such a double grid to leave grid marks on the bird?

Yes, but this is considered desirable by food connoisseurs.

●

62 A unique way of preparing frozen turkey is to cut the entire frozen bird using a band saw to cut cross sections of the entire bird 1—2 cm thick. These steaks or chops are marinated in oil and wine and allowed to thaw. The thawed steaks are easily boned, if desired. They may be broiled, sautéed or deep fried. The marinade can be used to baste the birds during broiling.

Would you use an old bird this way?

No, select young, tender, meaty birds.

●

COOKING BY MOIST HEAT

63 Young, tender fowl and other birds are usually cooked by broiling, roasting, or frying. Older birds are less tender—their flesh is higher in connective tissue. This tissue dissolves when in steam or hot liquids—

so-called moist heat. Dry heat only dries the flesh of
older birds and does not tenderize it.

We fry, broil or roast young, tender birds; use
.... heat to cook older birds.

moist

●

64   Simmering is an excellent way to cook older birds.
Cover the whole bird or portions in a stock pot or steam-
jacketed kettle with cold water, add one tablespoon of
salt per 5 litres of water and bring the temperature slowly
up to 85C (185F). Hold at this temperature until the
birds are tender. Then, remove and cool them quickly
by plunging the cooked parts in cold water. Quick cooling
prevents a hard, dark surface from forming on the outside and keeps the meat moist. Some cooks stop the heat
just before the poultry is done and allow the parts to
cool in the stock. This gives juicy flesh, but experience
is required to know when to stop the cooking.

Today's broiler is so tender that it needs only to be
brought slowly to a boil, simmered 5 minutes and then
cooled slowly in its own broth.

Why do we simmer rather than boil birds?

The heat of
simmering softens
the flesh; the heat
of boiling toughens
it. Boiling would
also tend to break
up the bird.

●

65   Birds cooked by simmering are done when the
'squeeze test' on the drumstick shows the flesh to be
soft and yielding or when no signs of blood are shown
in the juice issuing from the interior.

Why not use a thermometer for testing cooking when
simmering?

The thermometer
reading would
reflect the water
temperature rather
than the flesh
temperature.

●

66   Poultry can be steamed with about the same results
as achieved by simmering. Some cooks claim that higher
yields are obtained in steaming than simmering. High
pressures give a tougher product, however, than simmering. Overcooking can also be more of a danger under
pressure cooking than by simmering. Steaming is seldom
done to prepare poultry for direct service to the table.
Goose may be steamed for a while to get rid of the excess
fat, then finished by roasting. Steaming and simmering
both involve the use of what kind of heat?

moist

237

67   Coq au vin (cock in red wine) and Chicken à la Marengo are two popular braised chicken dishes. This dish was especially favoured by Napoleon, perhaps because it was invented by his chef on the day he won a famous battle at Marengo against the Austrians.

What advantages are gained by braising?

The flavour of the cooking liquid is blended into the birds and the moist cooking method tenderizes them.

●

68   More cooked turkey can be obtained by the poaching method than by roasting. One study showed 23 per cent less shrinkage by poaching over that of roasting. Also, the turkey was more moist, tender and better flavoured when cooked by this method.

To poach poultry breasts, thighs and legs, bone and brown at 171C (340F) for about 30 minutes. Water is added to cover the bottom of the pan about half a centimetre and the parts are poached for about three hours at 163C (325F). Turn frequently and add water as needed. A cover is not used. When fork-tender, remove the parts from the pan and plunge into cold water. Slice when chilled. Keep the drippings for gravy.

Why is it that the poaching method gives more satisfactory results?

The cooking time is less because the pieces are smaller and the cooking is done with moist heat rather than dry heat.

●

69   Boned bird parts may also be poached in stock pots or steam-jacketed kettles. Arrange the legs and thighs on the bottom, skin side up; then the breasts, and cover with water. Simmer for two to two and a half hours. When done, cool rapidly in the stock or plunge into cold water. Chill, then slice. Use the meat and stock within three days. The boned carcass parts— wings, necks, and tail sections—are simmered separately for stock. Use one tablespoon of salt and one teaspoon of pepper for every 3 kilogrammes of bird.

Does boning the turkey increase/decrease cooking time?

Decreases the cooking time because the flesh is cut open which allows faster heat penetration.

●

70   Chicken breasts are often poached. Frequently this is done in the oven, poaching in a rich chicken

stock, seasonings and white wine or lemon. The acid reaction from the wine or lemon produces a delicate white breast. The breasts are served with various sauces. Chicken fat is prized for making many delicate sauces such as a velouté.

Would it be reasonable to brown chicken breasts under a grill before serving?

Yes, if a browned surface is wanted. Mornay (cheese) sauce is a tasty accompaniment for chicken handled this way.

●

71   Almost every nation has a simmered chicken and rice dish. Poule Bouillie au Riz (boiled chicken with rice) is an example of one loved by the French people. Fowl is simmered in water with vegetables and seasonings. When the bird is almost tender, a part of the stock is removed and used to cook rice which has been sautéed in butter and onions. The remainder of the stock is thickened with *beurre manie* (kneaded butter and flour) and egg yolks, seasoned with lemon juice and nutmeg and finished with cream. The tender fowl and flaky rice is served with this delicate sauce.

Is it wrong to boil a chicken?

In cooking flesh foods the word 'boil' should be understood as simmer. A more tender, moist and flavourful product results when flesh foods are simmered rather than boiled.

●

72   Stewing is usually considered to be a cooking process in which flesh foods are covered with liquid and cooked by simmering. Vegetables and seasonings may be added for flavour. Browning may precede the moist cooking. Poaching is a method of simmering used to cook tender products, while simmering as such is often used to refer to cooking in water over a longer period to tenderize tougher flesh.

True or False: Poaching is a term preferred over stewing or simmering when tender foods are simmered.

True

●

73   Perhaps no dish exemplifies stewed chicken better than chicken and dumplings. Even an old rooster can be made to taste good when prepared in this manner. The bird is sectioned and placed with cut mixed vegetables (mirepoix) and a bouquet garni or small bag of seasonings (sachet garni) into cold water using one teaspoon of salt per litre of water used and simmered until the parts are tender. Dumplings are cooked on top

of the stock. To serve, some of the thin sauce is spooned over the steaming dumplings and tenderly cooked chicken.

In stewing chicken for chicken and dumplings add flavour to the stewing liquid by adding what items?

Mirepoix and sachet (bouquet) garni

●

74   A salmi or salmis is a dish prepared by using carried-over roast poultry or game. Boned sliced poultry meat (frequently game birds or duck are prepared in this manner) is reheated in a richly seasoned brown sauce made from the roast drippings of the poultry. Often, a salmi is finished at the table on a trolley using a gueridon to cook the item. Before serving, the sliced meat is stewed in the sauce and wine is added. Frequently, light flaky cooked rice is an accompaniment. Because a salmi is roasted (browned) and then stewed, it may be called a . . . .

Ragoût or stew

●

75   Left-overs of poultry with the skin and bone removed can be used for salads, cutlets, croquettes, vol-au-vent and bouchées.

76   Poultry meat can be used to make a *galantine* or a *chaud froid*, cold dishes suitable for service on a buffet. A galantine is a decorated dish of boneless poultry. The poultry may be combined with a force-meat and moulded into any shape, then coated with a chaud froid sauce or aspic. Or, it can be baked in a crust and served cold.

A chaud froid poultry piece is a whole bird which has been cooked until tender and covered with a chaud froid sauce (white sauce or mayonnaise to which gelatine has been added). The sauce is poured over the bird. The gelatine sets the sauce and after several coatings a decorative pattern is set into the coating, after which a clear aspic glaze is used to seal and cover the decorative materials. A boned chicken which has been pressed and formed into an oblong roll might be called a . . . .

galantine

REVISION

1. Young tender game birds can be roasted or fried. Older birds are braised in a pan with the cover on. How·can you tell if the bird is young?

Bend the backbone. If flexible and cartilaginous, the bird is young.

●

2. Ordinarily, using the conventional deep fat frying pan, chicken requires about how many minutes to fry?

Fifteen to twenty

●

3. When frying chicken on top of the stove what advantage is had by using a heavy pan?

It holds and distributes the heat evenly.

●

4. In what way is age in a bird related to cooking method used?

Younger birds are roasted, fried, grilled or broiled; older birds are cooked by moist heat.

●

5. Degreasing is a process of removing excess . . . . from the cooking utensil.

fat or grease

●

6. Why prick the thighs, breast and back of a duck or goose before roasting?

To allow rendered fat to escape.

●

7. Why 'hang' game birds?

To allow enzymes to tenderize the flesh and add flavour.

8. Chicken bone being hollow, transfers heat faster/ slower than the flesh surrounding it.

slower

9. When cooking, the flesh adjacent to the bone is likely to be more/less cooked than the rest of the flesh?

Less because the bone transfers heat more slowly.

10. To test if a simmering bird is cooked you do what?

Press the drumstick between thumb and forefinger for springiness and look for signs of blood in any juice issuing from the bird.

11. A roasting turkey which is not to be served until an hour after being cooked should be cooked to what internal temperature?

74C (165F).

12. Why is it that the roast-poach method of cooking turkey gives a higher yield than is obtained by roasting?

The bird is cut into smaller pieces which require less cooking and is braised instead of roasted.

13. Boned, braised birds served with a brown wine sauce would likely be called a . . . .

salmis

14. A cold, decorated, boneless cooked bird might be called a . . . .

galantine

242

15. Would you ever boil birds?

No, you would simmer them unless you wanted tough, stringy meat.

●

16. Why roast turkeys with the back uppermost (except for the last half hour of roasting)?

Fat from the fat glands in the back melts, bastes the turkey during roasting.

●

17. Why is deep-frying a faster method of cooking than sautéing (providing the food material is the same thickness)?

In deep-frying heat from the hot oil penetrates from all sides into the food.

●

18. What is the disadvantage of pre-cooking birds before final cooking?

The product is usually not as high in quality as if completely cooked from raw.

●

19. Southern Fried Chicken is nothing but fried chicken that has been coated with . . . .

seasoned flour

●

20. Why are birds that have been cooked by simmering plunged into cold water?

To stop the cooking and retain the moisture.

●

21. The term fricassée is used to refer to birds, veal or rabbit that have been cooked as a . . . . stew.

white

22. What advantage is there in boning birds before poaching them?

They cook quicker and give greater yield than if not boned.

●

23. Use high/low heat for roasting small birds and fat birds.

high

●

24. What precautions in handling poultry stuffing must be taken against germs causing food poisoning?

Bring to a temperature of 74C (165F) refrigerate in thin layers.

●

25. The process of removing drippings and sediment from a cooking pan for the purpose of making a sauce or gravy is called . . . .

deglazing

●

26. A barbecued chicken is a broiled chicken basted with . . . . sauce.

barbecue

●

27. Why should birds roasted in an oven be placed on a rack?

Portions of the bird on the bottom of the pan will burn because of the concentration of heat there.

●

28. Poultry is considered cooked when it reaches what temperature?

85C (185F)

29. Chicken that is breaded or floured is allowed to stand for 15 minutes before frying for what reason?

To allow the coating to tighten up and adhere to the bird.

●

30. Chicken Suprême uses what part of the bird?

Boned breasts

●

31. Chicken can be broiled completely in a broiler, but it can also be finished in an . . . .

oven

●

32. Coq au vin and Chicken à la Marengo are both prepared by . . . .

sautéing and braising

●

33. Small birds that are not larded and are roasted at low temperatures are likely to . . . .

dry out

●

34. Chicken fat can be used in making what sauce?

Velouté

●

35. When roasting small birds we can use high heat or a low heat. If we select low heat and the bird is lean we must do what to the bird to prevent its drying out while roasting?

Add fat by rubbing it in or by larding it with strips of fat such as bacon.

●

Salads and Salad Dressings

1   We usually think of a salad as a cold dish of greens or other vegetables dressed with oil and vinegar or some other dressing in which oil and vinegar predominate. Such a salad is served with a main course to give a crisp texture and flavour contrast to the other food. Salads can be made from just about any food material. They can be served in the form of an aspic, frozen, cold or hot. They can include meats, fowl, fish, fruit or vegetables. The food materials can be cooked or uncooked. The salad may be piquant or fairly bland. Salads are usually served as an accompaniment to a meal but they can be a separate course, a complete meal, or even served with a dessert to finish a meal. Salads are served at breakfast as for a wedding breakfast, at lunch or even at a very formal dinner.

What definition do you think best describes the salad? A salad is a food served with a dressing; the food can be:

a. A cold dish of green vegetables
b. A mixture of fruits
c. A hot mixture of piquant foods
d. A frozen mixture of bland foods
e. Chopped foods in aspic
f. A cold plate with slaw and potato salad
g. All of the above.

These are all 'salads'.

●

2   The word salad comes from the Latin word *sal* meaning salt. Our word salary comes from the same root because salt was once so valuable and rare that it formed part of the pay of Roman soldiers. Oil, vinegar and other seasonings became associated with salt because they all add flavour to the food.

The word *slaw* comes from the Danish word *sla*, a contraction of the French word *salade*. The word sauce is also derived from *sal* because sauces add flavour and zest to foods.

Salt is the root word for salary, sauce, slaw and . . . .

salad

●

3   Salads usually have four parts: an underliner of green leaves, a body, a dressing and a garnish. The underliner is frequently a leafy vegetable such as lettuce, romaine, escarole or endive, but could be an item such as sliced cucumber or fruit.

Not all salads have underliners. On a buffet salads are served from a bowl directly to the customers plate which has no underliner. Tossed salads are also served from bowls, which makes underliners unnecessary and saves time and labour.

True or False: A true salad rests on an underliner of a leafy vegetable.

Not necessarily

●

4   The most important part of the salad is the food which forms the body and gives salad its particular name. The body may be nothing but broken salad greens, fruit in a moulded aspic, sliced cooked potatoes, raw cabbage, wilted dandelion leaves, or tomato stuffed with cottage cheese. Exotic foods such as nasturtium leaves or hearts of palm are also used for the body. In fact almost any edible food may be so used.

The most important part of the salad is the . . . .

body

●

5   Salads are usually served with a salad dressing. The three basic salad dressings are: French, mayonnaise, and boiled or cooked. Thousands of variations of these dressings may be made from three basic ones. One authority states that 1300 variations are possible using French dressing and that nearly a thousand can be made using mayonnaise as a base.

Not every salad, however, must have a dressing just as every salad need not have an underliner.

True or False: We usually think of a salad having an underliner of green leaves and being served with a dressing.

True

6 Salad dressings are usually tart or piquant but there are also sweet salad dressings and some that are quite mild in flavour. A fruit salad, for example, may be dressed with a sweet, creamy, French dressing, and some vegetable or fruit salads maybe served with a dressing made from cream cheese.

Salad dressings include mild ones but are usually thought of as being . . . .

piquant or highly seasoned

7 The final part of the salad which may or may not be added is the garnish. It should be simple, edible and suited to the body of the salad. The garnish adds interest to the salad and complements the flavour of the body and the dressing. It should overwhelm neither.

True or False: When selecting a garnish for a salad pick one which is simple and edible.

True

8 Salads are *designed* to be attractive in colour, shape and height. For example, salads that are flat lose appeal. Ingredients should have definite form and not appear to be overworked. Foods which are difficult to eat should be bite size. Contrasts in colour, shape and flavour add interest.

Design should be planned but sometimes 'careful carelessness' is the best design just as with the wind-blown hair-do of a pretty girl.

Would you put a quarter piece of crisp apple into an arranged fruit salad?

No, since it would be too large to eat easily.

9 Crispness and freshness are quality factors in vegetable salads. Use young, tender vegetables and ripe but firm fruits. When using meats or fish be sure they

are well cooked, firm but tender. Since tender salad greens may be bruised in cutting, some experts recommend that they be torn rather than sliced with a knife. Sharp tools should be used to cut celery, cucumbers, tomatoes and fruits so that they have clean, sharp edges.

Why do some experts recommend tearing salad greens rather than cutting them?

To avoid bruising them.

10   Leftover meats, fish, poultry, cooked vegetables and the like are used in salads providing they are in good condition. Do not attempt to include foods of doubtful quality by working them into a salad. Shakespeare's comment that 'You can't make a silk purse out of a sow's ear' holds true for salads.

True or False: It is wrong to use 'leftovers' in salads.

Not if they are of good quality.

11   Many salad ingredients are living things. A head of lettuce picked from the field and shipped continues to live and breathe. A pear picked from a tree and shipped needs oxygen just as we do. Do not pack fresh fruits or vegetables together too tightly since they need oxygen to breathe. Refrigeration slows the rate of breathing and delays spoiling.

Some tropical fruits such as avocados and pineapples should be allowed to stand at room temperature if they need further ripening. Bananas should never be put under refrigeration.

True or False: All fresh fruits and vegetables should be refrigerated at once.

Not all of them.

12   Before serving salad greens and some vegetables, they can be crisped by immersing them into cold water and refrigerating with some moisture still clinging to them. If they dry, they will wilt and become limp.

To keep vegetables and greens crisp under refrigeration do we want them completely dry?

A little moisture helps to maintain their crispness.

J

13   Vegetable cells can draw in moisture and lose it by a process of absorption or loss known as osmosis. The more completely the tiny cells of a vegetable are filled with moisture, the crisper the vegetable will be. Therefore, moisture should be placed on their surface to be drawn in. Too much moisture will waterlog the cells.

Salt, vinegar and other seasonings on the outside of vegetable cells reverse the process and draw moisture from the cells, causing the vegetable to wilt.

Crisping of vegetables is accomplished by the cells drawing in . . . .

moisture

●

14   It is quite proper to soak vegetables and salad greens to clean them or to moisten them but it is not good practice to allow them to remain in water. Better crisping occurs if the vegetable or green is lightly moistened but not covered with water. Apparently, complete immersion in water suffocates the vegetable and it loses texture and perhaps flavour and quality.

Superior crisping occurs if the vegetable or green is placed in cold and lightly circulating air.

What happens if we leave vegetables soaking in water for some period of time?

They do not get the oxygen needed and lose quality.

●

15   Since salads require much labour in their preparation it is important to *line-up* the work by arranging it so as to save time in preparation. Timing is important so that salads are ready when needed, but only a short time before being needed. Some salads require last-minute assembly. Salad dressings can be made ahead of time and placed in easy-to-use containers. Vegetables can be torn or cut and placed in containers ready for use at the assembly point. Underliners and garnishes can be prepared ahead of time.

Frozen and aspic solids should be prepared 24 hours in advance of need.

Some salad materials such as meat, potatoes and cauliflower can be mixed ahead of time, along with their dressings because they do not wilt and lose quality. In fact, such salads increase in quality because the dressing has time to penetrate the food materials.

Crisp green salads should be assembled when?

As close to serving time as possible.

16   In arranging work, the tools, materials, plates, dressings and other items should be placed within 35 cm of the front of the worker. Nothing should be outside of the worker's maximum reach, which is 65 cm. Women's reach is about 10% less.

In arranging materials and equipment at a salad work station nothing should be placed further than . . . . in front of the worker.

65 cm

●

GELATINE BASED SALADS

17   Gelatine has some amazing properties. When dissolved in a liquid and chilled it has the power to bind and hold the liquid to form a semi-rigid structure known as a gel. Forces of attraction are set up between the long chain-like molecules of the gelatine which form a branched or 'brush heap' structure of cross-linked, molecular chains. The liquid is immobilized within these chains.

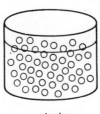

solution

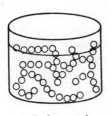

solution gel

A 2% solution of gelatine in water will 'set', becoming a firm gel at 15C (59F).

A 1% concentration of gelatine and liquid yields as firm a gel at 0C (32F).

The temperature at which a gelatine solution sets to a particular firmness . . . .

varies with the concentration of gelatine

18   A large variety of chilled salads can be made by using about 2% gelatine to liquid, which forms a gel when set and permits the gel to carry any fruits and vegetables desired. Powdered gelatine desserts contain sugar and acids which necessitate a greater percentage of the dry mixture to liquid.

Only about .... of a gelatine to water mixture is needed to form a gel in ordinary chilled mixtures.

2%

●

19   Gelatine is obtained from collagen found in bones, skin, and other collagen bearing parts of an animal. The gelatine powder is about 85% protein but is incomplete in that it lacks the essential amino acid, tryptophan. The 'biological value' is therefore low unless eaten with foods which supply the missing amino acids.

Since gelatine constitutes such a small percentage of the total of a gelatine salad or dessert its nutritional value is small/large.

small

●

20   The amount of sugar, the pH of a solution and the kind of liquid used affect gelling characteristics:

Milk, which contains about 13% solids, mostly protein and carbohydrates produces a firmer gel, probably because of the solids present and the fact that they are protein.

A medium amount of sugar increases the stiffness of gel but a large amount retards gel formation and weakens it.

Acids weaken gel structure.

More/less gelatine is needed when acids such as lemon juice or tomato juice are included in a salad.

more

●

21   More gelatine is needed when vegetables or fruits which are acid are included in a salad. The tendency is therefore to add enough gelatine so there will be no problem about gelling. The frequent result is that the product is rubbery and rigid rather than firm and delicate.

A rubbery gelatine is likely to be caused by ....

an excess amount of gelatine

22   Fresh pineapples and figs contain an enzyme which destroy the gelling power of gelatine. However, the enzyme can be destroyed by cooking.

Before using fresh pineapples or figs in a gelatine salad do what to them?

Cook them

●

23   The manner in which gelatine is put into solution and chilled affects the final product. To make a salad the plain gelatine is first soaked in a small amount of cold water. Then, only enough boiling water is added to dissolve the gelatine. The remainder of the liquid is added cold. (Gelatine will go into solution at 35C (95F) but the use of very hot or boiling water speeds the process.)

The first step in making gel is to . . . .

soak gelatine in cold water

●

24   The second step in the making of gel is to dissolve the moistened gelatine in hot water and then . . . .

add the rest of the liquid which can be at room temperature or cold

●

25   If gelatine sets at a temperature below 10C (50F) or is cooled too rapidly, the firmness of the gel may be weak. Therefore, it is recommended that the gelatine solution be cooled to below 38C (100F), and then placed in the refrigerator for the gelling action.

True or False: Rate of cooling and gelling temperature both affect the quality of the gel.

True

●

26   When chopped vegetables or fruits are to be distributed throughout a salad they must be added when the gelatine is in a syrupy stage. Otherwise, they will float on the top or settle at the bottom. If the gelatine is slightly firm the solids will remain where placed. The syrup stage is also right if the gelatine is to be whipped into a foam. Place the gelatine in crushed ice since the action raises the temperature of the gelatine.

If the gelatine is to be riced or diced it is allowed to become firm before processing.

If gelatine is to be beaten into a foam, more gelatine is needed than for a solid mass.

If gelatine is to be beaten, it should be at what stage?

The syrupy stage

●

27 Aspic salads are also firmed by gelatine, either that naturally present as in a reduced meat or fish stock or by the addition of gelatine.

Tomato aspic is probably the best known of the aspics and is made with cold tomatoes, tomato juice, or tomato purée with the addition of gelatine.

Aspics are also used decoratively as glazes to give a shiny surface to other foods, e.g. cocktail savouries, cold buffet dishes.

Aspic salads become firm by the setting action of the . . . . present.

gelatine

●

FROZEN SALADS

28 Frozen salads are usually made from a base which is $\frac{2}{3}$ by measure of mayonnaise and $\frac{1}{3}$ whipped cream. Sometimes, softened cream cheese is used in place of all or part of the mayonnaise. Fruits and vegetables are added to this mixture and the whole frozen and served frozen.

Some foods do not freeze well. Eggs, for example, become tough and rubbery, and processed or cottage cheese may lose their texture and flavour. Most thickening agents separate when frozen and a waxy maize type of starch which does not separate when frozen is used.

Would you guess that a tossed salad made of lettuce and a dressing of oil and vinegar would freeze well?

No, the cells in the vegetables would enlarge and rupture making the defrosted product mushy and without character.

254

TOSSED SALADS

29   Tossed salads are usually made completely or almost completely of salad greens which are tossed in a large bowl with the dressing added either before the customers or in the kitchen. They may contain celery, cucumbers, tomatoes, meats, cheese, other foods besides greens and herbs. One member of the onion family should be added.

The bowl in which the salad is tossed may be rubbed with a piece of garlic and a piece of onion. Croutons (cubes of bread, browned in butter and flavoured with garlic or cheese) may be added to give crispness. Dressings and seasonings that would destroy the texture of the salad are added just before service.

A mixture of chopped herbs, one of them a member of the . . . . family, is often added to a tossed salad before seasoning.

onion

●

30   To impart even more flavour to a tossed salad, a dry piece of bread is rubbed heavily with garlic and put into the salad until the time the salad is tossed. Then, it is removed. The bread adds flavour in a manner similar to what is accomplished when the salad bowl is rubbed with . . . .

garlic

●

31   A well-known tossed salad made from romaine (cos) lettuce, egg, greens, olive oil, anchovies and Parmesan cheese is the Caesar salad. It was originated either at the Marine Club in San Diego or in Tia Juana, Mexico, just south of San Diego. The bowl is rubbed well with garlic—or sometimes minced garlic is sautéed in the oil used in the dressing. A raw or coddled egg is added to crisp greens which have been torn and tossed. Olive oil is added and the mixture again tossed. Lemon juice and wine vinegar may be added or sometimes wine vinegar alone is used. Croutons, anchovy fillets, grated Parmesan cheese, dried mustard and freshly ground pepper are added and the mixture tossed again.

A well-known tossed salad using raw egg and anchovies is the . . . . salad.

Caesar

32   When oil and vinegar or other acid liquids are used separately for dressing, the oil is added to the salad greens first so that the oil will coat the salad materials. If the acid liquid is first added, the salad greens are moistened and when the oil is added it runs from the greens and is lost in the bottom of the bowl.

When adding oil and vinegar to a tossed salad add the . . . . first.

oil

●

33   Since some effort is expended in keeping salad greens chilled and crisp, it makes good sense to serve them on a cold plate. The same would be true of any cold salad. The salad can be plated and placed in the refrigerator or the plates themselves may be chilled in the refrigerator prior to use.

Will a warm plate draw heat from the salad placed on it?

Heat continually tries to equalize itself and will flow between any substances which are of different temperatures.

●

HOT SALADS

34   A hot salad of greens is usually made by wilting the greens with a hot fat such as chopped bacon and its dripping. The greens are then tossed and boiling vinegar is added and further tossing is done. The hot salad is served at once.

Another way to make a hot green salad is to boil the oil, vinegar and seasonings, and thicken them slightly with flour or starch. The salad greens are then tossed in this hot dressing a few moments while heat is applied.

True or False: A green hot salad can be made by either wilting the greens in hot oil or wilting them in slightly thickened sauce of hot oil, vinegar and the seasonings.

True

35 Other hot salad materials are cabbage slaw, sauerkraut, or cooked vegetables, such as potatoes, cauliflower, beetroots, string or dried beans. A hot salad can be made using any type of food that will not wilt when heated. An advantage of a hot salad made from such materials is that it can be held for a long time without loss of quality. A popular hot salad is the German potato salad which is served with cured meat or sausages or as a side dish.

Could you add the seasonings to a hot salad much in advance of the serving time?

Yes, the seasonings will combine with the hot foods and improve the salad.

●

FRUIT SALADS

36 Fruit salads are not tossed because the fruits would bruise or lose their shape. Fruits used in a salad are usually arranged in a specific manner on the salad plate. If the fruit will hold its shape the salad may be mixed and placed without arrangement on the plate.

True or False: Fruit salad materials are arranged unless the fruit can be mixed without breaking up, losing shape and appearance.

True

●

HIGH PROTEIN SALADS

37 Salads are often used as a main course by including diced or sliced pieces of meat, poultry, fish, egg or cheese. A ratio of about two parts of meat, poultry, fish, egg or cheese to one part of chopped vegetables such as celery, potatoes or other extenders is used. Any type of dressing may be served with this salad.

Would you serve such a salad as a side salad?

Not usually, since the salad is often large and contains enough protein food to be a meal in itself.

38   Carbohydrate food materials such as kidney beans
and macaroni may also be used to make substantial
salads.

The ratio varies
but is about 2 of
meat to 1 of the
extender.

If you were using meat and an extender such as
chopped celery in an entrée salad, what ratio of meat
to extender would you be likely to use?

●

FRENCH DRESSING

39   French dressing is one of the simplest and most
widely used for dressings. It consists of oil and vinegar
or other acid liquids such as lemon or fruit juice, plus
seasonings. Two or three parts of oil to one of vinegar
is the usual proportion, but this varies.

It is known as an unstable mixture, since oil and
vinegar do not mix to form a continuous solution. The
oil, being lighter, separates and floats to the top of the
vinegar or juices. Vigorous shaking mixes them again,
but they soon separate into two phases.

French dressing is an unstable mixture of oil and
liquid, the ratio of oil to liquid being about . . . .

two or three to one

●

40   The usual French dressing is an unstable mixture
but the addition of whole eggs, egg yolk, cooked starch
paste, agar agar, gum tragancanth, or gum arabic can
make French dressing into a stable emulsion. Instead of
the oil and water repelling each other they now attract
each other and the two liquids mix uniformly.

Oil and vinegar normally form an unstable solution
when mixed but can be made into an . . . . , if
eggs, cooked starches or some other ingredients are
added.

emulsion

●

41   French dressings are made differently for different
salads. Sweet dressings go well with fruit salads. Tangy,
well-seasoned dressings are desirable for vegetables or
salad greens. Roquefort cheese added in tiny bits to

French dressing also goes well with salad greens. Sour cream and chopped chives with French dressing produces a Bellevue dressing, excellent for citrus fruit. The addition of mango chutney, walnut catsup and finely chopped parsley, chervil or tarragon gives us a chutney dressing, perfect for a chicken salad. The addition of the mashed coral of a cooked lobster, Worcestershire sauce, and chopped parsley makes a dressing for fish or seafood salad.

True or False: Variations of the basic French dressing can be used with a wide variety of salads.

True

●

42   A marinade is almost identical with French dressing in that it includes an acid liquid such as vinegar or fruit juice plus seasonings and sometimes oil. Vegetables, fruits and other foods which will not wilt are soaked in the marinade to add flavour or to develop tenderness.

Recalling from an earlier section, how does an acid act to tenderize meat?

It breaks down the connective tissue.

●

MAYONNAISE

43   Mayonnaise is also one of the basic dressings, popular over the Occidental world. It is an emulsion of eggs, vinegar or lemon juice, oil and seasonings. The proportions of ingredients must be correct and properly mixed to form a stable emulsion. The eggs are the emulsifying agent that draws the oil and vinegar together and should be about 20% of the total weight. A more stable and firmer emulsion will be made if egg yolks only are used.

From the above would you guess that a lesser weight of egg yolks would be needed than if whole eggs were used?

Yes, the egg yolks are the important part of the egg as regards emulsification.

44 The moisture present in mayonnaise is held in suspension by the eggs. Therefore, the vinegar used must not exceed about 10% of the final weight or half the weight of the eggs.

The weight of the oil is about 65—70% of the total, which leaves about what percentage of the total for other seasonings?

Up to five per cent of the total weight can be in salt, paprika, mustard, pepper, and other seasonings.

●

45 The oil must be added slowly to the eggs and seasonings—almost a drop at a time—so that the oil can be incorporated into the eggs.

Beating should not be too hard since air might be incorporated, making the mixture unstable.

Once an emulsion is started by finely dividing some of the oil into the egg, the oil can be added more rapidly.

After half the emulsion is made, the vinegar or acid liquid can be added and the rest of the oil blended in.

The reason for dribbling the oil into the egg yolks at the beginning of making mayonnaise is to . . . .

be sure to start a good emulsion by incorporating the oil into the egg yolks

●

46 Sometimes mayonnaise breaks: the emulsion does not hold and the oil separates from the egg. When this happens, the emulsion can be reformed by adding a bit of the broken emulsion a little at a time to some stable mayonnaise and beating. Increase the quantity of broken mayonnaise added until all of the broken batch has been reformed. One can also reform a broken emulsion by beating it slowly into whole egg, egg yolk, vinegar, a starch paste or other liquid.

A broken emulsion can/cannot be reformed.

can be

●

47 Commercial mayonnaise is much more stable than that made in the kitchen because the oil and emulsifiers have been homogenized, divided into tiny particles. Such mayonnaise can hold a higher proportion of oil to liquid and emulsifier. However in the United States, government regulations require that commercial mayonnaise

contain not less than 50% edible oil and that the combined percentage of eggs and oil be not less than 78% of the total weight.

Commercial mayonnaise is more/less stable than mayonnaise made in our own kitchens?

More, it can even be frozen and the emulsion will remain stable when thawed.

●

48   Mayonnaise, like French dressing, is basic and has numerous variations. Roquefort or blue cheese may be added to mayonnaise to make a roquefort or blue cheese dressing. Use of the mayonnaise produces a creamier and slightly thicker dressing than that made with a French dressing. Chopped chutney added to mayonnaise can be mixed with chicken salad. Mayonnaise with caviar, chopped chives, a touch of hot mustard, and finely chopped egg white is delicious for an egg salad.

The well known, 1000-island dressing is made using two parts of mayonnaise to one part chili sauce and adding chopped pickles, olives, hard cooked eggs, onions and pimento.

Russian dressing is made using two parts mayonnaise with one part chili sauce and seasoning with a few drops Worcestershire sauce and cayenne pepper.

Russian and 1000-island dressings are both variations of . . . .

mayonnaise dressing

●

COOKED OR BOILED SALAD DRESSINGS

49   Remember, it was said that there are three basic salad dressings: French, Mayonnaise and Cooked or Boiled Salad Dressings. This last is the only one which is thickened with a starch. Eggs, too, are added and they help in the thickening when they coagulate during cooking. The liquid used in boiled dressing may be milk, or vinegar, or water, or fruit juice, or other liquid.

Two thickeners used in cooked or boiled salad dressings are . . . . and . . . .

eggs, starches

50   In the best cooked dressing, about one-fourth to one-third of the total weight is oil or fats such as butter or margarine. Seasonings are salt, pepper, mustard, paprika and others.

A boiled dressing contains more/less fat than mayonnaise.

less

51   Boiled dressings are usually thick, which means that they may be thinned with other ingredients. This permits the boiled dressing to be used as a base for a number of other dressings. Sweet, creamy dressings for fruit salads, a tangy dressing for potato salad, or a smooth, creamy dressing for cole-slaw are some of the variations possible.

True or False: Boiled dressings, being thickened with starch, can be made into several other creamy dressings.

True

52   An excellent dressing for fruit salad can be made from a boiled dressing which includes orange or lemon juice, egg yolks, flour, butter, sugar, and a few seasonings. It is thinned with milk or orange juice and then sweetened whipped cream is folded in. An excellent boiled dressing for potato salad is made using milk, butter or margarine and seasonings which are thickened with flour and eggs, and then thinned with vinegar or cream or evaporated milk. If maple syrup is added, this same dressing is excellent over a tart fruit salad.

What distinguishes a boiled dressing from other dressings?

It has been thickened with flour and cooked.

REVISION

1. What happens when a vegetable draws moisture into its cells until all of the moisture possible is held in the cells without breaking them?

The vegetable is crisped.

2. If water is drawn from the cells of the vegetable by a substance such as salt or salad dressing, what happens to the vegetable?

It wilts.

●

3. Name the four parts of the salad.

1. underliner
2. body
3. dressing
4. garnish

●

4. Name the three basic salad dressings.

1. French
2. mayonnaise
3. cooked or boiled

●

5. What are the two principal ingredients and their proportions in French dressing?

2 or 3 parts oil, 1 part vinegar

●

6. Why is mayonnaise called a stable emulsion?

The oil in the mayonnaise is surrounded by liquid which will remain that way unless seriously disturbed by heat, salt or agitation.

●

7. The proper proportion of mayonnaise to whipped cream in frozen salad is . . . .

two to one

●

8. Would you add more or less gelatine to a mixture when:
   a. acid is added to it.
   b. much sugar is added to it.
   c. chopped vegetables are added to it.
   d. it is made into a foam.

a. more
b. more
c. more
d. more

9. Why should oil be added to the greens in a salad before the vinegar?

So that the oil will adhere to the salad greens.

●

10. Some experts insist on tearing the salad greens instead of cutting them. Why?

They believe the greens are less bruised in tearing than in cutting.

●

11. To develop a tender gelatine of quality, cool it quickly/slowly.

slowly

●

12. Gelatine is weakened by the presence of . . . .

acid

●

13. Excessive gelatine in a salad makes the product . . . .

rubbery

●

14. A small quantity of sugar strengthens a gelatine mixture but an *excess* of sugar weakens it. Why?

The excess sugar competes with the gelatine for the moisture and the gelatine cannot get enough moisture to set.

●

15. If a gelatine is to be whipped to a foam more/less gelatine is needed.

more

16. Fresh pineapple should/should not be added to a gelatine salad.

should not

●

17. Within limits, the more gelatine present the higher/lower the temperature at which the gel forms.

higher

Vegetable Cookery

1   The principal reason for cooking vegetables is to break down their cellular structures so the vegetables are more palatable and digestible. The compound that makes vegetables tough or hard, cellulose, can be softened by cooking. The amount of cellulose in a vegetable often determines its cooking time and how it is best cooked. Spinach has very little cellulose compared with a carrot.

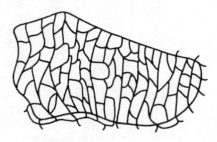

cellulose network in a carrot

Therefore, spinach would be cooked a longer/shorter time than carrots.

shorter

●

2   Cooking tends to change the flavour of vegetables. Raw carrots, for example, have a different flavour, besides a different texture, from cooked carrots. Different cooking methods can make the same vegetable quite different. Steamed, boiled and baked marrow, for example, are quite different in flavour, texture and vitamin content. Cooking may or may not increase

palatability in a vegetable. For instance, some people may prefer the flavour and texture of raw to cooked celery.

A vegetable is cooked to change its . . . .   taste, texture
and . . . .

●

3   The choice of preparation methods for vegetables is frequently cultural. People tend to prefer vegetables prepared in manners to which they are accustomed. In the Southern States of America, for example, vegetables are prepared with bacon, pork or other fat and cooked to a state of limpness or mushiness, considered over-cooked by people from other sections of the country. Large numbers of British people also prefer vegetables cooked until very well done and limp. The Chinese like their vegetables underdone and slightly crisp. Europeans usually cook their vegetables in a stock, often adding fat of one form or another. The Italians like their fat to be olive oil, the Bretons of Northern France like butter, and the French and Germans of Alsace like to use fat pork. Vegetable cookery therefore is/is not standard in various regions of the world.   is not

●

4   The method generally considered best for cooking mild flavoured vegetables such as peas, spinach, beans, corn, is to cook them as little as possible while retaining as much of their original flavour, colour and nutrients as is possible. Vitamin C (ascorbic acid) is the principal vitamin lost in vegetable cookery, it being water soluble and easily leached into the cooking water. It is also heat labile (destroyed by heat) and is easily destroyed   Steaming, since
by oxidation. Thiamine chloride (vitamin B_1) is also   leaching is less
heat labile and is quickly destroyed in an alkaline   and cooking time
medium. Other vitamins such as vitamin A can be   shortened.
destroyed by wilting or long standing of the vegetable.   However, the higher
Minerals can be lost by their being leached out of the   temperature of
vegetable in soaking or cooking in water. Because of the   the steam may
ease with which nutrients can be lost by solubility, heat,   bring about a
chemical reaction, and so forth, which method would you   loss of heat labile
think would best preserve these compounds, boiling   vitamins greater
or steaming?   than by boiling.

5   The colours in vegetables are changed by different cooking methods and chemical reactions. Green vegetables are green because of the presence of *chlorophyll* which can be degraded by heat. As cooking continues magnesium in the pigment is lost and green turns to green yellow. After twenty minutes in a steam table, green vegetables show a loss of colour. This destruction is speeded up in cooking by the presence of acids.

Chlorophyll is destroyed by . . . . and . . . .   heat, acids

●

6   To cook green mild flavoured vegetables, therefore, we have four problems: (1) to retain the nutrients, (2) to retain the colour, (3) to obtain a desirable texture and (4) to obtain a desirable flavour. We want much/little water present so that the nutrients and flavour will not be leached away.

Little; however, we see later that some green vegetables are best boiled in a large quantity of water when they are strong flavoured.

●

7   Most vegetables are slightly acid, and these are soluble in water and volatile in cooking—that is, they are leached out into the cooking water and escape easily in the steam. For this reason, then, it makes good sense to get rid of these acids to cook green vegetables in water with the lid on/off.

Lid off, to allow the escape of the volatile acids which affect the chlorophyll present.

●

8.   Vegetables are one of the few foods which should be cooked by boiling. Would it matter if the water is at a slow boil or a fast boil?

The temperature in both instances is 100C (212F). The fast boil may fragment the vegetables unnecessarily.

9   Practically all of the loss of ascorbic acid occurs from the time that vegetables are added to boiling water and when the water returns to the boil. This destruction of vitamin C is probably due to enzymes present in the vegetables whose action is increased by the heat, and are destroyed at somewhat below the boiling point.

True or False: In cooking vegetables have the cooking water boiling and try to return it to the boil as quickly as possible after the vegetables have been added.

True

●

10   We should leave the lid on up to a point where the salted water *begins to boil;* then we should add the vegetables, put the lid on and *remove the lid just before boiling starts again.* This permits the escape of the volatile acids which would destroy the green colour (chlorophyll).

True or False: It is proper to leave the lid on all the time during the cooking of green vegetables.

False; leave the lid on only to speed the cooking up to the point where the vegetables boil; then, take the cover off so that volatile acids can escape.

●

11   Professional chefs ordinarily leave the lid off so they can observe what is going on in the cooking utensil. This way, they see the progress of cooking and allow the acids to escape so that the colour in green vegetables known as . . . . is not destroyed.

chlorophyll

●

12   Once vegetables are cooked should we remove the vegetables from their cooking water?

Yes, to prevent further cooking and nutrient loss.

●

13   Calcium, magnesium salts and other compounds may be present in the cooking water which cause the water to be 'hard' or alkaline in reaction. A water having less than 50 parts per million of these salts is called 'soft' water, but water having 100 ppm is said to be

hard. This hardness or alkalinity can change the colour pigments in vegetables to undesirable colours. It can also react unfavourably on nutrients and texture. For instance, if a vegetable is cooked in hard water or water to which soda has been added, nutrients are destroyed. The alkaline reaction also softens cellulose so that the vegetable becomes over soft and mushy. Some vegetables develop an objectionable slipperiness.

An alkaline reaction in the cooking water may cause cellulose or the structure of a vegetable to become . . . . or . . . .

soft, mushy

●

14 Since acids destroy chlorophyll, green vegetables cooked in an alkaline medium will not lose colour as rapidly as when cooked in a water that is slightly acid or neutral. However, because of the unfavourable effects of an alkaline reaction on vitamins and to the texture of a vegetable it is wise to avoid the addition of alkaline compounds such as bi-carbonate of soda to cooking water for vegetables.

A vegetable that has an objectionable slipperiness in the mouth and has lost a great deal of its vitamin C and B_1 has probably been cooked in an . . . . water.

alkaline

●

15 Since the retention of vitamin C and other nutrients in vegetable cookery depends in part on the amount of water in which the vegetables are cooked, the minimum amount of water possible is used for some mild flavoured greens, and just a little more for peas, beans, corn and other items which contain more starch. Greens should be turned from top to bottom several times during the relatively short cooking time to provide even cooking. All vegetables are cooked until tender but not soft. The minimum or moderate amount of water applies to the mild flavoured vegetables such as peas, spinach, broccoli, beans, carrots, asparagus and arti-chokes. Vegetables with strong flavours e.g. cabbage, onions, turnips, parsnips, Brussels sprouts and wild greens may be cooked in large amounts of water for what reason?

To allow for strong flavours to pass from the vegetable into the cooking water.

270

16   When cooking red vegetables, the problem is to retain vitamins and to brighten the red pigments which are called *anthocyanins*. Acids are helpful in brightening red colours while alkalis turn this red colour to a dirty blue or purple. The acid in most red vegetables—beetroots, red cabbage and rhubarb—helps to retain the red colour providing the cooking water is not hard. If hardness exists, cream of tartar, lemon juice, vinegar or some other acid ingredient may be added. This is why red cabbage may be cooked with sour apples or vinegar may be added or other acid foods combined with the beetroot.

When the cooking medium is acid, the colour of a red vegetable is kept . . . . but when the cooking medium is alkaline, the colour becomes a dirty . . . .   red, blue, purple
or . . . .

●

17   Cauliflower and other white vegetables owe their whiteness to pigments called *flavones*. These pigments are white in an acid medium and yellow in an alkaline medium. The flavones are soluble in water; therefore, when onions or some other vegetable containing a large quantity of flavones are cooked in an alkaline water, the colour of the water turns yellow as well as the vegetable. White vegetables when cooked in an alkaline   yellow
medium turn yellow/white.

●

18   If a very small quantity of cream of tartar is added   As we learned,
to hard water, an acid reaction results and keeps the   the acid might
cauliflower white. However, if the water is too acid,   develop strong
what might happen?   flavours and in
a green vegetable
would destroy
chlorophyll;
therefore, we try
to have the reaction
only *sightly* acid
or neutral, that
is, neither acid
nor alkaline.

271

19   *Carotenoids* are the pigments which provide most
of the yellow and orange colours of fruits, vegetables and
flowers. The carotenoids themselves are little affected
by acid or alkaline and they are insoluble in water.
However, they are always accompanied by chlorophyll,
about 3 to 4 parts chlorophyll to each part carotenoid
and in some cases if the chlorophyll is degraded the
yellow colour appears brighter since it is not obscured
by the green. This apparently happens when cooking
carrots in an acid medium.

Most of the oranges and yellows in vegetables are from
pigments known as the . . . .   carotenoids

●

19a   Carotenoids range in colour from yellow to red
and the redness in tomatoes, peppers and radishes   No, this would
is from a carotenoid pigment rather than anthocyanins.   only be true if
Would you expect tomatoes and red peppers to lose   they were
their colour if cooked in an alkali?   anthocyanins.

●

20   To review what was said about the four sets of
pigments with which we are concerned in cooking vegetables, here are the pigments. What colours do they
represent in a neutral medium?

anthocyanins   . . . .   red
chlorophyll   . . . .   green
flavones   . . . .   white
carotenoids   . . . .   yellow or orange

●

21   The table below summarizes information about the
colour pigments in vegetables, noting the effect of an
alkaline or an acid medium on them, their solubility in
water and how they are affected by heat.

	Colour in Alkaline medium	Colour in Acid medium	Soluble in water	Destroyed by heat
Anthocyanins	blue or purple	red	X	
Chlorophyll	green	olive		X
Flavones	yellow	white	X	
Carotenoids	yellow or orange	yellow or orange		

Would you expect the cooking water in which we cook carrots to turn yellow?

Not much, carotenoids are not soluble in water (they are soluble in fat and alcohol).

●

21a Suppose you are cooking beetroots and they turn blue or purple, what do you know about the water?

It is hard water, alkaline in nature.

●

21b Suppose the water in which you are cooking cauliflower turns yellow, what would you know about the water?

It is alkaline since the alkalinity turns the white pigments, the flavones, yellow.

●

22 A cook boils red cabbage, which contains both flavones and anthocyanins, in alkaline water. The water itself and the cabbage turn green. Explain the reaction.

The flavones turn yellow and the anthocyanins turn blue in an alkaline water; the green colour is the result of the blending of these two colours.

●

THE ONION AND CABBAGE FAMILIES

23 While it is desirable to use as little water as possible with most vegetables, those that contain strong flavours such as broccoli, Brussels sprouts, cabbage,

turnips and onions may be cooked in a large quantity of water and the lid of the cooking utensil should be left off so that the strong flavours as well as the acids can escape. If acids are allowed to get too strong in the cooking water, they assist in the development of strong sulphur tasting compounds or other undesirable flavours. Thus, in cooking onions, we can use a large quantity of water to dilute the excessive flavour of the onions and keep the lid on/off.

Off, to allow the strong flavours and acids to escape in the steam.

●

24   The strongly flavoured vegetables should be separated into two groups because different cooking methods should be used with each. The onion family which would include besides onions, leeks, garlic, shallots, chives, and scallions (young onions), should be cooked by one method, and the cabbage family which includes swedes, broccoli, turnips, and kohlrabi may be cooked by another method. There are two separate classes of strongly flavoured vegetables, the . . . . family and the . . . . family.

onion, cabbage

●

25   Vegetables in the cabbage family and in the onion family should both be cooked in a fairly large quantity of water which is neither strongly alkaline nor strongly acid. If vegetables in either family are stored for long periods of time, the flavour will be stronger. The time of cooking should be short for the cabbage family but the time of cooking for the onion family should be long. This is because the flavour compounds in each behave differently in cooking.

The development of flavours in vegetables in the cabbage and the onion family are different/the same.

different

26　Onions and other members of that family develop sharp flavours rapidly after they start to cook but longer cooking dissipates this strong flavour, leaving a milder, subtler flavour. On the other hand, cabbage and other members of its family develop strong flavours when cooked a long time. Therefore, these vegetables are cooked for as short a time as possible. Early green cabbage which is boiled six minutes in salted water is delicious and has a good texture and appearance while the same cabbage cooked for 45 minutes will have a strong flavour, soft, slippery texture and a poor appearance. Would you sauté diced onions, shallots or minced garlic previous to putting them in an item such as bread stuffing, sauce or other dish, or would you add them raw and expect them to cook while the item itself cooked?

Usually, we sauté these items in butter or fat without colour to dissipate the strong flavours. Then, we add them to the item to be cooked. This longer cooking gives a milder flavour (except for shallots which become bitter if browned).

●

27　Vegetables of the onion and cabbage families are both cooked in a quantity of water. Those of the cabbage family are cooked for a relatively short time; those of the onion family for a relatively . . . . time.

long

●

28　In preparing onions with skins on them there is the problem of removing the skins and cutting up the onions easily and with a minimum of tears from the worker caused by volatile products given off. To avoid irritation to the eyes first put onions into boiling water for several minutes, the time depending upon their size. This softens the skin and some of the acrid gases are dissipated. Remove from the water and slice off the root and top ends. The remainder of the skin is easily removed, since it is no longer anchored to the body of the onion at the ends. If onions are to be cooked whole, push a knife up into the root end twice to form a cross incision. Why?

To allow the heat to penetrate up into the centre of the onion more quickly.

●

29　Said writer Dean Swift '. . . lest your kissing should be spoiled, your onions must be thoroughly boiled . . .'. He was partly right. Do not boil onions. High temperatures develop sulphuric off-flavours when cooked at too high a heat. Should the utensil cover be on or off when cooking onions?

Off, to allow the volatile flavours to escape easily into the atmosphere.

275

PREPARING AND COOKING OTHER VEGETABLES

30 Some vegetables are soaked before cooking to remove soil and insects. Salted water encourages the tiny mites in cabbage, Brussels sprouts and cauliflower to leave. From what you know about water soluble vitamins would you think that soaking should be done in minimum time?

If the cells are not damaged little leaching will occur over a reasonable period of time.

●

30a Dried beans are ordinarily soaked in cold water overnight to allow the beans to take up the water which was lost in drying and to soften.

A quicker method of cooking dried beans is to bring the water to a boil and add the beans (one cup beans to one quart water). Let them boil for two minutes and then set off heat for one hour. They can then be cooked. One cup dried beans yields $2\frac{1}{2}$ cups of cooked beans.

True or False: Heating the water in which beans are to be cooked lessens the time necessary for them to soak.

True

●

31 Some vegetables such as kale, have strong flavours. To dissipate some of these strong flavours, blanch or parboil the vegetables first; then add to fresh water and complete cooking. Blanching and parboiling are terms used interchangeably to indicate the same cooking procedure. To blanch may also mean to dip quickly into boiling or cold water. To blanch may also be a method of subjecting to steam for a very short period in order to partially cook.

A few of the strong vegetables may be . . . . or . . . . to rid them of strong flavours, after which they are cooked.

blanched, parboiled

276

32   Most vegetables lose their natural sugars rapidly following harvesting. Corn and peas, for example, lose 25 per cent or more of their sugars within 24 hours after harvesting. In cooking, sugar is leached into the cooking water. Therefore, it is reasonable to add some sugar to vegetables to replace that which has been lost. This, of course, is a matter of individual taste. If starch is formed in a vegetable such as peas or corn after it is harvested, what would you think is happening in view of what has been said here?

The sugars are turning to starch; this gives a far less sweet and tender vegetable and one that tastes much less fresh than when just harvested.

●

33   To facilitate the removal of vegetables easily after boiling in water, cook them in a colander or salad basket and set this down into cold water. In this manner, they can be removed quickly once they are done, preventing overcooking. Would you do this with potatoes?

Probably not; often the water is drained from them and the heat is left on so that the potatoes lose their excess moisture by evaporation.

●

34   Fine division of a vegetable aids in reducing cooking time. It also aids in dissipating strong flavours in vegetables belonging to the onion and cabbage families. Fine division, however, results in a higher loss of nutrients because more surface area is exposed for leaching out of the nutrients. Because the tips of broccoli and asparagus are much more tender and require a shorter cooking time than the tougher stalks, how would you treat these in preparation to give even cooking times?

Split the stalks.

●

35   Generally speaking, it is best for nutrition and flavour to cook vegetables in larger pieces, and where practicable for root vegetables in their skins. Following this reasoning, would you cook beetroots unpared and whole, and skin them after cooking?

Yes, the beetroots peel easily after cooking and retain more flavour when cooked in their skins.

36 Vegetables should be cooked as close to the serving time as possible. To accomplish this, vegetables are cooked in small quantities known as small batch cookery or progressive cookery (the cooking progressing along with the serving of the food). Vegetables should be served within 20 minutes of cooking. Is cooking going on in vegetables that are being held in a steam table?

Yes, heat is being transferred to the vegetables and they are cooking slowly, losing their form, colour and vitamin content.

●

37 It is especially important that vegetables have the cooking stopped once they have reached the desired point of cooking. When the vegetables are to be served later, many chefs place the vegetables in a colander under running cold water (called 'refreshing' them) which accomplishes this purpose, but it also tends to wash away some of the flavour and nutrients.

Another way to accomplish the same purpose is to transfer the vegetables from the cooking utensil to a shallow pan and spread them out so that they are not more than 2 cm in thickness. Add six or seven chips of butter to every kilo of vegetables. By shaking the pan or stirring the vegetables from top to bottom, the butter melts and the cooking process largely stops. Now, add, after cooling, some of the cooking water to a depth of about $\frac{1}{2}$ cm.

Another way to prevent overcooking is to undercook the vegetables initially, cool them in the refrigerator, and finish the cooking just as they are needed for serving. However, if at all possible, cook and serve immediately after cooking.

To prevent overcooking of vegetables, cook in small batches, keep the holding time as short as possible, and stop the cooking process by spreading them in a shallow pan or by placing them under . . . .

cold water

38   Sometimes the broccoli and asparagus for cooking are tied into bunches and the bunches set, stalks down, into boiling water for cooking a short time. The string is then cut, removed and the entire vegetable is submerged and cooked. This precooking of the stalks cooks them and avoids overcooking the tender tips. Beans are often sliced into thin strips to speed cooking. Cauliflower may be broken up into small flowerettes for the same reason. Fine division, therefore, does three things in cooking: (1) . . . . (2) . . . . (3) . . . . . .

Shortens cooking time; dissipates flavours quickly in vegetables belonging to the onion family; and causes a higher loss of nutrients.

●

39   From what has been said about cooking vegetables, what advantages do you see in removing the tough stems from spinach or other leafy vegetables before cooking them?

Removing the stems takes time and effort but permits the vegetables to cook in less time. Less time in cooking means more colour, flavour and nutrient retention.

●

40   The most common method of cooking vegetables is by boiling. We have noted the factors involved and the recommended procedures. There are several other ways of cooking vegetables.

The French ordinarily cook all vegetables as rapidly as possible by boiling. They use a large kettle of rapidly boiling, salted water: 7−8 litres of salted water ($\frac{1}{3}$ cup of salt to this quantity of water) to 1−1$\frac{1}{2}$ kilos of vegetables. The more boiling water is used in proportion to the vegetables, the quicker the water returns to the boiling point after the vegetables are dropped in. This rapid cooking permits the greatest retention of colour. While the larger amount of water leaches out more flavour and nutrients, the more rapid cooking assists in counteracting this undesirable action and the resulting product has good colour, texture and flavour.

To cook in this manner, the proportions of water and salt to two or three pounds of vegetables would be . . . . . .

7 to 8 litres of water and $\frac{1}{3}$ cup of salt.

41 Unless the vegetables are served at once, the French chef may drain them immediately after they are cooked and 'refresh' them by plunging them into a large quantity of cold water for a few seconds and then spread out evenly into shallow pans. These vegetables can then be reheated in their own liquor saved when they were drained. Some chefs do not like to refresh by plunging into cold water but drain and then spread the vegetables out about 1 cm deep and cool them quickly. They claim there is less flavour and nutrient loss when this is done.

What do you think is the purpose of refreshing?

To stop the cooking process and prevent the vegetables from being overcooked.

●

42 Many vegetables may be baked. Some, such as potatoes or sweet potatoes, tomatoes, and so forth, may be baked in an oven from the completely raw state; others, e.g. parsnips, marrow, onion should be par-boiled or partially cooked before baking.

True or False: All vegetables should be baked from the raw to done state without any previous cooking.

False

●

43 Vegetables may also be steamed. Some vegetables are better steamed than boiled or baked. Usually the nutrient losses are less in steaming than in boiling because the steam leaches out less of the nutrients. However, some vegetables such as greens and peas that pack together tightly in a steam pan may not steam well. In such cases, boiling is a preferred method. Vegetables such as potatoes, carrots, cauliflower and beetroots that leave spaces between items steam well. Would you say that steam would be a good way to cook most root vegetables?

Yes, steam cooks these vegetables very well.

●

44 For steaming vegetables in compartment steamers use shallow steam table pans which permit the steam to circulate more easily. Use only $\frac{1}{2}$ cm of water for green beans and peas; 1 cm for the cabbage family. If you steam leafy greens, use no water at all except that which clings to the leaves after washing them. (Most vegetables are 80−95 per cent water when fresh

and supply their own water once cooking starts.) In cabinet pressure cookers the same procedure is used except that the cooking time is much reduced, two to eight minutes. Broccoli, for example, reaches the optimal colour, texture and flavour after two minutes in a $103 \cdot 4$ kN/m^2 (15 lb/in^2) pressure cooker. Boiling requires ten minutes for the same results.

Since the use of pressure steamers results in faster cooking, timing must be more exact than cooking on top of a stove. With tender vegetables, a few seconds too long in the steam pressure cooker means overcooking. Asparagus, for example, tends to fall apart if overcooked in a steamer.

Would you expect that it would be a good idea to open the door of a compartment steamer for a few seconds during the cooking process of strong vegetables. tables.

Yes, but not practical. This would permit the strong flavours in some vegetables to escape, but the door of a steam cooker should not be opened until all steam has dissipated or the pressure gauge registers zero.

●

45 Can vegetables be cooked in high pressure chambers such as chambers having $137 \cdot 9$ kN/m^2 (20 lb/in^2)?

Yes, but only a few seconds are required. Thus, frozen peas can be cooked in 20 to 30 seconds. Fresh beans cook in one to two minutes or even less.

●

46 Vegetables are also prepared by braising, frying and broiling. In braising, fat in some form is used and the vegetables are also partially steamed.

Is this braising the same method as used in braising meat?

Yes, the time is shorter, however.

●

47 Leafy vegetables such as spinach, lettuce, chicory (also known as endive), red and white cabbage, and sometimes celery, are braised (steamed in a little liquid, cover on the cooking utensil).

Braised leafy vegetables have little flavour of their own and are usually braised along with blanched bacon

281

K

(simmered 10 minutes separately first to remove the strong bacon flavour and to render some of the fat), onions, carrots, beef or chicken stock and seasoning of thyme, parsley and bayleaf.

What is the reason for cooking bacon, stock, flavourful vegetables and seasoning with braised leafy vegetables?

To provide flavour to the vegetables which lack flavour.

●

48 Some vegetables such as diced potatoes, sliced tomatoes, cooked sliced parsnips or carrots are sautéed.

To review what we learned earlier about cooking methods, sautéing is a method of . . . .

frying in shallow fat

●

49 Some vegetables are excellent deep fried. This is especially true of potatoes. Other vegetables, however, deep-fry well, especially breadcrumbed items such as tomato slices, onion rings, egg-plant or cauliflower that has been parboiled, breaded and then deep-fried. Other vegetables that have been parboiled may be breadcrumbed and fried, such as asparagus, carrots or parsnips, etc. Do you think fresh corn-on-the-cob could be deep-fried?

Yes; do not, however, cook frozen corn-on-the-cob without first defrosting it.

●

50 Can some vegetables be grilled?

Yes, tomato parboiled eggplant (aubergine) and mushrooms.

51   As noted previously, some vegetables deep-fry well. The Italian 'frito misto' is an assortment of deep-fried meats and vegetables such as cauliflower, artichokes and apples. The Japanese 'tempura' is a similar assortment of fried items including carrots, shrimp, and seaweed.

52   Tempura is a batter-fried food that is deep-fried at about 163C (325F), usually in vegetable oil. The batter is an egg-flour-water mixture.

Foods usually used for tempura include shrimp, pieces of fish and various vegetables such as thinly sliced carrots and green pepper. Immediately after frying, the foods are dipped for eating into a tempura sauce containing among other ingredients soy sauce and saké (rice wine).

If 204C (400F) were used to fry tempura would we have less fat soakage?

Yes, it is said that the Orientals use the higher temperature for quick browning and cook only a few items at a time so that the fat temperature drops only slightly.

●

53   The Chinese are well known for their vegetable cookery which is done by sautéing quickly in peanut oil. The method appropriately enough is known as the *hot-fry* or Chao method.

Before sautéing, fibrous vegetables and those with strong odours are blanched. Vegetables which they feel are fibrous enough to need softening include string beans, asparagus, broccoli, cauliflower, carrots and the green pea for which they are best known, the snow pea. These are blanched for two to three minutes in boiling water, rinsed in cold water, then drained. Cabbage, celery and bean sprouts are scalded quickly in boiling water to remove objectionable odours, rinsed in cold water and drained.

Tender vegetables such as green peas, lettuce, spinach, tomatoes and green peppers are merely washed and sliced prior to the 'hot-fry'.

All vegetables are then cut or sliced into small pieces and sautéed in a few tablespoons of peanut oil which is 177C (350F). While sautéing the vegetables are stirred continually. Sometimes a sauce of cornflour and chicken or other stock is then added and the whole sautéed for a minute or two longer.

We see that the French and the Chinese both blanch their vegetables and that they both then stop the cooking process by a quick rinse in cold water which is called what by the French?

'Refreshing the vegetables.'

●

54   What is the difference in preparing vegetables by the hot-fry method and by the tempura method?

The tempura method includes the use of a batter and deep fries rather than sautés.

●

55   You have noted that the recommended method of cooking vegetables is frequently the result of a compromise. To get rid of strong flavours we cook in a large quantity of water or divide finely. This results in a great loss of nutrients. We may cook in steam to obtain a lower loss of nutrients and speed cooking by a higher heat. However, this higher quantity of heat will destroy some nutrients more quickly. It may also destroy green colour more rapidly.

In the last analysis, we should cook vegetables in the way which is most pleasing to our . . . . and to ourselves.

guests

●

56   Serving temperature of vegetables, entrées, hot beverages and soups should be about 65 to 71C (150—160F). This allows for about a 4 to 5C (8—10F) temperature drop during the service and before eating takes place, 60C (140F). Food and beverages lose about 2C (4F) each minute after being dished up on pre-warmed plates or bowls at room temperatures of about 24C (75F).

Would you expect some individual differences regarding preferred serving temperatures for food?

Yes, studies show a 28C (50F) range in preferences. 'Some people like it hot, some like it cool.'

284

CANNED VEGETABLES

57 If an entire can is not used, leave the vegetables in the opened can and refrigerate. There is more danger of bacterial contamination in pouring the contents into another container. Can you guess why?

The insides of cans holding canned vegetables have been sterilized at high temperatures and have fewer live bacteria than even a newly washed pan. The inside lining of the can will prevent rusting for several days.

●

58 To cream canned vegetables, would you use the liquor from the vegetables in the cream sauce?

Yes, the liquor contains much of the flavour, vitamins and other nutrients. If there's too much liquor, it can be reduced by boiling, or use only what you need.

●

FROZEN VEGETABLES

59 Would you expect that frozen vegetables would be somewhat tenderized by the freezing process and therefore require a little less cooking?

Yes, this is the case. Frozen vegetables require less cooking. Most are partially cooked before freezing.

60   Most frozen vegetables are best cooked from the frozen state with the exception of corn-on-the-cob which should be thawed and then cooked. If this is not done to frozen corn, what do you think happens to it?

The corn is cooked on the outside while the inside is still frozen.

●

61   To boil frozen vegetables, have the salted water boiling vigorously. Break the frozen chunk of vegetables into smaller pieces as they are dropped into this water. Cover for a few minutes and bring back to a boil, and *just before boiling begins remove the cover and cook with the cover off.*

Is the cooking of frozen vegetables much different then than cooking of fresh vegetables?

Not much; once the vegetable is thawed, the cooking is almost the same.

●

62   Vegetables that are frozen may be steamed but if tightly packed such as peas, spinach, and so forth cooking will not be even, the outsides of the package will overcook while the insides remain uncooked. Such frozen vegetables are best boiled.

Would frozen whole Brussels sprouts steam well?

Yes, because this product has spaces between pieces which will allow the steam to surround each piece and cook it evenly.

●

63   Since freezing tenderizes vegetables slightly and almost all frozen vegetables have been blanched before freezing they, therefore, require a shorter cooking period.

Would you expect frozen vegetables to have more colour after being cooked than other vegetables?

More colour; this is especially true of frozen peas. However, many authorities feel that canned green beans stand up better in a steam table than frozen green beans.

RICE COOKERY

64   Rice is cooked differently depending on the preference of the eater and how it will be served. Orientals who eat rice daily add a number of seasonings and other food materials for variety.

For plain fluffy rice 5 litres of water are used per $\frac{1}{2}$ kilo of uncooked rice. The water is brought to a boil and two tablespoons of salt added. Stir while the rice is added and simmer until nearly tender as tested by pressing a grain against the side of the kettle or pressing between the fingers.

The excess water is then drained and the cooking completed over low heat until the remaining water has evaporated.

It is either served at once or refreshed by running cold water over it and refrigerated until needed.

Would you expect $\frac{1}{2}$ kilo of uncooked rice to swell and produce a greater volume?

Yes, rice is about 80 per cent starch and the starch granules take up water as gelling occurs. Half kilo of uncooked rice ends up as $1\frac{1}{2}-2$ kilos of cooked rice.

●

65   Would you expect high cooking temperatures to rupture the rice cells, releasing the starches and making for a sticky cooked rice?

Yes, this does happen.

●

66   Short grain varieties of rice usually are not as soft when cooked and tend to stick together more than the long grain varieties. Waxy or glutinous rice is useful in making rice cakes and the like. It contains almost all amylopectin fraction, very little of the amylose fraction (see item 21, page 343).

Newly harvested rice tends to leach more into the cooking water and to cook into a pasty mass than does rice that has been stored for a time.

To get light, fluffy rice use long grain rice that has been stored and use what kind of cooking temperatures?

Simmering rather than boiling.

67   Would it be reasonable to add a small amount of salad oil to rice before cooking to prevent the grains from sticking together?

Yes, this is frequently done.

●

68   Orientals usually wash the rice in several waters to remove surface starch. The water from the first wash is often used in other foods. About four tablespoons of oil are added per kilo of uncooked rice.

Less water is used—$3\frac{1}{4}$ litres per kilo of rice. The same amount of salt—2 tablespoons per kilo of rice is added to the water along with the rice. The kettle is covered and low heat used. As the rice becomes tender the cover is removed so that the rice steams dry. More water can be added if needed but too much water produces rice which is overcooked and too soft. If cooked in a steam kettle, the kettle is covered for about 40 minutes, uncovered during the last 10 minutes.

In the Oriental method less water is used, lower temperatures and longer/shorter cooking time than with the simmer-steam method.

longer

●

69   To add flavour, rice is often sautéed in margarine, butter or other fat or oil and sometimes sautéed onions added. Stock is often substituted for the cooking water.

When seasonings and meat are added, the dish is known as rice pilaf.

True or False: Coating the rice with fat helps to assure individual rice grains when cooked in water.

True

●

69a   Rice is available as long grain and short grain. Brown rice is the whole grain, only the husk removed, more nutritious than white rice, but takes longer to cook. Converted rice is rice processed by a patented method of parboiling which retains more vitamins and requires longer to cook than regular polished rice. Instant rice has been precooked and requires only about 5 minutes to cook.

True or False: Since rice is available in various forms, the best way to cook it is to follow instructions on the package.

Yes, especially as regards cooking time.

CHESTNUTS

70 Chestnuts are used as a vegetable substitute, especially in France. In this country purée chestnuts are sometimes served instead of mashed potatoes; whole chestnuts are served with pork, duck or turkey.

Since chestnuts have little flavour they are simmered in stock and other flavouring added.

They can be purchased whole and shelled in cans (expensive), or bought fresh to be peeled in the kitchen. The shell and inner skin fit tightly but can be removed by first slicing off a sliver of shell and skin, then placing them on a pan of cold water which is brought to a boil. The nuts are peeled while still hot.

They require about 30 minutes to cook in stock, 45 minutes to cook in an oven.

Why is it necessary in shelling to cut into the shell, then bring to a boil in water?

The slit in the shell allows water and heat to penetrate to soften the kernel and free the shell and inner skin.

●

GLAZING

71 Vegetables, especially carrots, onions, and turnips, are sometimes glazed before serving. Glazing as applied to vegetables means that after they are nearly cooked they are finished by tossing in butter, sugar or a sugar substitute such as syrup or honey. The surface of the vegetables becomes shiny and semi-transparent.

The term 'glaze' comes from the French 'glacer' to freeze and is used with frozen desserts, called glaces. The term is also used whenever a shiny surface is formed on a food, hot or cold. Fish and eggs are glazed when a white sauce is applied to them. Meat and fish are glazed when a sauce or syrup is spread on the surface, then heated to give a brown or semi-transparent effect. Fruit glazes are made with cornflour and sugar to give a fruit a shiny, transparent appearance, as in a strawberry glaze. Sweets and confectionery are glazed by sprinkling them with sugar and subjecting them to high heat. Yeast breads are often glazed with an egg wash (egg plus water or milk).

Glazing, then, is the formation of a shiny surface on food or a frozen food. As applied to vegetables, glazing is accomplished by using butter and what else?

Sugar

●

72 Glazing fruits and vegetables by cooking them in a sugar solution gives sheen and firmness. Osmotic pressure created by the difference in pressure between the liquid in the fruit or vegetable and the more concentrated sugar solution surrounding them forces some of the liquid out of the item. Cooking drives off some of the water and the sugar forms shiny crystals.

True or False: Osmotic pressure forces liquid out of a fruit or vegetable which is surrounded by a heavy sugar syrup.

True

●

SALAD GREENS

73 Vegetables for salad greens can be prepared several hours before needed for serving and improved in the process. They should be washed and drained, broken (not cut, which will bruise the greens) into bite-size pieces, and placed into a large-sized colander (bowl-shaped sieve or strainer). The colander is then stored in a refrigerator, placed on a towel, and covered with a damp towel.

The air moving through the greens dries off excess moisture, cools the vegetables and leaves them cold and crisp, ready to be served when needed.

Would you expect the air in a refrigerator at 1C (34F) to be of lower humidity than a vegetable-holding box at a temperature of 7C (45F)?

Yes, the lower the temperature, the less moisture it can hold.

74 When moisture evaporates what happens?

Heat is required and so some slight bit of evaporation of water on a vegetable in holding can assist in cooling a vegetable.

●

75 Remember, do not soak greens. They can become water-logged. Allow enough moisture on them to dampen them. Is a slight amount of moisture absorption beneficial?

Yes, by a process called 'osmosis' the vegetable cells will draw in moisture causing the cells to be swollen with moisture. This reaction causes crispness. Contrarily, a vegetable or green that has lost moisture from the cells is limp.

●

POTATO COOKERY

76 Potatoes, contain about 80% water, 18% starch and sugar and 2% protein. Even slight differences in the total solids content or sugar content affect their cooking character.

Potatoes for deep-frying and baking should have a high starch content (more than 1·07 specific gravity). Those for deep-frying should be low in sugar.

For baking, select a potato that looks good and is high/low in starch.

High

76a   Store potatoes at about 7C (45F) in a well-ventilated space at about 85—95% humidity.

At lower temperatures starches present turn to sugar or the potatoes may freeze.

Higher temperatures lead to sprouting and bacterial spoilage.

Keep them away from sunlight to avoid the formation of green spots (containing chlorophyll and a bitter tasting alkaloid).

Store potatoes at about what temperature?

7·5C (45F)

●

77   Most people buy baking potatoes according to variety, purchasing mature large, regular-shaped King Edwards or Desirée potatoes for baking, French frying or mashing. For boiling or pan frying select King Edwards or Golden Wonder or other potatoes high in moisture and sugar, lower in starch.

Why would a potato with less starch be better for boiling?

Less swelling occurs in the potato with less starch, which means less swelling of cell walls and less sloughing off of the potato into the cooking water. The waxy potato remains intact.

●

77a   A simple test discriminates between the baking types and boiling types. It reflects the degree of maturity, growing conditions, variety and hence the water-solids ratio. Place sample potatoes from bags of potatoes to be tested into a litre of water in which has been dissolved 120 grammes of salt. Those that sink are good bakers and fryers; those that float should be used for boiling.

(The test measures their specific gravity, a comparison of the weight of a material with an equal volume of water.)

If you get the kind of mealy, crumbly, dry product you want in buying large King Edwards, why bother with the sink or float test?

Many less expensive potatoes can be used as bakers and you can be more certain of your choice.

78 Baking potatoes are scrubbed and, when baked in quantity, are started in a 260C (500F) oven. After 15 minutes the oven temperature is cut back to 204C (400F) and the potatoes baked for a total of 60 to 90 minutes, depending upon their size.

They are done when an internal temperature of 91C (195F) is reached, or when a fork easily pierces their centres.

Is it reasonable to sort potatoes and bake those that are of the same size together?

Yes, by doing so all will be done together, some not over cooked as happens when unsized potatoes are cooked together.

●

79 Since all potatoes are high in moisture, steam is generated during the baking. To allow it to escape and avoid sogginess, the potatoes are pierced at their ends with a fork before baking and after baking are slit lengthwise. They may be served with butter or sour cream and chives dressing in the opening.

Is there any advantage in wrapping potatoes in aluminum foil before baking as is often done?

None at all. The foil delays the baking and holds in the steam.

●

80 Can you see any advantage in wrapping potatoes in aluminum foil once they have been baked?

Yes, immediately after baking wrap in foil; this retains the heat. Wrapped potatoes will hold up to 60 minutes before becoming soggy, turning grey and losing their mealy character.

●

81 If the skins of baked potatoes are to be eaten some cooks rub the scrubbed potatoes with butter or margarine before baking them. The fat adds flavour, softens the skin and some people like the browned appearance.

The yield after baking is 91 per cent on potatoes oiled before baking and 81 per cent on potatoes that are un-oiled before baking.

Small, new potatoes are not baked but are simmered in their scrubbed jackets for about 20 minutes. The salted water in which they simmer is first brought to a boil. Why?

So that the cold potatoes will not drop the temperature below the cooking point and slow up the process.

82   Baked potatoes 'hold' satisfactorily for up to one hour after being baked. After that time they become soggy, turn grey, lose their mealy characteristics.

After one hour of holding, sweet potatoes become soggy and shrivelled.

Mashed potatoes from fresh potatoes lose quality after twenty minutes. Those made from potato flakes should not be served after thirty minutes of holding.

What is the maximum period for holding mashed potatoes made from potato flakes?

One-half hour

83   To provide variation and a tasty product, and also to make baked potatoes easier to handle for the eater, scoop the cooked interiors of the potatoes out of the shells, being careful to preserve the shells. The removed portion is whipped along with hot milk, butter and salt. This mixture is then placed back in the shells by use of a pastry bag. These are then reheated in a hot oven or under a grill.

When preparing baked stuffed potatoes would you expect to end up with some extra whipped potato?

Yes, in whipping the potatoes their volume is increased considerably, but pile this extra up on top.

84   The amount of yield from potatoes is related to the method of preparation. Small potatoes should be boiled or steamed in their jackets (skins on) and peeled before they cool. Yield is high, by boiling 94 per cent and by steaming 98 per cent.

Medium-sized potatoes are usually peeled in a mechanical, abrasive-type vegetable peeler or purchased already peeled. Eyes are removed by hand. Yield is about 70 to 80 per cent.

Large mealy-type potatoes are often scrubbed and baked. Waste is negligible. If pared in an abrasive peeler the yield is around 75 to 84 per cent.

These large potatoes are also peeled and cut into thin strips (Julienne, allumette and shoe strings), into larger strips of French frying, and sliced for puffed potatoes (pomme soufflé), O'Brien, Anna and other potato dishes.

The kind of potato in large part determines the method of preparation. What other factor in the potato plays a part in the method of preparation used?

The size of the potato.

●

85   Which methods of cooking potatoes give the greatest yield?

Steaming, followed closely by boiling in the jacket; baking is next.

●

86   In making mashed potatoes from fresh potatoes, it is important that the mashed potatoes do not get cold while they are being mashed. Because of this, the container in which they are mashed should be heated by running it under the hot water tap. Another way to ensure fluffiness in mashed potatoes is to add scalded cream or milk. Would it be satisfactory to use a food mixing bowl for mashing potatoes which is at room temperature?

No, not if you want the best product possible.

●

87   Some potatoes develop dark spots and others are grey or lack whiteness because of oxidation taking place. Any potato darkens if the peeled surface is exposed to air. We can overcome this darkening by adding a bit of cream of tartar. Why?

You learned earlier that the acid reaction given by cream of tartar or other acid ingredients whitens flavones and since these pigments are in potatoes, the cream of tartar gives a whiter potato.

88 Mashed potatoes usually have hot milk or cream added to them in the mashing process (about $1\frac{1}{2}$ litres of milk to each 5 kilogrammes of potatoes). Be sure that the potatoes receive some pre-mashing before adding the milk so that lumps do not occur. Solid butter or margarine broken into small pieces improve the flavour ($\frac{1}{2}$ kilo of butter to 10 kilos of potatoes). The last minute of whipping should be done at high speed to insure fluffiness and break up all final lumps.

If potatoes are mashed with egg yolks, they are known as duchesse potatoes. These are used for making potato borders, toppings and patties. If whipping cream and egg yolks are added, they are known as mousseline meaning light and fluffy. Would you guess that the yolks should be at room temperature?

Yes, since the potatoes will whip better when warm.

●

89 Potatoes, the most widely used of all vegetables, are prepared in dozens of ways. Some of the more popular ways which are used in restaurants are:

Au gratin: literally 'crusted'; these are made from boiled potatoes placed into a cheese or cream sauce topped with crumbs, paprika, melted butter and baked. (The term au gratin is usually associated with cheese, but may refer to a top coating of bread, cracker crumbs or finely ground nuts placed on top of scalloped or sauced dishes.)

Roast or Franconia: peeled whole and baked brown with a roast.

Hashed brown (sauté) potatoes: boiled potatoes, diced or sliced, and pan fried.

O'Brien: hashed brown (sauté) potatoes garnished with onions, green peppers, and pimentoes.

Lyonnaise: hash brown (sauté) containing onions.

Maître d'hôtel: boiled or steamed in skin, peeled, cut in slices, covered with hot milk, sprinkled with parsley and nutmeg.

Cottage Fried: Raw, thin potatoes sautéed in fat or butter until tender and browned.

Noisette: cut with a round ball cutter, seasoned and sautéed in butter. If cut into smaller balls and deep-fried they may be called Parisienne potatoes.

Rissolé: either whole or large potato pieces cut into oblong or egg-shape, boiled and sautéed in butter and then browned in an oven. The word rissolé means browned. Sprinkle with parsley just before serving.

Escalloped or Scalloped: layers of thickly sliced potatoes, dredged with flour, milk and butter or cream added and baked at 175C (350F). The term 'scallop' originally meant to cook in a scallop shell.

Anna: thin raw slices of potato baked brown in a special pan.

What would potatoes be called which are in the shape of a hazelnut and sautéed in butter?

Noisette (in fact, noisette means hazelnut in French).

●

90   Potatoes which are sautéed with onions might be called . . . .

Lyonnaise

●

91   If potatoes are first formed into egg-shaped balls and browned in an oven, they would be known as . . . .

rissolé

●

92   Potatoes which are roasted or browned along with a roast are known as . . . .

roast or Franconia

●

93   The preparation of French fried potatoes is best done without interruption from the raw stage. (See the chapter 'The Frying Process'.)

Blanching before frying is often done when large quantities of French fries are needed or when the potatoes are cut large (9 mm to 1 cm in thickness). They should be blanched for a particular meal, never blanched and stored in the refrigerator.

Blanching is pre-cooking and can be accomplished by these methods:

Simmering for one minute after the water has reached a boil.

Steaming in a compartment steamer for two minutes, then drying.

Steaming in a pressure steamer for one minute, then drying.

Deep fat frying for one and a half to three minutes at 150C (300F), using $\frac{1}{2}$ kilo of potatoes to 3—4 kilogrammes of fat. Before frying, the outside moisture on the potatoes should be dried by towelling.

Baking in a 205C (400F) oven for five or six minutes. The potatoes should be dried and coated with fat by dipping them before being placed in the oven.

Pre-cooking or blanching of potatoes can be done by baking, frying, steaming, and by what other method of cooking?

Simmering

●

94   The quantity of sugar in potatoes for deep-frying is important to quality. If the potato has less than a half of one per cent or over three per cent sugar in it, it will not perform well in French frying. Most potatoes have a half of one per cent but some potatoes such as new potatoes and potatoes stored for a long time below 10C (50F) may have as high as a six per cent sugar content. To de-sugar the latter kind, 'condition' by storing at a temperature above 10C (50F) for three weeks. The higher temperatures cause the sugar in the potatoes to return to starch.

Storing raw potatoes below 10C (50F) raises/lowers their sugar content, while storing these potatoes above 10C (50F) raises/lowers their sugar content.

raises, lowers

●

VEGETABLE FORMS AND SIZES

95   Most of the terms which relate to the size and form of vegetables are of French origin. Gradually they are becoming a part of the English language and are already a part of the culinary lexicon around the world.

Here are some of the more important terms:

Allumette: match shaped, similar to shoestring.
Bouquetière: a garnish of vegetables arranged around
        roasted meat to appear as flowers. Carrots and tur-
        nips are cut into balls and glazed. Potatoes are cut

into balls and browned in butter. Cauliflower is divided into flowerettes and covered with Hollandaise sauce.

Brunoise: in the style of Brunoy, a district in France; tiny or fine dice, cut about 3 mm thick.

Jardinière: Gardener's style; mixed vegetables cut in batons.

Julienne: finely shredded; smaller than shoestring but similar shape about 2 cm long.

Mirepoix: sliced about 9 mm thick; a mixture of carrots, onions and celery or other vegetables used to season meats, fish, poultry sauces, soups or gravies.

Noisette: hazelnut sized, about 1 cm diameter. Also refers to a brown colour and to the best part of a fillet or to a type of sauce.

Olivette: olive sized.

Pearl: round and small.

Printanière: spring-grown, young, tender, thinly sliced. The word means 'spring-like'.

Salpiçon: any ingredient diced into about 3 — 6 mm cubes; can refer to a dice mixture of almost any vegetables, meat or seafood. When bound with a sauce the mixture is known as a compound salpiçon.

What is the difference between Brunoise and Julienne?

Brunoise is cut in small dice, Julienne is cut in fine strips.

●

96 Potatoes which are cooked, mashed with egg yolks and formed by squeezing out a pastry tube are known as . . . .

Duchesse

●

97 Shredded vegetables can be called what?

Vegetables Julienne

●

98 What would you know about a soup brunoise?

That it contained finely diced vegetables.

99 A garnish of vegetables placed around a roast and made to look like flowers could be called what?

Bouquetière

100 In cooking potatoes or any other vegetable, can you see any advantage in preparing the vegetables for cooking so that all of them are about of equal size?

Cooking time will be more equal when items are of the same size. Some items will not be overcooked, others undercooked.

101 Would there be any possibility that the way a vegetable is cut would affect its nutrient loss during cooking?

This is true for carrots, which should be cut on the bias, rather than square cut. Less of the cell structures are ruptured by cutting on the bias. Also cutting vegetables finely is apt to cause a higher loss by oxidation and leaching.

GUIDELINES TO VEGETABLE COOKERY

Preserve red colour in vegetables by adding acid.
Preserve green colour in vegetables by cooking quickly and with a little or moderate amount of water.
Preserve green colour in vegetables by removing the lid (to allow volatile acids to escape) once the water has returned to the boil.
Quick blanching of strong green vegetables removes the strong flavour. Use a quantity of water for cooking vegetables having a strong flavour. Cook

only that quantity of vegetables needed for immediate service.

Potatoes that float in a properly prepared salt solution are best for boiling and mashing. Potatoes that sink in a similar solution are best for baking and frying.

Add flavour to vegetables by cooking them in a stock.

Add flavour and shiny appearance to vegetables by glazing them (adding butter to them; evaporate off all the liquid by boiling, then toss them continuously over fierce heat).

Cook vegetables in the onion family slowly; cabbage and green vegetables quickly.

Select vegetables of approximately the same size to cook together.

Flavour and nutrients are more likely to be saved when the vegetables are cooked whole and without peeling.

To produce fluffy, dry rice use a long grain variety, a little oil, drain off excess water when the rice is tender and evaporate the excess moisture by further cooking in a double boiler.

Add salt to the cooking water of vegetables and bring the water back to the boil quickly after vegetables are dropped in.

Serve vegetables at about 65C (150F).

REVISION

1. What is progressive cookery as applied to cooking vegetables?

Vegetables are cooked in small quantities, as needed for serving.

●

2. Is it desirable to add a little bicarbonate of soda to the water in which green vegetables are to be cooked?

No, while a little soda improves the green colour, too much softens the vegetables and soda destroys nutrients.

3. Which vitamin is most likely to be lost in cooking vegetables?

Vitamin C

4. What would you add to red vegetables if you wanted to retain the red colour?

Vinegar, lemon juice, cream of tartar, apples or some other tart item.

5. Would an orange sauce go well with beetroots?

Yes, the acid from the orange would brighten the red in the beets.

6. Would you cover the pot in which swedes are boiled?

No, you let the strong flavours escape by leaving off the cover of the cooking utensil.

7. What is meant by 'refreshing' vegetables?

Pouring cold water over them or dipping them into cold water to stop the cooking process.

8. Do vegetables continue to cook when held on a steam table or in a bain marie?

Yes, even though the temperature is quite low.

9. For what reason would you add sugar to cooked carrots?

To replace the natural sugars lost in the cooking process, or to glaze the surface.

●

10. In cooking broccoli or asparagus should the stalks be cooked differently than the tops?

Yes, the tops are more tender and should be steamed rather than simmered or the stalks given longer boiling than the tips.

●

11. If you added whipped cream and egg yolks to mashed potatoes, what would you have?

Potatoes mousseline

●

12. Matching:
a. Anna Potatoes
b. Franconia Potatoes
c. Lyonnaise Potatoes
d. O'Brien Potatoes
e. Potatoes Noisette

1. Sauté (Hash browned) with onions, pimentos and peppers
2. Baked brown along with roast
3. With onions
4. Thin slices baked in a special pan
5. Round balls cooked in butter

a. 4
b. 2
c. 3
d. 1
e. 5

●

13. Scalloped vegetables contain what sauce and are cooked by what method?

A milk or cream sauce; cooked by baking.

14. An au gratin dish would likely be topped with cheese or what else?

Bread crumbs and butter, or grated cheese or grated cheese and crumbs.

●

15. What is the best way of stopping the cooking process when vegetables are done?

Spread them out in a shallow pan to cool or by a quick cold blanch.

●

16. Acids help to develop bright red colours in vegetables but destroy what in green vegetables?

Chlorophyll

●

17. What is the purpose of cooking vegetables which contain strong juices in plenty of water?

The strong juices leached into the water can be discarded with the water.

●

18. For what reason are potatoes sometimes stored at a temperature above 10C (50F)?

To change their sugars back to starch. Excessive sugar in potatoes is undesirable for French frying.

●

19. Vegetables are blanched to get rid of some of their undesirable surface flavours and for what operational purpose?

To partially cook them so that final preparation during rush periods is shortened.

20. Glazing as applied to vegetables does what to their surface?

Makes them shiny or gives a semi-transparent coating.

●

21. The sink or float test for potatoes distinguishes between those suitable for baking, mashing and frying and those suitable for . . . .

boiling

●

22. In the sink or float test potatoes suitable for baking and frying . . . . while those suitable for boiling . . . .

sink, float

●

23. The bakers contain more/less solids than do the boilers.

more

●

24. Do not hold baked potatoes or sweet potatoes for longer than . . . . after being cooked.

one hour

●

25. The oriental method of cooking rice to achieve a fluffy product uses more/less water initially than the method we usually use.

Less; more water is added later if needed.

●

26. True or False: Potatoes can be blanched by either moist or dry heat.

True

●

27. Onions should be cooked slowly; cabbage and green vegetables . . . .

quickly

28. The reason we should remove the lid of the cooking utensil when cooking green vegetables is to allow the escape of the . . . .

volatile acids which destroy the chlorophyll in the vegetables

●

29. To *ensure* that rice cooks dry after it has become tender what is done?

Low heat is used and the cover removed so that the excess water evaporates.

●

30. The Chinese sauté their vegetables in peanut oil, the Japanese tempura method includes the use of batter and cooking by . . . .

deep-frying

●

31. A dish with the title of Printanière included in it would have what in it?

Young or spring vegetables.

●

32. The greatest yield from potatoes is achieved by cooking by what method?

Steaming

●

33. To speed the cooking of vegetables having heavy stalks peel the stalks and do what to them?

Cut them up or cut incisions into their ends to allow quicker heat transfer.

●

34. The four pigments with which we are concerned in cooking vegetables are chlorophyll (green), flavones (whites), anthocyanins (reds) and . . . .

carotenes (yellows)

35. Since chlorophyll is lost rapidly at temperatures above 65C (150F), the serving temperature for vegetables, it is desirable to reduce the holding of green vegetables to as short a time as possible. Therefore, do not hold cooked vegetables more than .... minutes.

20

●

Bakery Products

1   Baked products are basically wheat flour and milk or water mixtures to which eggs, sugar, shortening and an aerating agent may be added.

During baking, the mixtures are expanded by air, steam and/or carbon dioxide. The proteins present (in eggs and/or as gluten) coagulate and the starch takes on water and sets (gelatinizes). The problem in baking is usually one of obtaining proper expansion with the aerating agent and then firming of the structure by coagulation and gelatinization to retain this aerating development. In the baking the surface is dehydrated and the sugars and proteins there brown.

What ingredients give baked products their structure?

The coagulated proteins and gelatinized starches.

●

2   From what you know about temperatures, do the interiors of baked goods exceed 100C (212F)?

No, not as long as they are moist. The dehydrated surfaces do exceed 100C (212F) and browning occurs.

●

3.   Baked products may be divided into doughs, pastes, and batters. Batters are beaten during preparation and can be dropped or poured. Examples are cake, pancake, and crumpet batters. Doughs are too thick to be beaten and require handling or kneading which can be done manually or by machinery. Mixtures for making yeast bread, sweet rolls, pastries and biscuits are examples of doughs. Puff or pie paste are smooth

pastes, between a dough and a batter in consistency. Eclair paste is like a thick batter.

Doughs, pastes and batters contain flour and milk or water; a dough has greater/lesser consistency than a batter.

greater

●

4   Pastry includes a wide variety of products made from doughs containing medium to large amounts of fats. Sweet rolls, for example, contain a medium amount of fat and are aerated with yeast. Danish or other rolled-in sweet doughs have butter, margarine or shortening spread between layers of dough and puff paste contains so much fat that a portion of it is also folded or laid into the dough. Pie crust contains 50 to 100% as much shortening as flour.

Pastry doughs are identified by the fact that they contain more/less fat (shortening) than other doughs.

more fat

●

5   A wonderful property of wheat flour is that when water is added and it is mixed *gluten* is formed. Gluten is mostly a protein or complex of chemically related insoluble proteins which stretch and form continuous strands in a baking product. The gluten is then coagulated in baking to form a firm structure in the baked product.

One of the principle substances that gives baked products their volume and firmness when baked is . . . .

gluten

●

6   The amount of gluten present in flour is related to the amount of protein in the flour. Wheat flour ranges in protein content from about 7 to 15 per cent. If a baked item is to rise and assume a new enlarged form some gluten must be present so that the dough will stretch and harden when in the expanded form. The amount of gluten needed for a product varies considerably. Bread, eclairs and pound cake may contain high amounts of gluten to give the desired structure, while cake, biscuits and some pastries may require

much less because less structure building properties are desired. In a product such as pie dough low gluten is wanted so that the crust will break easily.

Soft wheat flour (low in protein or gluten) is used in cakes, hard flour (high in protein) for bread and blends of each may be used in other products to give the desired structure or strength.

Hard wheat flour is often used for making puff paste but the gluten is retarded from forming because the shortening lubricates the gluten stopping it from sticking together and forming a strong, continuous structure.

The amount of gluten present in flour partly determines its use in baked dough products.

Less/more gluten is desirable for bread than for pie dough.

more

●

7 Would you think that bread flour (high protein) could be used for making pie dough?

It is sometimes used; however, a higher proportion of fat is needed to shorten the dough, that is, keep it tender by hindering the formation of the gluten strands. Pastry flours which have a medium protein content are widely used to produce pastries that are both tender and flaky. Cake flour contains so little protein that it is almost impossible to form a rolled dough with it.

8 Much of baking knowledge is concerned with the amount, nature and control of the gluten which is developed in a particular flour.

Breads baked on the hearth (on stones and not in pans) require high protein flour which when baked will be strong enough not to flatten under the weight of the dough and to withstand the strong aerating action of the large amount of carbon dioxide gas developed by the yeast.

Cake flour, on the other hand, must be made from a soft wheat (low protein content). If bread flour were used the cake would be tough. You can make a cake with bread flour if you increase the fat but the product is never as good as when cake flour is used.

Flours intermediate between those needed for cakes and biscuits are necessary for pastries and hot breads such as rolls and muffins.

The protein content and gluten development of flour which is best for pastries and hot breads are more/less than those contained in bread flours.

less

9 Muffins are characteristically light and fluffy and the problem in making them is to avoid developing the gluten in the flour. Mix the dough as little as possible. Even in putting the dough into a pan too much manipulation causes a tough muffin. In a baking powder biscuit dough we want a stronger structure and so we will work the dough more than a muffin dough. However, too much kneading or working will destroy quality in the biscuit.

If we mix biscuit dough too much we will get what?

A heavy, tough biscuit.

10 For Danish and sweet rolls bread flour can be used but some formulae call for the addition of some pastry flour. Why?

So that gluten development will be less.

THE AERATING ACTION

11   Baked dough products rise or are aerated by the action of a gas-usually carbon dioxide—which expands the dough. CO_2 is formed by the action of yeast which breaks down sugar to CO_2 and alcohol and by the action of an acid or heat on soda which releases CO_2. Baking powders contain soda plus an acid ingredient that reacts with the soda when moistened and the product is heated. Double acting baking powders are called this because they release from a fifth to a third of their gas while at room temperature when moistened. The remainder of the gas is given off during the baking process; hence the baking powder acts twice and its name, 'double-acting'. A single acting baking powder will give all of its gas in the cold stage when moistened. This makes it difficult to handle in quantity baking. In using soda alone as an aerating agent we may add an acid such as sour milk, molasses or buttermilk. Soda that develops carbon dioxide alone in a product without an acid ingredient to react with it (by heat alone) may leave a soapy flavour in the baked product. Sometimes we add an excess of soda to a chocolate cake so an alkaline action is developed and this causes the chocolate to turn a nice reddish colour. However, we do this at the expense of the flavour for we may get this soapy flavour in such a cake.

What gas is responsible for most of the aerating action in baked dough products?

Carbon dioxide gas (CO_2)

●

12   Double acting baking powders give off CO_2 twice—when first mixed into a product and at what other time?

During the baking when heat is applied.

13 Carbon dioxide performs what task in a baking powder biscuit?

The gas which is released from the baking powder or soda expands with heat, stretching the gluten which coagulates and firms, giving the biscuit its shape and texture.

●

14 Steam and hot air are other gases which also expand dough. When water changes to steam, its volume increases 1600 times which accounts for almost all of the aerating action in the baking of cream puff shells, crackers, and in pie crust.

Is it necessary for carbon dioxide gas to be present for a dough to rise?

No, air and steam also act to expand the dough.

●

15 Yeast is used to make bread and sweet dough rise. Yeast action begins during the time the dough is allowed to ferment and ends in the oven when the internal temperature of the dough reaches around 60C (140F), at which temperature yeast action is killed.

Ethyl alcohol is produced by the action of the yeast acting on some of the sugars in the dough. The yeast also releases carbon dioxide. The carbon dioxide is the main aerating agent in a yeast dough, although gases from water (steam) and ethyl alcohol may help to aerate the dough.

Carbon dioxide gas is formed by the action of baking soda, baking powder and what other common baking ingredient?

Yeast

L

16   Still another aerating agent used, but not widely, is baking ammonia vol (ammonium bicarbonate). In the presence of heat, baking ammonia changes to carbon dioxide, ammonia gas and water vapour. It is used in making cookies and choux pastry (for making the shells of cream puffs, eclairs and the small cream puffs known as profiteroles). Ammonia does not discolour the dough as would baking soda. The word choux means cabbage in French; the choux pastry probably takes its name from the fact that some of the pastries look like little cabbages. 'Vol' is recommended as an aerating agent only in dry goods such as biscuits. Ammonia odour will be retained in moisture (or moist eating confectionary).

Would you think that in using ammonia as a leavening agent the residual gas would be dangerous?

Most of the gas escapes; and when the shells are opened so that the fillings can be inserted, any gas that is left escapes.

●

17   To achieve an aerated product, we need a gas acting on the dough, paste or batter and the presence of what substance in the dough which stretches and forms the structure for the raised product?

Flour containing gluten.

●

FATS AND OILS IN BAKING

18   Fat or oil used in baking is selected to perform a particular function. Shortenings are fats which are used to shorten the gluten strands, to surround them and make them more easily broken. In the language of baking, the product is made more *tender*. Shortenings also add flavour, colour and help to aerate the product when it is creamed. Creaming is working the fat until it is soft and creamy; air is added to the fat during this process which helps in the aerating.

Shortening shortens what?

The gluten strands, making the gluten strands less continuous and the product more tender.

314

19   Gluten development is necessary in bread to allow the bread to rise, give it enlarged form, and firm texture.

Is shortening needed in a bread formula?

Some, to give a bit of tenderness and to give richness and a sheen to the crumb.

⬤

20   The plasticity of fat determines its ability to cream, that is to incorporate and hold air, increasing the volume of cake batter or creamed icing. Fat also imparts a sheen or gloss to the crumb of a product.

What would you expect to result if fat used is too hard for creaming?

The product will not cream well and will have a heavy crumb.

⬤

21   We want tender moist cakes so we need a shortening which will separate the gluten strands. Emulsifiers are added to the fat to permit greater dispersion of the shortening in the batter. Higher ratios of sugar, eggs and liquid to flour can be used when good dispersion of the fat occurs.

Such shortenings are known as *high absorption shortenings* because the fat is held in suspension which allows more of what ingredients to be absorbed?

Sugar, eggs and liquids.

⬤

22   Fat serves to lubricate batters and doughs, allowing them to 'slip' and move easily. The fat must be of the right degree of plasticity for a particular purpose. For example, soft poultry fats shorten gluten well but blend too easily with flour to produce a flaky crust for pies. Too much fat mixed with flour gives a greasy crumb of an oily quality.

Since fat shortens a baked product what would you expect would happen to a cake which has excessive fat in the batter?

The cake will fall while baking—it is too tender.

315

23   Fats and oils which contain a high percentage of unsaturated fats have more shortening power than saturated fats. Shortening power is also increased as free fatty acids increase. Thus, animal fats such as butter, lard and chicken fat make tender baked products because they contain large quantities of free fatty acids. Vegetable fats contain fewer free fatty acids and therefore do not make a tender product. However, it is possible for a fat to have too much shortening power and this is why we prefer vegetable fats for some baking uses. Butter and margarine contain water (butter and margarine are only 80% fat).

Can we substitute one fat for another to achieve a particular shortening effect?

Not kilo for kilo because of differences in saturation, free fatty acids, and water content in various fats and oils.

●

SUGAR IN BAKED PRODUCTS

24   Sugars vary in their sweetening quality. Beet sugar has the same sweetening quality as cane sugar. Compared to table sugar honey is 97% as sweet, corn syrup made by the acid process 30%, maple syrup 64%, molasses 74%, saccharine (a non-sugar) is 300 times as sweet as sugar.

Corn sugar is sometimes used in pie dough for the reason that it browns well.

Is it possible to substitute one sugar for another in a baking formula?

Yes, but allowance must be made for the difference in sweetening effect and for other effects mentioned in the next item.

●

25   Honey which contains a particular kind of sugar, invert sugar a mixture of glucose and fructose, retains moisture better than does other sugars and for that reason is used in items to be stored, such as Christmas cookies. However, cakes made with honey are heavier and more compact because honey holds more moisture in the cake than would other sugars.

Honey can be substituted for as much as half the sugar in cakes if corrections are made for the moisture difference. Honey lowers the pH of the batter, causes a loss of volume and some undesirable browning.

Molasses is like honey in that it contains moisture, draws moisture into the baked product and is slightly acid.

In substituting honey we must also consider the effect that it has as the result of a changed ....

pH or acidity

●

PASTRY DOUGHS AND PIE BAKING

26   We defined pastry dough as being a flour and water mixture containing more fat than most other doughs (puff paste and Danish dough contain even more).

In making pastry an attempt is made to produce *tenderness* and *flakiness*. Tenderness is the quality of being easily chewed or broken as measured by the breaking strength. Flakiness is measured by the height between layers of dough in a baked sheet. The blisters in flaky pastry make it higher than it would be if it lacked flakiness.

The added fat in pastry dough provides flavour, ... and flakiness.

tenderness

●

27   Flakiness is achieved in pie dough, puff paste and rolled-in yeast doughs by developing a thin sheet of fat between layers of dough. In baking, this fat melts, steam forms where the fat was and the steam lifts the dough forming blisters.

Do flaky products require more shortening than non-flaky ones?

Yes, because a part of the shortening must be used for the development of flakiness.

●

28   The development of flakiness opposes to some extent the development of tenderness. For tenderness we want a minimum of gluten development but to achieve flakiness some gluten development is necessary. As we have seen, during the baking the gluten layers are separated by the fat and steam develops to produce the blistered or layered effect.

Tenderness and flakiness are/are not perfectly correlated.

are not

29 Would you expect that adding fat to a pastry dough would increase tenderness?

Yes, this will happen if the fat is sufficiently mixed in to surround the gluten particles since the fat separates the gluten. Too much fat produces excessive tenderness so the dough becomes too tender and crumbles.

●

30 Fats that are the most plastic and become softest while being incorporated into a dough seem to make a more tender product. Lard, highly plastic, and high in free fatty acids since it is an animal fat, usually makes a more tender dough than hydrogenated vegetable fats.

Excessive water causes toughness in pastry doughs, possibly by excessive hydration of the gluten. Butter and margarine are fats which contain up to 20 per cent water. Would this fact influence the tenderness of pastry doughs?

Yes. An equivalent quantity of butter and margarine make less tender doughs than lard or hydrogenated vegetable oils.

●

31 Pastry is 'relaxed' by storing the dough before rolling or adding flour during the rolling process. The gluten in the stored dough absorbs water and becomes more pliable and tender.

True or False: To relax a pastry dough store before rolling.

True

●

32 Other factors that affect quality in pie dough are the manner and amount of mixing. Use fat at 15·5C (60F) and blend it as desired with the flour, but once the water is added, mix as little as possible. If the fat is left in large pieces, a flaky crust is obtained because the chunks of fat spread out between layers of dough. Additional mixing spreads the fat around the gluten and yields a mealy crust.

To achieve flakiness in pie dough should the fat, flour and water be thoroughly mixed?

No, this spreads out the fat destroying the chances for flaky crust development and the mixing develops gluten, toughening the dough.

33   Can you guess why ice water is often recommended as the liquid in pie dough rather than warm or tap water?

Ice water keeps the shortening in plastic form. Gluten also develops faster in a warm dough than in cold dough.

●

34   Since the amount of mixing after water is added is critical in making a pie dough many experts insist that pie dough be mixed by hand. They feel that it is too easy to overmix by leaving the dough a few seconds too long in a mechanical mixer. What kind of pie crust will be produced if the fat is thoroughly mixed into a dough?

A mealy dough which is preferred for under crusts of fruit and berry pies and custard and pumpkin pies since this crust resists soaking.

●

35   Is it possible to mix a flaky pie crust using a mechanical mixer?

Yes, using a special pastry knife blade in the mixer which cuts the dough with little rise in temperature.

●

36   A cafeteria chain well known for their pastries uses a rich pie dough formula of seven kilogrammes of shortening to ten of unbleached pastry flour. The flour and fat are hand mixed until marble-size balls are formed. The result is a rich, flaky dough for use for the tops of all fruit pies and cobblers (a kind of pie with only a top crust which is cut and served in squares).

Scraps of dough left over are machine mixed and though the dough then becomes mealy it is satisfactory for use in under crusts of these pies of for open face pies such as pumpkin, custard and cheese. The mealy dough is also good for making pastry shells for ice box pies using cream and custard fillings.

A flaky dough becomes what kind of dough when mixing is continued?

Mealy

37 What kind of dough, mealy or flaky, is usually preferred for open face pies and ice box pies?

It depends. While a mealy crust resists soaking of the filling, many like the flaky quality in a flaky crust. If they use a flaky crust, they may fill their pies only just before service, holding back the shells and filling these closer to serving demand.

●

38 Single crust pie shells have pin holes made in the dough before baking—a process called *docking*. These holes allow steam generated during baking to escape and prevents raised portions of crust— blisters—from forming.

An even more effective method for avoiding blisters is the practice of double-panning. An empty pie tin is placed on top of the dough in the pan. Double-panning holds the crust in place, retaining its form as well.

Will double-panning tend to produce a brown inside crust?

Yes, the inside tin is a good conductor of heat and allows the crust to brown. If desired, the double pan can be removed about five minutes before the shell is completely baked.

●

39 The bottom crust of fruit pies has a tendency to become soggy, the fruit juices soaking into the crust while the pie is baking. The bottom crust should be brushed with egg-white before baking.

To avoid this the crust dough can be mixed until a mealy texture is reached, or the pie can be baked on the bottom shelf of the oven which will accomplish what purpose?

The bottom of the oven is hotter than the rest of the oven since the heat originates there and as a result the bottom layer bakes quickly, sealing out the juices.

●

40 Use of a shiny pie tin can also assist in forming a soggy bottom crust. Would a shiny surface absorb or reflect heat?

A shiny surface reflects heat rather than passing it through to the crust inside.

41   Often, frozen pies when being baked should be moved to a different spot in the oven after 10 minutes. Can you think of the reason for this?

The frozen pie chills the spot it sits on. The cold spot does not recover its heat in time to bake the lower crust before the top is brown.

●

42   Will carbon deposits on the oven shelf slow down the browning of the bottom crust?

Yes, carbon deposits are poor conductors of heat.

●

43   To prevent soaking a bottom crust bakers sprinkle dry cake crumbs in the bottom of a baked pie shell before filling it. What is the effect of the crumbs?

They absorb excess liquid from the fruit, liquid which would otherwise soak into the crust.

●

44   Fruit pie fillings are thickened to prevent their running when cut and to provide desirable texture. Various thickening agents are used such as wheat flour, waxy maize-starch, cornflour and tapioca.

Flour produces a cloudy, milky gel which hides the colour of the fruit.

Waxy maize starch and cornflour both give a clear, shiny gel but the waxy maize gel is soft while the cornflour produces a firm gel.

Is wheat flour a suitable thickening agent for cherry pie?

No, flour yields a dull lustre and tends to hide the cherries.

●

45   Is waxy maize starch suitable for thickening cream pie fillings?

No, the gel it forms is too weak to provide structure for cream fillings and the filling runs. Cornflour is better.

321

46   Cornflour forms a firm gel—too firm by itself—while tapioca forms a weak gel. Used together they can be excellent for cherry pie and similar fruit pies. Researchers at Cornell University recommend the use of 3 parts of tapioca to 2 parts of cornflour. For a 20 centimetre pie the proportions are one cup of sugar, three tablespoons of tapioca, two tablespoons of cornflour.

What is the principal reason for using the tapioca?

To prevent the cornflour from making a gel which is too firm.

●

47   For a clearer filling what would you use?

Waxy maize which gives a soft paste and a very clear gel.

●

48   In making cherry pie would you drain the juice from the cherries and thicken the juice, then add the cherries—or would you thicken the two together?

Separately. Additional heat on the fruit only serves to destroy flavour, colour and texture. Mix the two together after the juice has been thickened. If you wish, you can thicken the juice of berries and fruit with a cold setting starch (see the section on starch cookery).

●

49   If a sweet pie is desired the amount of sugar needed may be so much that it prevents gelling. Can you think of a way to avoid this happening?

Withhold some of the sugar until gelling occurs, then add the rest of the sugar.

50   The kind of filling used in a pie determines the temperature used in the oven for baking. Fruit pies are baked at 204—218C (400—425F) for 25—30 minutes. Some bakers prefer 177—191C (350—375F) for 45 minutes. Pies with a quantity of milk and eggs cannot stand such a high temperature for so long a time. Fruit cobblers (a top crust only) are baked at 121C (250F). Bake single crust pies in a 204 to 218C (400—425) oven for 15 minutes.

Custard pies baked directly in the shell are baked for ten minutes only at the 232C (450F) temperature, then the temperature is reduced to 149C (300F) and the baking continued for 45 to 50 minutes to cook the custard. Fruit pies are usually baked at . . . . for 25 to 30 minutes or . . . . for 45 minutes.

204—218C (400—425F), 177—191C (350—375F)

●

51   One of the most popular of all baked desserts is apple pie. Fresh, frozen, dehydrated or canned apples are used for the filling, depending upon the price of the apples, their texture and taste desired. The amount of sugar or other sweetening also varies widely.

True or False: the apple fillings used in apple pie should always be made from fresh apples.

False; more labour is involved in peeling fresh apples and they may not be as desirable to some people as canned or frozen apples.

●

DANISH, PUFF AND ECLAIR PASTRY

52   Danish is a yeast bread product that is made from a rolled-in, rich, high-fat dough. All purpose or a combination of bread and cake flour is used. Some bakers buy a special Danish shortening; others use margarine or butter, or a combination of both. The shortening is placed in a thin slab or dotted over part of the dough. The dough is then folded over the shortening and the whole rolled. This procedure is repeated three or four times. The dough is *rested* in a refrigerator for at least twenty minutes between each rolling so that it becomes firmer, more elastic and holds together better.

The finished dough is a series of layers of fat and dough which expands in baking to form the characteristic Danish texture.

Danish pastry requires considerable/little time to prepare.

considerable

●

53 What would happen to Danish pastry if the fat melts while it is being rolled?

The dough becomes soaked with fat, and does not become flaky or layered.

●

54 Puff pastry is not a yeast dough but is similar to Danish pastry in that it is rich in fat, but more flaky. It is a basic dough used for pastry shells and their larger brothers, the vol au vent (literally 'gone with the wind') cream slices and similar light, crispy pastries.

Puff pastes are made of bread flour because the gluten is needed to provide the 'stretch' or puff and to hold the new puffed form.

Puff paste recipes call for a 1 to 1 ratio of fat and flour. Water, cream of tartar and salt are added ingredients. The fat must be highly plastic and a special puff paste margarine is available.

Puff paste doughs use what kind of flour?

Hard or bread flour

●

55 A vol au vent is a large . . . .

puff pastry case

●

56 Eclair paste (also called choux—paste) is a paste which is between a batter and a dough consistency. It is made of bread flour, butter or shortening, eggs, water and salt.

The paste is used for making cream puff and eclair shells, their small cousins the profiterolles.

Eclair paste is also known by its French name, ...

choux paste

57   What do you suppose gives eclair shells their yellow colour?

The eggs contained in the paste.

●

58   An aerating agent in puff paste and choux paste batter is steam. Steam develops in the areas where fat exists, between the sheets of dough in the puff paste and causes the flaking. In the choux paste the steam formed inside pushes the paste or batter up or out making a large hollow inside. Continued baking causes the shell around the hollow to form due to coagulation and gelatinization. Baking must continue until this wall is quite firm and will not collapse when the product is removed from the oven and the steam pressure subsides. Actually the shell is partially dried in the baking to give it strength.

What oven temperatures would be used for products such as this that are leavened by steam? High or low?

High to start 232C (450F) is used for some items) to secure rapid steam development before the product sets and then when full expansion has occurred, the temperature is dropped to complete baking.

●

CAKE BAKING

59   Cakes may be divided into those that contain no fat and include beaten eggs to develop volume and those that include fat and a chemical aerating agent, usually bicarbonate of soda or soda. Examples of the unshortened cakes are sponge and angel food cakes.

Carbon dioxide is a gas which expands the shortened cakes. What is it that gives volume to unshortened cakes?

Air beaten into the eggs and expanded during baking. There is also some steam development.

●

60   In the shortened cakes butter, eggs and sugar may be *creamed* to incorporate air. Some small quantity of air may be obtained in beating or stirring. During baking the air obtained from creaming and beating is joined by the carbon dioxide given off by the baking powder or soda. Steam also is an aerator. A true pound cake is a shortened cake aerated by air incorporated in creaming and contains no aerating agent. Why is it called a pound cake?

Because the proportion of ingredients was a pound of shortening, a pound of sugar, a pound of eggs and a pound of flour.

61   A cake batter contains gluten and starch. With the application of heat the starch gelatinizes (the molecules take in water and swell) and the gluten coagulates. Egg proteins present also coagulate to give structure to the cake.

During the baking of chemically aerated cakes, the air bubbles expand with carbon dioxide and the cell walls become firm because of the coagulation of .... and the gelatinization of ....

proteins, starch

●

62   The size of the crystals in the sugar used in cakes affects its texture. Small crystals give better cake texture than coarse sugars. Powdered sugar, however, which would appear to be even better, is not recommended because the crystals have been ruptured by grinding and give too fine a crumb or cell structure.

Fine, whole sugar crystals used in cake recipes result in better/poorer cakes?

better

●

63   Emulsifier-type shortenings give results superior to other fats in cake baking. These hydrogenated fats include mono- and diglycerides added to give spread to the fat in the batter. The mono- and diglycerides increase the emulsifying property of the fat in the cake batter which produces larger volume, finer grain, improved texture and tenderness.

Emulsifiers in cake shortenings have what effect?

They spread the shortening out into finer globules giving a smoother batter and improved texture. Higher ratios of fat and sugar can also be used.

●

64   Compared with strong bread with some chew we want a tender cake. With this in mind what kind of flour should be used for cakes, one high in protein or low in protein?

Cake flour is low protein flour.

●

65   Angel and sponge cakes owe their structure and lightness to air in beaten eggs. The eggs furnish structure when they coagulate but the structure is not nearly

so firm as that produced alone by gluten so these cakes must be treated more carefully.

They are often baked in tube pans, a tube running up the centre of the pan which aids in transferring heat to the batter and also supports the cake as it rises and firms.

Would it be well to grease angel or sponge cake pans before the batter is added?

No, greasing allows the cake to slip and fall. Instead, the pans are dampened and left damp before adding the batter.

●

66   Chiffon cakes are leavened by beaten eggs and some baking powder. They contain oil instead of fat. The large quantity of beaten eggs used give them the characteristic of sponge cakes. The beaten eggs are folded into the batter at the end of the mixing period so that the eggs will attain volume for aerating.

Would you grease the pans used for baking chiffon cakes?

No, for the same reason that angel and sponge cake pans are not greased.

●

67   Fast heat penetration is desired in cake baking. What kind of metal pan would be best for baking cake: one made of iron with a dull finish or a bright aluminum pan?

The dull iron one absorbs and transmits heat faster and more effectively than the pans having a shiny surface. Dull pans result in faster browning.

●

68   It is reasonable to suggest that when placing cakes in an oven the pans be placed so that they do not touch the sides of the oven; or placed directly over another?

Yes, allow free air circulation around the pans. If they touch each other or the sides of the oven the rate of heat transfer is increased where they touch.

69 Knowing that a warm, freshly baked cake breaks easily if handled, would it be wise to allow the cake to cool before removing it from the pan?

Yes, it is recommended that cakes be allowed to cool to 60C (140F). This may take a long time. At least let them cool for 10 to 15 minutes so that their centres will be partially cooled.

●

70 A sheet cake, baked as a large unit, retains its moisture and freshness longer than if the same amount of cake were made in smaller units. The smaller units have proportionately more surface area exposed to the heat source. The sheets can be baked and stored, then cut into a variety of squares, bars and other shapes.

    True or False: Sheet cakes are less likely to dry out than smaller sized cakes.

True, because of the proportionately smaller surface exposure.

●

GLAZING

71 Differences in surface sheen are produced by glazing, adding butter, water or sugar to the surface and heating. Sweet rolls and tarts are often glazed to produce colour and sheen on their tops. Apricot preserves are used for glazing the various French pastries. Egg mixed with milk, cream or water is frequently used as a glaze. A deeper brown develops when cream is used.

    If a soft crust is wanted on a dough the product is brushed with butter *before* baking.

    For crisp crusted bread or rolls, steam is injected into the oven *during* baking. To develop these surface finishes use what methods?

    1. A brown glaze . . . .
    2. A crisp crust . . . .
    3. A soft crust . . . .
    4. A yellow, sweet glaze . . . .

1. eggs and cream
2. steam
3. butter
4. apricot preserves

72 The French frequently use apricot preserves, apricot jelly or red currant jelly as a glaze on tarts and cakes and as a waterproof lining for pastry shells. The preserves or jelly are boiled to between 107·2 and 108·8C (225 and 228F). Upon cooling the pectin present stiffens and the glaze can be easily handled.

Glazing adds sheen to a surface but may also serve what other purpose?

As a waterproof lining.

●

YEAST DOUGHS

73 Yeast doughs get their name from the fact that they are aerated largely by bakers' yeast, one celled, microscopic plants which break simple sugars into carbon dioxide and ethyl alcohol.

The CO_2 is trapped in the gluten and aerates (raises) the dough.

Aerating in yeast dough is caused by CO_2 formed by the action of . . . . on sugar.

yeast

●

74 Yeast doughs may be divided into rich and lean. Both contain flour, liquid, fat, salt and are aerated by yeast. A conditioner containing sugar may be added on which the yeast can feed.

The rich doughs contain greater amounts of sugar and fat, and sometimes eggs. Doughs to which any amount of sugar is added are called sweet doughs.

Lean dough products—bread, rolls, pizza—are characterized by a chewy texture and will therefore use what kind of flour?

Hard wheat flour, high in protein and gluten.

●

75 Rich dough products such as coffee cakes, cinnamon rolls, butter horns, Danish pastry and crescent rolls are made to be more tender and would use what kind of flour?

Some pastry or soft wheat flour is used with bread flour to achieve tenderness, less chewiness.

76 Yeast products are made in this sequence of operations: *mixing, fermentation, knock-back, rest, scale and shape, proof, and bake.* Before mixing the ingredients are weighed, 'scaled off' as the baker says, then formed into a smooth paste and the gluten is thoroughly developed.

What is the next step?

Fermentation

●

77 During fermentation enzymes in the yeast known as zymase change the sugars dextrose and levulose into carbon dioxide and ethyl alcohol:

$$C_6 H_{12} O_6 + yeast \rightarrow 2CO_2 + 2C_2H_5OH$$

Dextrose or levulose	carbon dioxide	ethyl alcohol
100 parts	47·9 parts	51·1 parts

Temperatures of about 29 to 32C (84—90F) are best for fermentation. Above 43C (110F) yeast action is slowed and at about 60C (140F) yeast is destroyed.

Enzymes in the yeast act on simple sugars to produce .... and alcohol which causes the dough to rise. This is the fermentation process.

CO_2

●

78 As fermentation proceeds, the gluten hydrates (absorbs water) and the dough becomes more pliable and smooth.

Fermentation is considered complete when the dough has doubled in bulk.

The dough is 'taken to the bench young', in other words, the dough is taken from the container where it is fermenting when fermentation is about $\frac{3}{4}$ complete.

Fermentation causes the dough to rise and become more ....

pliable and smooth

79 The next step is knocking-back. The dough has expanded to a point where the gluten cannot support the structure without the firming action of heat. If it is pushed or 'punched', it collapses at that point.

In the 'knocking-back', the dough is folded over on all sides causing it to collapse and return to its original bulk. The knocking back allows the CO_2 formed to escape and redistributes the food available for the yeast so that a vigorous secondary leavening can take place.

Is the term 'knocking-back' misleading?

Yes, the dough is actually folded and pressed rather than knocked-back. When folding is complete, the dough is turned upside down in the container

●

80 The 'make up' comes next. The dough is taken to the bench where it is allowed to 'rest' a short time. It is then divided (cut), shaped and panned as desired. Rolled-in doughs have shortening spread over them and are folded and rolled at this point.

So far, the dough has been mixed, fermented, knocked-back, rested, and . . . .

scaled and shaped

●

81 The next step is 'the proof'. Made up products are placed in an area where the temperature is about 37·7C (100F) and the humidity is high. In a bakery a 'proofer' or proofing cabinet in which steam or hot water produces a high humidity may be used.

Aerating action increases, the yeast grows quickly giving off CO_2, and the products swell to at least twice the original make up size.

The 'proof' follows what step?

Scale and shape

82   Now—finally—the dough is ready to bake. As heat is applied, the final aerating occurs before the heat reaches 60C (140F) and the yeast is destroyed. The steam and CO_2 produced rapidly expand the dough to produce 'oven spring'. The top crust of a loaf is pushed up because of the spring.

Would you guess that oven spring might be too vigorous if some of the gases were not allowed to escape?

Yes, to avoid too much 'oven spring' hearth and rye breads which develop hard, unyielding crusts are 'docked', sliced across the top to allow for expansion and to permit some of the gases to escape. If docking is not done, the crusts would burst.

●

83   Should small rolls be docked (scored)?

No, their smaller size produce less spring and except for crisp rolls their crusts are soft, which permits expansion.

●

84   To review, we see that yeast dough products are made in a series of steps: mixing, ... , ... , ... , ... , ... , and . . . .

fermentation, knockback, rest, scale, shape proof, bake

●

85   We mentioned crisp crusted breads. These are produced using a lean dough and applying steam to their surfaces during the early part of the baking. Or the bread can be brushed with water several times during the early stages of baking.

Crisp crusts in breads are produced by using lean/rich doughs and applying . . . . to the surfaces during the early stages of baking.

lean, steam or water

86 Baking temperatures are related to size of the product and to richness. Lean rolls and small products bake at 204—218C (400—425F). Richer products and large, lean ones are baked at lower temperatures.

Pizzas which are a lean, thin product topped with tomato paste and cheese require a high/low temperature.

A high temperature —up to 315C (600F) to dry the tomato paste and quickly brown the dough.

●

87 Depanning and cooling of yeast dough products should allow for the escape of steam and alcohol developed during baking. To allow for this, large products may be removed from their pans so that free air circulation can occur.

Crisp crusted breads and rolls are not wrapped so as to prevent softening of the crusts. Does this mean that crisp crusted bread and rolls will keep longer?

No, they must be baked daily if a quality product is desired.

●

88 Quality of bread is well kept if it is wrapped and frozen. However, refrigeration produces more staling than if the bread were kept at room temperature. In hot muggy climates refrigeration does prevent mould growth and may be necessary.

1 kilogramme of unsliced bread that is frozen requires about 4 hours to thaw at room temperature.

Ordinarily we should/should not refrigerate bread.

should not

●

89 Yeast is also used to aerate such items as Babas, English muffins and crumpets. Sour dough and old fashioned hot cake batter is 'started' by use of an old dough or batter in which fermentation is quite complete. Such 'starter' is highly acid or sour—hence the name 'sour dough'.

A sour dough is a dough which has been well . . . . .

fermented

REVISION

1. Why is the use of wheat flour so important in baking?

It contains 7 to 15% gluten which, when developed, can stretch and firm, forming the enlarged product.

●

2. Pastry doughs can be identified by the fact that they contain large quantities of . . . .

fat or shortening

●

3.
Product	Kind of Flour
Bread	a. . . . .
Pastry	b. . . . .
Cake	c. . . . .
Biscuits	d. . . . .
Danish pastry	e. . . . .
Eclair paste	f. . . . .
Puff paste	g. . . . .

a. High protein (bread flour)
b. Usually medium protein (pastry)
c. Low protein (cake flour)
d. Medium protein (pastry)
e. Medium protein (pastry)
f. High protein (bread flour)
g. High protein (bread flour)

●

4. Soft wheat flour makes for a tender/less tender product.

tender

●

5. The principal gas formed by growing yeast is . . . .

CO_2

●

6. Gases active in aerating include CO_2, ammonia, hot air, ... and . . . .

steam, ethyl alcohol

334

7. Creaming fat means incorporating . . . . into it.

air

8. High absorption shortening allows greater amounts of . . . . to be used in cake.

sugar, eggs and liquids

9. A well worked pie dough results in a flaky/mealy crust.

mealy

10. A shortening shortens what?

Gluten strands

11. Honey has what advantage in baking?

Holds more moisture longer than other sugars. Brown sugar is superior in this regard to refined cane sugar.

12. When pastry dough is allowed to relax it absorbs . . . . and becomes more tender and pliable.

water

13. The critical time for making a pastry dough flaky or mealy occurs before/after water is added.

after

14. Mealy pie doughs are recommended for . . . .

open face and soft pies

15. If a flaky pie is wanted for soft cream pies, the filling is added when?

If possible, just before serving to minimize soakage into the flaky crust.

16. A combination of thickening agents, tapioca and ...., is recommended for cherry pie filling.

cornflour

●

17. Custard pies baked at lower/higher temperatures than fruit pies.

Lower, because of the eggs in the custard.

●

18. Resting Danish Pastry dough has the effect of making it more ....

firm, elastic and able to hold together better

●

19. A vol au vent is made of ....

puff paste

●

20. Choux paste—bread flour, butter, eggs and water—is used in making cream puffs and .... shells.

eclair

●

21. What gas makes eclair shells rise?

steam

●

22. In cake baking the cake forms a new larger structure supported by gelatinized starch and ....

coagulated protein

●

23. In a chiffon cake .... is used in the recipe instead of fat.

oil

●

24. The tube in the middle of an angel food cake pan serves to pass heat quickly into the batter and to ....

support the cake in its expanded form

25. Cakes should be allowed to cool before handling; otherwise they are likely to . . . .

break

●

26. The yellow glaze which appears on most French pastry is made of strained . . . .

apricot jam or preserves

●

27. In making bread dough, it gets two periods during which yeast action is strong: during fermentation and while . . . .

proofing

●

28. Yeast action is also strong while the doughs are in the oven before the temperature reaches . . . . in the dough, destroying the yeast.

60C (140F)

●

29. Oven spring is caused by . . . .

the expansion of CO_2 formed during the fermentation of the yeast and the formation of steam in the hot oven

●

30. Knocking-back procedure permits the gases present to escape, returns the dough to its original size and also effects yeast action in what way?

Redistributes yeast foods so that the yeast thrives.

●

31. Docking (scoring) is done to pie shells and to crisp crusted breads for the purpose of allowing . . . .

gases to escape

The Uses of Starch
in Cookery

The cooking of starch has been discussed briefly in relation to sauce making on pages 67—71 and elsewhere. This more detailed section on the subject is for those who wish a better understanding of starch cookery.

1   Starch is the reserve carbohydrate of plants and is found abundantly in such common foods as corn, rice, wheat and potatoes. Rice is about 80% starch, wheat 70%, and potatoes about 19% starch.

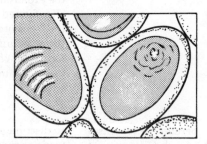

Starch granules (potato) greatly enlarged

Starch provides body for baked goods and is a food in its own right providing the body with calories for energy and heat.

When we speak of starch cookery, however, we usually refer to cooking those starches used for thickening such foods as sauces, gravies, soups, creamed vegetables, salad dressings, candies, puddings, pie fillings, and fondues.

Starch is found in most foods, but when we say starch cookery we usually refer to starch being used as a .... agent.

thickening

2 ' Cornflour is a starch used for thickening. All-purpose or pastry flour is also widely used, especially for thickening sauces and gravies. Rice flour, rice starch, wheat starch, arrowroot, tapioca, potato starch and more recently the waxy and modified starches are being used to a limited extent. As cooking becomes more precise the selection of a particular starch for a particular purpose will become more common.

The two most widely used starches in the kitchen are
. . . . and . . . .   cornflour, flour

●

3 Each starch has its own character and limitations. Regular cornflour should not be used in foods that will be frozen and thawed since the water separates from the starch in the freeze-thaw process. Cornflour is of little value in foods high in acid since the acid thins out the starch. In some foods the firm texture formed by a cornflour gel is desirable; in others, such a firm texture is not wanted. In some foods, a clear paste is wanted so that other ingredients in the mixture can be seen. Cornflour gives an opaque paste which is not suitable for berry pies or glazed fruit.

True or False: Although cornflour is a popular starch for thickening foods, it is not acceptable for several   True
products.

●

4 Starch is white and almost tasteless and odourless when cooked. This is an advantage in that it blends well with almost any food material. When uncooked, starch has a 'raw starch' or cereal flavour which is eliminated by proper cooking.

Unlike protein, most starches must be cooked to a temperature close to boiling to thicken and to get rid of the raw starch flavour.

We usually think of using low heat for cooking protein, but need comparatively . . . . heat for   high
cooking starch.

5   Starch as seen under a microscope is composed of granules of various sizes each granule containing many molecules. The size of the granule is measured in millionths of a metre. The average size of a rice granule is about 5 millionths of a metre, that of corn 15 millionths of a metre, and potato is the largest in size, up to about 100 millionths of a metre.

When cooked the larger granules pick up water and swell first, then finally the smaller ones.

Would you expect potato starch to thicken at a lower temperature than rice starch?

Yes, because the potato starch has the largest granule, but there are other factors to be considered as well.

●

6   Can you see a starch granule with the naked eye?

No, you need a microscope. Under a microscope each starch is seen to have granules that are distinctive from other starches.

●

7   The granules in a particular starch vary in size. During cooking the larger granules gelatinize first, then finally the smaller ones.

Knowing this, would you expect starch to thicken at one temperature or over a range of temperatures?

Over a range of temperatures.

●

8   The root starches—tapioca, arrowroot and potato—begin to thicken at lower temperatures than needed for the cereal starches. The root starches start to thicken at about 65·5—71C (150—160F), and thicken completely much below the boiling point.

Cereal starches—corn, wheat and rice—begin to gelatinize at about 71C (160F) but require about 85—96C (185—205F) for maximum thickening.

Tapioca thickens at a lower/higher temperature than cornflour.

lower

9 Cooked and cooled pastes made from cereal starches are opaque and tend to form a gel. In contrast pastes made from root starches such as potato, tapioca and arrowroot remain fluid, cohesive and non-gelling.

True or False: Cereal starches when cooked and cooled tend to gel while most root starches do not.

True

●

10 The swelling of starch granules as they soak up water when heated is known as gelatinization. This is not the same as gelling.

Let's stop a moment and distinguish between some basic terms: colloids, sols, gels and gelatinization.

Colloids: substances holding in suspension particles ranging from ·001 to 1 millionths of a metre. Only the largest can be seen with the ordinary microscope. Colloids are distinguished from solutions.

Sols: colloidal dispersions that flow.

Pastes: cooked starch and water that flows.

Gels: colloidal dispersions that do not flow but are rigid or semi-rigid.

Gelatinization: a process whereby starch when cooked in water soaks up water and thickens.

Starch and water cooked until the mixture barely flows and yet is not rigid enough to be called a gel is a paste. If it sets up so that it stands without support it would be called a . . . . (solution—a liquid containing a dissolved substance.)

starch gel

●

11 We cook starch and water and when the mixture thickens we know that the process of . . . . has taken place. It is now called a starch paste. When the starch mixture becomes semi-rigid, we have a . . . .

gelatinization, gel

●

12 Raw cornflour added to water in a ratio of about 1 to 20 and cooked in water that is close to boiling produces a starch-water mixture known as a . . . .

paste

13 If this cornflour paste is allowed to cool it sets and becomes a . . . .

gel

14 Heating starch in water causes the granules to take on water and swell to many times their original size. If we continue to cook and stir we end up with a starch-water mixture of swollen granules and granule fragments.

We can also expect what else besides these oversized granules and fragments?

Some free starch in water, leached from the granules.

15 In cooking a starch-water mixture, it is usually stirred during the early cooking stage to disperse the starch uniformly in the liquid. Continued vigorous stirring after thickening occurs ruptures the starch cells and causes the mixture to thin out.

True or False: In thickening a mixture with starch, stir at first but stop stirring unless you want a thin paste.

True

16 Many cookbooks recommend continued cooking of water-starch mixtures to 'get rid of the starch flavour'. Many starches used today do not need this extra cooking because the objectionable flavour has been eliminated during the original processing of the starch.

Once a mixture has reached the desired viscosity, stop the cooking/continue cooking it at least another ten minutes.

stop the cooking

17 The greater proportion of starch present in a mixture, the greater the viscosity (resistance to stirring) developed when cooked. Cereal starches have more thickening power than root starches. Cereal pastes are more cloudy than root starch pastes.

Cornflour has high thickening power and its gel is relatively cloudy.

Would cornflour be good for thickening a berry pie?

Not if you want to see the berries and wanted a tender gel.

18 Since a temperature close to boiling is needed to thicken cereal starches to their maximum, is it wise to cook them in a double boiler?

No, it takes too long and at high elevations they would never thicken to their maximum because the temperature does not go high enough.

19 Adding up to 50% sugar to a starch paste increases its viscosity but decreases the strength of the gel which is formed. Adding sugar to a cereal starch paste such as cornflour increases the clarity of the paste.

Up to a point adding sugar to a starch paste makes for a stronger/weaker gel and a clearer/less clear gel.

weaker, clearer gel

20 Acids break down starch pastes by hydrolysis.

The variations often observed in the consistency of lemon pie filling may be due to the fact that the egg yolks have not completely coagulated. Even so, would it be wise to withhold the lemon juice until after the filling has been thickened?

Yes, allow the gelatinization to complete and then add the acid. Cool quickly because pastes low in pH thin out if cooled slowly.

21 Most starch contains two fractions or parts called amylose and amylopectin.

A high-amylose starch forms a firm gel and a cloudy paste. A low amylose paste forms a weak gel or does not gel at all.

Corn and wheat starch contain 20–25% amylose as compared with 20% or less in the root starches.

Would you expect corn and wheat starch gels to be more firm and cloudy than a potato or tapioca starch gel?

Yes, because they contain more amylose.

343

22   Some starches *retrograde* when frozen or stand for a time. Retrogradation is seen as the separation of water from the starch or the formation of a skin or film on the surface.

Retrogradation of starch means that the granules try to go back to the original structure they were in before being cooked. The molecules become less soluble and tend to aggregate and partially crystallize.

Retrogradation is a desirable/highly undesirable feature of some starches.

highly undesirable

●

WAXY STARCHES

23   Waxy corn, grain sorghum and rice——called waxy because their seed coats appear waxy——contain almost all amylopectin. Amioca, a trade-named starch, one such waxy corn starch, contains only the amylopectin fractions. Pastes made with it are thick and clear but have little tendency to gel.

Pastes containing about 5% of the regular starches gel when cooked, but most of the waxy starches require as much as 30% in a paste to gel when cooled.

Would amioca be useful in thickening a fruit pie filling?

Not by itself unless you want a runny pie. Cornflour or gelatine can be added to provide stiffness. A special waxy maize starch can also be used.

●

24   Waxy starches do not break when frozen and thawed as do pastes thickened with eggs or regular cornflour.

To prevent syneresis (weeping) in frozen products use what type of starch?

A waxy type (or modified starch as we shall see).

●

MODIFIED STARCHES

25   Modified starches are those which the processer has changed chemically so that some cross-bonding or cross-linking between molecules has taken place.

Some of the starch molecules are tied to adjacent molecules and in some instances into a cellulose network or matrix.

Would you expect a modified starch to cost a little more?

Yes, since some additional processing is necessary by the processer.

●

26   Modified tapioca starch is ideal for thickening fruit pie fillings. It is sparkling clear, fluid and free from the stringy quality of natural tapioca and does not weep when frozen and thawed. Neither does it set to a firm gel.

Would it make good sense to combine tapioca starch with cornflour to achieve a tender gel?

It can be done but the result is not as good as using a special starch.

●

27   Starch has been developed which is almost all amylopectin containing the branched polymers while other starches contain 55% or more amylose, the straight chain polymers. The amylose starches set very rapidly and gel firmly upon cooling. In fact, the high amylose starches set so firmly that they are excellent for use in batters for deep-frying. The batter adheres so completely to the food that it is almost impossible to remove without pulling off a portion of the food material along with the batter.

The high amylose/amylopectin starches have been found to be very useful in food batters.

amylose

●

28   Cross-linking reduces stringiness in starch paste, increases resistance to thinning in the presence of acid and helps to prevent separation when the paste is frozen and thawed.

A regular potato starch, for example, is not used for thickening pie fillings because the acids present break it down. A modified potato starch, however, can be used for the same purpose.

Cross-linked starches are more/less resistant to acids.

more

M

INSTANT STARCHES

29 Pre-cooked starches (also known as instant or pre-gelatinized starches) are available. They have been cooked and dried and need no further cooking to absorb water. Instant puddings now on the market contain instant starches.

In using pre-cooked starches be sure to mix them with sugar (about 1 part starch to 4 parts sugar) before adding liquid.

Can you guess why?

The pre-cooked starches absorb water so quickly that they lump. The sugar separates the granules permitting them to disperse in the liquid.

●

30 Suppose you wanted to make a cherry pie using canned cherries and a pre-baked pie shell, could you finish the pie without further cooking?

Yes, by thickening the cherries with pre-cooked starch and using a whipped cream topping instead of a pastry top.

●

31 If frozen fruit is used in 'instant' pies, you will need to cook the fruit to inactivate the enzymes present. Once thawed the enzymes continue to effect changes in the fruit.

How about canned fruit for use as the filling in an 'instant' pie?

Yes, the canned fruit has been cooked. In fact, further cooking as in a pie causes loss of quality.

●

32 Pre-cooked starch thoroughly mixed with sugar can be used to stabilize whipped cream. The starch gives body and the whipped cream will not separate for several days if refrigerated.

Remember we must mix the starch with . . . . before adding it to avoid lumping.

sugar

SELECTION AND USE OF STARCHES

33 Many cooks prefer flour to the other starches for thickening gravies, sauces and soups. The protein in the flour gives the sauce or soup more body and when cooked adds a nutty flavour. The other starches have very little flavour and for this reason are excellent thickening agents for pie fillings where you want to keep the flavour of the berry or fruit predominant. The neutral flavour is excellent in custards and puddings which are bland and have subtle flavours. In using flour as a thickener for sauces would you prefer bread, pastry, or cake flour?

This is somewhat a matter of opinion, but most chefs prefer pastry or all-purpose flour which contains a medium amount of protein. Such chefs claim that bread flour produces a stringy product because of its high protein content.

●

34 Flour can be mixed directly with cold water to form a slurry or uncooked paste, which can be added to hot liquid without lumps forming. Pure starches are more likely to lump if handled the same way.

A cold water and flour mixture used for thickening is called a . . . .

slurry (also called 'whitewash' or jayzee)

●

35 Flour is usually added to soups and sauces in the form of a roux, cooked fat and flour.

To make a stiff roux use (540 grammes) of all purpose or pastry flour per $\frac{1}{2}$ kilo of butter. Using a wooden spoon, heat and stir the mixture for about 3 minutes. The roux can then be placed in a 93—121C (200—250F) oven for 7 minutes to cook away the starch flavour.

This roux can be held and used for any sauce. No further cooking is needed if the stock and the roux are both hot when blended together using a whisk.

Most chefs use flour/cornflour in thickening sauces.

flour

36 Why not put the flour directly into the hot stock and stir?

You'll get lumping. The fat separates the starch granules allowing them to disperse into the stock.

●

37 White or cream sauce is one of the most widely used sauces. It is milk or cream thickened with flour and fat. Thickness depends upon the amount of flour and fat added.

A thin white sauce is made by using $\frac{1}{2}$ litre milk, 30 grammes each of butter and flour.

A medium white sauce uses 45 grammes of butter and flour to $\frac{1}{2}$ litre of milk.

A thick white sauce uses 60 grammes of butter and fat to $\frac{1}{2}$ litre of milk.

For a litre of medium thick sauce what ingredients would you need?

Multiply the basic recipe by 2: 1 litre milk, 90 grammes butter, 90 grammes flour.

●

38 Cost of a white sauce can be cut sharply if margarine is used instead of butter and nonfat dried milk substituted for fluid milk. Here is a good recipe for
5 litres of white sauce of (50 servings):
Margarine—$\frac{1}{2}$ kilo
Flour—$\frac{1}{4}$ kilo
Salt—1 tablespoon
White pepper—2 teaspoons
Liquid instant milk—$3\frac{1}{2}$ litres
1. Melt margarine. Add flour and seasonings. Stir until smooth. Cook over low heat until smooth and bubbly.
2. Stir in liquid instant milk gradually. Cook, stirring constantly, until sauce is smooth and thickened.
Suppose margarine sells for 30p a kilo, butter 60p a kilo, instant nonfat milk—4p a litre, fluid milk—9p a litre. How much money can be saved per 5 litres of white sauce using margarine and nonfat milk?

About $17\frac{1}{2}$p saving on milk, about 15p on the fat. Whole milk contains 36 grammes of fat per litre which means that $3\frac{1}{2}$ litres of whole milk would contain about 120 grammes of fat and only 360 grammes of butter would be needed for the milk and butter recipe.

39   The proper thickness of a white sauce depends on its use; for cream soups we use a very thin sauce. A thin sauce is also used for scalloped potatoes and macaroni dishes. Why not use a thicker sauce for these dishes?

The starch in the macaroni and potatoes helps to thicken them.

●

40   A thin or medium sauce is used for fish pie and cheese sauces while thicker cream sauces are used for soufflés.

Would you want a very thick sauce for croquettes?

Yes, you need a heavy sauce to bind the pieces of food together to form the croquette.

●

41   A thin white sauce is used for thickening cream soups. The roux in the white sauce serves to prevent curdling in the milk. How?

The fat in the flour serves to separate the milk protein and keep it from coagulating.

●

42   The thickening power of various starches varies greatly.

About the same thickening effect results in the use of these amounts of thickeners:

Waxy maize—60 grammes
Cornflour—82·5 grammes
Tapioca—105 grammes
Dry bread crumbs—105 grammes
Pastry flour—120 grammes
Bread flour—150 grammes

Why does bread flour have less thickening power than pastry flour?

It contains less starch (more protein).

●

43   The thickness of a gravy depends upon the amount of flour added. One tablespoon of flour per cup of liquid gives the gravy the consistency of heavy cream. Two tablespoons per cup produces medium consistency and 3 or 4 tablespoons per cup—a heavy consistency.

Would we use the same amount of cornflour as flour?

No, cornflour has greater thickening power. 1 T. of corn starch equals about 2 T. of flour in thickening quality.

44   Starchy vegetables that have been puréed thicken soups of which they are part. Potato and split pea soups are examples of such soups.

Potatoes contain about 18% starch. Would they have as much thickening power as flour?

No, flour contains about 70% starch

●

45   In making brown sauces or gravies some cooks brown the flour first. Browning can be done by heating the flour in a pan over direct heat or by baking and stirring flour in a thin layer in a 204—232C (400—450F) oven. Roux can also be browned.

As flour browns some of the starch is converted to dextrin and some of the starch granules are broken up. As a result the flour looses its thickening power. More than 3 times as much heavily browned flour is needed as compared with unbrowned flour.

Browning flour increases/reduces its thickening power.

reduces

●

46   Recipes which include wine and a starch thickener usually calls for reducing the wine before adding it to the mixture.

Can you guess why?

The wine dilutes the mixture and the low pH thins the starch.

●

47   Macaroni and spaghetti (pasta) are flour and water products which in the dry form contain about 75% starch. The problem in cooking is to prevent pieces from sticking together and to avoid cooking until too soft. Cook in rapidly boiling water (1 litre of pasta to 5 litres of water plus 2 T. of salt). Oil is sometimes added to the cooking water.

Why 'rapidly boiling water' and oil?

To prevent the pieces of pasta from sticking together. The oil also prevents boiling over of the cooking water.

48 Wheat starch is flour with the protein removed from it. Would you think that substituting some wheat starch for flour in pastry dough would increase the tenderness of the dough?

Yes, it is reported that if wheat starch is substituted for 30% of the flour in pastry dough about $\frac{1}{3}$ of the shortening can be left out and the pastry will even be more tender. The question is if enough protein is left to form a continuous dough.

●

49 It is said that if wheat starch is substituted for 30% of the flour in biscuits it increases the spread of the biscuits. Oddly enough, if pregelatinized wheat starch is substituted, the spread is decreased. Spread in biscuits has to do with how much the dough flattens out on the biscuit pan during baking.

Substituting wheat starch for flour in biscuits makes for a more/less tender biscuit.

more

●

50 Rice starch produces a more tender gel than corn or wheat starch. Potato and arrowroot gels (from root starches) are even more tender.

Which gel is more translucent and tender, one made using cornflour or potato starch?

Potato starch (a root starch).

●

51 Compared with cereal starches, root starches gelatinize at lower/higher temperatures, produce more tender/rigid gels, and gels which are more opaque/translucent.

Gelatinize at lower temperatures and their gels are more tender and translucent.

52   Potato starch sells at about the same price as cornflour and is more widely used in Europe than in this country. It is used in Swedish and German style bread, crackers and matzoh (unleavened bread) and as thickeners in soups and gravies.

Potato starch and other root starches (fecula) are called for in some French recipes for delicate sauces. Knowing that potato starch is a large-granule root starch, why do you think that it is often specified?

Because it cooks at a lower temperature, is more transparent and does not set as much on cooling as do the cereal starches.

●

53   Most recipes for pie fillings call for from 4 to 7% starch. The kind of starch, the amount of cooking, stirring, time of cooking, amount of acid, and sugar all affect the viscosity of the paste and the strength of the gel formed.

True or False: In making a pie filling feel free to substitute one kind of starch for another in the recipe.

False, feel free if you don't care how the product comes out.

●

REVISION

1. If a recipe which includes a protein food such as cheese or eggs is to be thickened with a starch, would you cook the protein and the starch separately?

Yes, if protein is cooked at the temperature necessary to gelatinize the starch, the protein will coagulate and toughen.

●

2. Factors which affect the viscosity of a starch paste include the cooking time and temperature, the amount of stirring, the effects of other ingredients especially sugar and . . . .

the pH

3. Would a waxy starch be a good thickener for a starch pudding?

No, the pudding would be runny, lacking gel strength but some waxy starches have been modified so that they are suitable.

●

4. The most widely used starch for thickening in this country is . . . .

cornflour

●

5. A modified starch is one that has been changed so that it is more/less resistant to breakdown when frozen and thawed.

more

●

6. The cereal starches need a higher/lower temperature for gelatinization than the root starches.

higher

●

7. Which one of the starches that are commonly used has the smallest granules?

Rice

●

8. Which granule, the large or the small ones, gelatinize first when heated?

The larger ones

●

9. With the usual starch used for thickening what per cent of starch to water is needed to form a gel when the starch cools?

About 5%

●

10. The root starches are more/less cloudy when they gel than the cereal starches.

less

11. The more amylose present in a cooked starch the more/less cloudy they are and the more/less firm the gel is which results.

more, more

●

12. Retrogradation (to revert) is an attempt on the part of the starch granule to return to a pattern similar to what it was before it was . . . .

cooked

●

13. What percentage of waxy starch is needed in a paste to form a gel when cooked and cooled?

About 30%

●

14. In using instant starches, why is it so necessary to separate the starch granules by adding sugar before adding the starch to a liquid?

To prevent lumping.

●

15. Why do most chefs prefer flour over other forms of starch for thickening sauces?

Flour gives more body and flavour.

●

16. Is it possible to substitute margarine and dry milk for butter and fluid milk in making a sauce?

Yes, and cheaper

●

17. Browning flour reduces/increases its thickening power.

Reduces

●

18. Why is it that adding vinegar to spaghetti when cooking prevents the drains from clogging with starch?

The vinegar prevents a gel from forming.

Control of Sugar and Ice Crystallization

1   The size of the sugar or ice crystals in several food products determines whether or not it tastes smooth or gritty. We all know the grainy feeling in the mouth when sherbert has sat around in a refrigerator too long, the granular taste of fudge when it has been stirred at high temperature and the sandy taste of some frostings. The cause of these unwanted textures is the presence of comparatively large crystals of sugar or ice. To develop a creamy smooth texture where these crystals are involved means to ensure that many small ones are produced rather than fewer large ones.

Large crystals, be they ice or sugar, result in a . . . .

gritty or grainy texture

●

2   A crystal is a pure substance composed of a closely packed mass of molecules arranged in a definite pattern. The size of sugar or ice crystals produced depends upon the rate at which they are produced. If crystallization takes place rapidly, the crystals are relatively small.

The size of sugar and ice crystals depends on the . . . . at which they are formed.

rate

●

3   Stirring a sugar solution which can crystallize or a mixture to be frozen causes crystals to form rapidly and to be small in size.

Stirring ice cream, mousses, ices, or sherberts, candies, or fondants helps to ensure a creamy smooth texture by producing . . . .

smaller crystals

355

4   Crystals are pure substances and the introduction of foreign substances interferes with crystallization. The foreign substance adheres to the crystal preventing the addition of the crystal forming substance. For example, paddles churn air into an ice-cream mix and the air interferes with the growth of ice crystals. In home-made ice-cream, fat in the cream used coats the crystals and keeps them small and also adds richness. Starch, egg, or egg white also adhere to the sides of the crystals as they form preventing them from getting too large. If this is true, would the addition of egg white as used in divinity fudge help to ensure that it was creamy?

Yes, the egg whites serve the purpose of interfering with large crystal formation and produce the delightful divinity fudge texture.

●

5   Most of the package mixes for homemade ice-cream contain gums, starches, and gelatines which accomplish the purpose of inhibiting large crystal growth. Recipes for making fondant frostings (creamy sugar-water mixtures made up of tiny sugar crystals) are designed for keeping the crystals small in the frosting. Corn syrup contains dextrins, maltose, and glucose—sugars different than the sucrose (table sugar). These 'foreign' sugars interfere with the formation of large sucrose crystals in the frosting.

From the above, would you say that the reason corn syrup does not form grainy sugar crystals is because it is made up of several types of sugars?

Yes, this is one of the reasons.

●

6   Some recipes for candy call for vinegar or cream of tartar. These acids break down the sucrose (the most common type of sugar used) into more simple sugars, glucose and fructose. These 'foreign' sugars interfere with the crystallization and a soft candy is produced.

Acid added to a syrup of water and common table sugar (sucrose) produces simple sugars which serve to interfere with . . . .

large crystal formations

7   Cream of tartar, an acid salt, is usually used in candy making to keep the candy soft and noncrystalline. Being a solid it is more easy to control than acids such as vinegar or lemon juice which also can be used. The more acid, the more of the simple (called invert) sugar formed and the softer the fondant produced.

Sugar and water which is cooked and stirred will produce a softer, finer textured product if what is added to it?

Cream of tartar or other acids.

●

8   In some candies we want a soft sugar centre, a fondant. Fondant, we recall, is a sugar solution to which has been added an acid which changes some of the sucrose to simpler forms of sugar. When this is stirred, smaller crystals are formed and a creamy texture is maintained rather than a hard crystalline texture found in hard candies.

The addition of acid to a sucrose solution that is boiled and stirred ensures . . . .

a softer, more creamy texture

●

9   For sugar crystals to form, a solution must be supersaturated which means that there is more sugar dissolved in the solution than it normally can hold at a particular temperature. When this condition takes place, sugar crystals are likely to form rapidly.

For sugar crystals to form the sugar solution must be . . . .

supersaturated

●

10   A supersaturated sugar solution is ready to form crystals and care must be taken so this does not happen when the supersaturated solution is hot. Even a small crystal formation on the side of a pan or a drop of foreign matter such as a speck of dust can 'seed' the formation of crystals.

The presence of a single crystal in syrup after boiling may start a chain reaction of crystal formation.

The reason we wipe the sides of a cooking utensil down, when cooking a sugar syrup is to . . . .

prevent the crystallization of the same sugar

11   When candy syrup has been cooked to a desired concentration, it is poured from the pan without scraping. Either scraping or stirring may start the formation of large crystals. Large crystals mean . . . .

a gritty or grainy texture

●

12   The extent to which syrup is allowed to cool also is a factor that determines the number and size of crystals that form at one time. If syrup is beaten while hot, it is less supersaturated and crystals do not form as rapidly. Therefore, the syrup is allowed to cool until lukewarm—40C (104F)—before it is beaten. If this is done, many tiny crystals form at one time; and the product is smooth and creamy. Beating is continued until all the sugar present forms into crystals.

If we beat a supersaturated syrup at high temperatures we are likely to get what kind of crystals?

Large crystals, a grainy product.

●

13   In making a candy item such as fudge, one way to avoid the problems of forming crystals at all is to cream and cook only the chocolate, milk and butter and other ingredients. Then add confectioners sugar after the mixture has cooled. The crystals of confectioners sugar have been mechanically broken up into fine pieces and produce a velvety smooth texture product (provided they aren't cooked and crystallized).

Fudge can be made without any crystallization of sugar taking place by using confectioners sugar and adding it cooked/uncooked.

uncooked

●

14   Various recipes call for a particular temperature of cooking sugar and water together which is another way of saying that a particular concentration of sugar has been attained. We know that we cannot heat water above 100C (212F), if it is at sea level. However, a 10% sucrose solution (10% sugar in water) boils at 100·5C (213F). A 50% solution boils at 102C (216F) and an 80% solution at 112C (234F).

The boiling temperature (a boiling point) of a sugar solution is an indication of . . . .

the percentage of sugar in the solution

15 The more sugar in a solution the more viscous it is when pressed between the fingers or dropped into cold water.

For example, a small thread will form of sugar if it boils at 101·5—102·5C (215—217F). A large thread forms if the boiling temperature is at 102·5—104·5C (217—220F).

A small ball will form if the boiling temperature is between 113—115C (236—239F).

The sugar is said to be at the 'crack' stage when it will spin a thread and it snaps between the teeth, or breaks off. This occurs when the boiling temperature is between 132—143C (270—290F).

As the boiling temperature of a sugar solution rises, the concentration of the sugar in the water also . . . .

rises

●

16 These boiling temperatures are not precise because of variations due to differences in altitudes and also due to humidity in the air. On humid or rainy days the boiling temperature should be increased by about 2 degrees to get the same concentration of sugar as on normal days. The added temperature adjusts for the moisture which is picked up from the air.

Boiling temperature is decreased 1 degree for each increase of 150 metres in elevation.

Adjustments in boiling temperature must be made in sugar cookery for both altitude and . . . .

humidity

●

17 To review, in most candy and frozen dessert food items we want tiny crystals rather than large ones so that the texture of the product is smooth and creamy rather than coarse and grainy.

One way to ensure that only tiny crystals grow is to add certain other materials to the pure sucrose——(or water in the case of frozen desserts) which inhibit the growth of large crystals. Some of these 'foreign' materials are air, cream, fat or oil, eggs, and what type of sugars?

Those that are different than sucrose, usually simple sugars which can be formed from sucrose by the addition of an acid such as cream of tartar.

359

18 Stirring and beating also inhibit the growth of large crystals but in the case of syrups the beating should take place at a temperature of . . . .

about 40C (104F)

●

19 A supersaturated syrup is one that . . . .

has more sugar dissolved in it than it can hold easily in solution at that temperature and is ready to crystallize

●

20 The boiling temperature of a syrup is an indication of the amount of . . . . in the water.

sugar (the concentration of sugar in the solution)

●

21 Jams, jellies and marmalades owe much of their character to the sugar present. For the best gel the sugar concentration must be 67·5%, the pH between 2·5—3·5 and pectin in the amount of 5—1% must be present.
Must we always have sugar present to form a jelly?

No.
A no-sugar gel can be made using a low methoxyl pectin and calcium)

●

22 Can honey be substituted for sugar in a recipe?

Yes if the recipe calls for liquid. Reduce the recipe by $\frac{3}{4}$ cup sugar and $\frac{1}{4}$ cup of liquid for each cup of honey used.

Action Words In The Kitchen

Rather than present a glossary of terms which is likely to be read about as frequently as a dictionary, the verb vocabulary—the key words—of food preparation is presented.

Let's begin with those verbs that relate to the processing or manipulation of food prior to cooking it. Most of these words are generally known and need no explanation: peel, pare, shred, stir, mix, grind, measure, roll, and blend. Other terms may not be so familiar.

1   Consider the methods of mixing.

We mix ingredients before cooking by sifting, stirring, beating, kneading, folding and creaming. Fat is added to a flour mixture either by mixing, cutting or rolling in. We *cut in* fat into flour or other dry ingredients by dividing and distributing it by chopping or breaking the fat into the flour using a knife or knives, spatulas, hands, or a pastry blender, the latter being a special device with wires that act as cutters. This is continued until the fat is uniformly divided in the desired size into the flour. Complete blending of the fat and flour is minimal by this method. Fat is cut into pastry dough for making pie crusts.

Cutting in fat means to mix fat into flour or other dry ingredients by chopping it in to give maximum/ minimum blending.

minimum

●

2   We know that to roll something is to turn it over or to wrap it around something else. We may also *roll* pieces of food in flour, corn meal, or crumbs to coat

them prior to deep-frying the food. This process may also be called 'flouring' or 'coating pané'. But to *roll-in* refers specifically to the blending of fat into a dough in layers such as is done in making Danish pastry. The fat may be 'dotted', placed in small lumps on the dough, before the dough is folded over it. We use the rolling-in method when we make puff paste, sweet rolls, or Danish pastries.

Rolling-in fat distributes the fat into thin layers whereas *cutting-in* distributes the fat into lumps surrounded by flour. Later when the flour in the cut-in mixture is moistened it forms a paste around the fat. While both methods give a somewhat similar mixture, the rolled-in dough gives a much more flaky product because the fat is spread in larger quantity between sheets of dough. The fat acts as a lubricant minimizing the formation of a strong gluten structure and producing a tender product when baked. We roll in fat when making Danish pastry but . . . . fat when making pie pastry.

cut-in

●

3   Flakiness results because the thin layer of fat melts in baking forming a pool between sheets of dough preventing these sheets from sticking together. Steam forms here and puffs up the dough. Cooking firms the dough and we have a final product that is flaky.

Rolled-in pie doughs become flaky because fat separates layers of dough and . . . . acts as an aerating agent to further separate the layers.

steam

●

4   Air is incorporated into several food materials but the terms used to describe the process vary with the product. We *beat* or *whip* eggs to add air and to increase their volume; we *whip* cream or butter for the same reason and we *cream* fat to add air and to develop a smooth creamy texture.

Creaming also means to mix fat and sugar while at the same time incorporating air. Also a food to which a cream sauce has been added or which has been cooked in a cream sauce is said to be creamed.

A fat and sugar mixture which has been beaten or well mixed together is said to have been . . . .

creamed

5   Many whipped food materials are *folded* into other ingredients so that air which has been incorporated does not escape. Folding consists of two gentle motions, one by which the implement used cuts vertically down through the mixture on one side of the container, the other which turns over the mixture by sliding the implement across the bottom of the container and up the other side and folding over the whipped material until it is well blended into the mixture. The instrument used can be a spatula, a spoon, a whip, or the hand. If carefully done, folding can be accomplished by using a whip in a mechanical mixer.

We beat or whip whites to obtain a foam, whip cream to develop whipped cream and . . . . such ingredients into other ingredients so as to preserve the incorporated air.

fold

●

6   The word *toss* is used when lightly mixing two or more ingredients and is often used when referring to combining salad ingredients. We mix the ingredients of a batter—but the ingredients of a salad are more likely to be . . . .

tossed

●

7   In bread or biscuit making, one *folds* dough over itself after mixing and after knocking-back (a process explained in the next item).

Foods containing air are mixed by folding in to preserve air; in bread making folding is simply a process of . . . . a part of the dough over on itself.

laying or folding

●

8   After yeast action has expanded a dough until little more CO_2 (carbon dioxide) gas can be retained, the dough is knocked-back. It is lifted up on the sides and folded over into the middle until most of the gas is expelled. In other words, knocking-back is not knocking-back but rather a folding process to expel what gas?

CO_2 (carbon dioxide)

9   *Kneading* is a method of mixing dough to develop gluten in a dough or to force out excessive carbon dioxide to prevent over-stretching the gluten strands and to distribute yeast cells throughout a dough. Kneading is done with the palms down, fingers over the farthest edge of the dough, pressing the dough flat with the flat back part of the hand and folding it over, then turning between each kneading.

A dough hook in a mechanical mixer accomplishes the same purpose. Athough kneading a dough further mixes the ingredients, kneading is also done to remove some of the . . . . (a gas) or to develop . . . .

carbon dioxide, gluten

●

10   The surfaces of food materials are gashed or slit for various reasons. The edges of some food such as the fat covering of a steak is *scored* (cut) which prevents the meat from curling when the heat strikes it and the proteins are contracted by coagulation. Thick fish such as herring and mullet are scored in order to allow heat to penetrate more quickly. Rye, French, and Italian, the hearth breads, are frequently *docked* by making slashes across the top of the loaf about $\frac{1}{2}$ cm deep. Docking allows steam to escape without bursting the crust.

Docking pie crusts is pricking the dough with holes to prevent blisters from forming in the crust.

Docking is a term used in baking whereas scoring is used with . . . .

meats and fish

●

11   The top surface of baked products is often *washed*, which means to wet with milk, cream, evaporated milk, eggs or melted shortening. Usually one of these is brushed over the top surface to give extra colour to the product.

When we wash a dough we are not cleaning it but are covering it with . . . . to give colour to the crust.

liquid or fat

●

12   *Glazing* of baked items by adding sugar or sugared and puréed fruits produces a shiny surface which adds to the appearance. Glazing also occurs when egg white is

brushed on the inside of a raw pastry shell to prevent liquid from the filling causing softening of the pastry, when the pie is baked. Glazing of vegetables, meats, fish or poultry is done by basting during cooking or by adding sugar or syrup to the surface and heating.

Washing and glazing of baked dough products both accomplish the purpose of . . . .

adding colour or sheen to the surface

●

13   *Deglazing* is the removal of meat drippings from a cooking utensil usually for use in a gravy or sauce. Liquid, usually stock or wine, is added to the utensil, the utensil heated and the liquid swished and swirled (swept around) until the drippings dissolve.

To deglaze a pan one must add a . . . . and apply . . . .

liquid, heat

●

14   Several other terms are peculiar to the manipulations necessary in making bread and rolls. We have already mentioned kneading, washing and glazing. Here are the other common terms of manipulation:

Divide—to size dough into appropriate segments, approximating the size and appearance of the finished product.

Shape—to put into desirable form.

Scale—to size by weight by using a weighing device.

Pan—to place a dough or batter in appropriate metal containers for baking.

In the process of scaling, what instrument must be used?

A weight measuring device, a scale.

●

15   *Rounding* is shaping a dough piece by hand or machine into a firm ball with a smooth unbroken skin over its entire surface prior to allowing the dough to proof; while *moulding* is the forming of dough pieces by hand or machine into the shape desired for the finished loaves of bread just before panning. Rounding occurs before moulding.

True or False: Moulding differs from rounding in that in moulding the loaves are shaped for panning.

True

16   In meat cooking several manual operations are involved in addition to cutting and boning it. If meat is too lean it may be *larded* by inserting strips of fat into the muscle or it may be *barded* by placing strips of fat on the surface or tying them to the surface. Another way of adding fat is to rub fat, usually butter, over meat or poultry before cooking. Deep-frying, cooking the food immersed in fat, is an excellent method of adding fat since some of the fat is soaked up by the food during the cooking.

True or False: Larding and barding both have the purpose of adding fat to lean meat before cooking.

True

●

17   While larding, barding, and basting add fat to meat, *degreasing* is a process of removing fat or grease from stews, stocks, sauces and the like. Degreasing can be done by using a spoon to skim off melted fat from collected liquids. A bulb-baster normally used for basting—pouring juices or fat over the surface of a meat while it is cooking—can also be used for sucking up accumulated fat in the degreasing process. Another way to degrease is to refrigerate the product, congealing the fat which then can be easily removed.

Degreasing is the process of removing . . . . from pans or stews, sauces, stocks and the like.

fat

●

18   Several terms are used in connection with cutting—brunoise = small dice; julienne = fine strips; jardiniere = batons; paysanne = roughly but uniformly cut.

How would you expect to see vegetables cut in a consommé brunoise?

In small neat dice.

●

19   *Ricing* refers to forcing food through a device called a ricer, which contains perforations and produces particles about the diameter of a rice grain. A *China cap* (chinois) is a cone shaped sieve which strains liquids. A *sieve* also can be used to do this.

True or False: Ricing produces separate food particles

while a China cap (chinois) or sieve separates particles of food from a liquid.

True

●

20   Various foods are coated with flour or flour liquid mixtures, especially before deep-frying. *Dusting, flouring, coating* or *dredging* refer to the use of flour to cover a food with a thin layer of flour but food items may also be sprinkled or coated—in other words, dredged—with sugar or meal. Dusting refers particularly to distributing a film of flour on a work table or on equipment to prevent dough from sticking to them. We would dust a work bench but . . . . (apply) flour on a veal cutlet before sautéing it.

dredge

●

21   *Breadcrumbing* (pané) is the process of covering a food item with a bread coating. The usual process is to flour food, then drop it into a wash of egg and milk and then into fine bread crumbs or other suitable dry material.
     True or False: We can bread a food item by coating it with meal or other materials than bread.

True, bread-crumbing is a term which can refer to the use of coating materials other than bread.

●

22   *Batter dipping* is a term applied to dipping foods into a prepared batter before sautéing or deep-frying them.
     A food item such as tender chicken can be floured or breaded before frying or it can be battered—dipped, drained, and then fried. A flour or bread coating is allowed to tighten (become firm) for about 15 minutes before being fried, but batter-dipped foods are allowed to drain only a moment and then are fried. Items which are floured or breaded should be allowed to tighten for . . . . before they are deep-fried.

about 15 minutes

●

23   We speak of coating foods to be fried but *mask* a food by covering it with a sauce. When a food is covered with a sauce it is described as being . . . . rather than coated.

masked

367

TERMS RELATING TO COOKING PROCESSES

As heat is applied to various food materials, cooking takes place. A number of verbs relate to these processes and rather than discuss each separately, they are listed below. Read them over and see if you can answer the questions which follow the list.

Bake —to cook by dry heat—convected or radiated— usually in an oven. When applied to meats, baking is synonymous with roasting. Baking is usually used in referring to the cooking of flour and liquid mixtures—doughs, pastes and batters.

Blanch—to partially cook food in either hot fat, steam or boiling water. Blanching in deep fat is usually done to precook foods so that they may be finish-cooked later when time is at a premium. Vegetables, fruits, and nuts are blanched in boiling water to remove their skins, to remove off flavours, to inactivate enzymes and to shrink the foods prior to canning. The word 'blanch' comes from the French, 'blanchir', to whiten.

Boil—to cook in a liquid in which bubbles rise and break at the surface, 100C (212F) for water at sea level.

Braise—to cook covered in a small quantity of liquid. Meats are usually browned in the presence of some fat and then braised.

Broil or Grill—to cook under or over direct heat some or much of which is radiant heat. Broiler temperatures begin at about 232C (450F) and go as high as 982C (1800F). Temperatures on the food surface may be as low as 149C (300F) and still good broiling action occurs.

Caramelize—to heat sugar or foods containing sugars until a brown colour and characteristic flavour develop. Barley sugar is very lightly browned sugar. Black sugar is sugar that is almost burned.

Clarify—to heat for the purpose of removing unwanted solids. Butter is clarified by melting it, removing the butter fat from the top leaving the solids to collect at the bottom of the utensil. Soup stock is clarified by adding raw beef and egg whites and often fresh vegetables. The liquid is simmered until the solids present rise to the surface and form a raft which is then removed.

Coddle—to cook below the boiling point; usually applied to cooking eggs by pouring boiling water over them.

Fricassée—is a white stew of poultry or meat in which the meat is cooked in with the sauce.

Fry—to cook in hot fat. When a small amount of fat is used in frying, the process is known either as sautéing, griddle frying, grilling or pan frying. Deep-frying occurs when the food is completely immersed in hot fat, usually at temperatures between 149 and 196C (300—385F).

Glaze—to cook in such a way as to produce a shiny or a coloured surface. For meats and poultry the glazed surface is produced by basting. For vegetables the shiny surface is the result of heat applied to a mixture of butter or margarine and sugar or syrup. Glazing also refers to coating meat, poultry, or fish with a meat essence containing a high amount of gelatine. Glazed surfaces are also produced with icings or concentrated sweets such as jams or preserve purées. 'Glacer' is French for to freeze or chill. The noun 'glaze' refers to stocks reduced to one fourth volume or to the cooked syrup used in glazing pastry items.

Griddle—to cook on a griddle, a flat metal heating surface. Food is placed directly onto the griddle, fat may or may not be added according to the fat content of the food.

Grill—to cook by radiant heat either from below or above.

Pan Fry—To fry in a small amount of fat in a pan.

Pan Broil—to cook in a dry, hot frying pan pouring off fat as it cooks out of meat. The meat must contain sufficient fat to prevent sticking to the utensil.

Parboil—to boil until partially cooked. Usually cooking is completed by another method.

Poach—to cook by simmering in a small quantity of water that barely covers the item. See 'simmer'. The term 'poach' is usually used when simmering tender foods for a brief time.

Poeler or Pot-Roast—to roast joints of meat or poultry on a bed of root vegetables using butter as the fat and covering the joint with a lid during the cooking process.

Plank—to broil fish or meat on a plank of special hard wood then surrounded with vegetables and a border of Dutchess potatoes.

Jugged—braised and usually served in a casserole as in 'jugged hare'.

Reduce—to cook a liquid by simmering or boiling until part of the liquid has evaporated.

Render—to melt and separate fats from meat by heating slowly at low temperatures.

Rissoler—to toss in hot fat or to coat with fat and brown in an oven to produce a brown colour. It is most often used to indicate oven-browned potatoes.

Roast—to cook by dry heat usually in an oven. The same process as baking. Meats are 'roasted' whereas dough and batter products are 'baked'.

Sauté—to fry lightly and quickly in a small amount of fat turning the food frequently.

Scald—to heat liquids or milk just below the boiling point when tiny bubbles form at the edge; to dip certain foods in boiling water.

Sear—to brown the surface of meat by short application of intense heat.

Simmer—to cook in a liquid between 85 and 91C (185—195F). Bubbles form slowly but collapse below the surface. (In boiling, the bubbles break at the surface.)

Steam—to cook by the action of steam by exposing food to the steam.

Steep—to soak a substance in a liquid just below the boiling point for the purpose of extracting flavour, colour, or other qualities.

Stew—to cook by simmering in a small amount of liquid; also the dish or brew that results from standing after hot liquid has been poured over a food.

REVISION

1. Poaching, coddling, steeping, and simmering all are done at what temperature?

   Just below the boil, about 85 to 91C (185—195F).

   ●

2. When sugar is browned it is said to be . . . .

   caramelized

   ●

3. Pot roasting is cooking accomplished by what method?

   Braising

   ●

4. Grilling is the same cooking process as . . . .

   Broiling

   ●

5. A fricassée is closely related to what other cooking process?

   Stewing

   ●

6. If we were to brown the meat and cover it with liquid so it could stew, we would be cooking it by what method?

   Braising

7. We roast meat, fish, and poultry but . . . .
   flour and water mixtures.

   bake

   ●

8. Simmering differs from boiling in that the temperature is about . . . . in simmering instead
   of 100C (212F) as in boiling.

   85 to 91C (185—
   195F)

   ●

9. Most cooking is done by simmering rather than
   boiling. How can we tell which is taking place without using a thermometer?

   In simmering the
   bubbles break
   below the surface;
   in boiling, they
   break at the surface.

   ●

10. The volume of liquid can be . . . . (de-
    creased) by applying heat and evaporating some
    of the water present.

    reduced

    ●

11. What is the process called by which we achieve a
    shiny surface on foods?

    Glazing

    ●

12. When carefully mixing two food materials so as
    to preserve the incorporated air, they are . . . .
    rather than stirred or whipped.

    folded

    ●

13. Foods are . . . . to achieve a shiny top
    surface.

    glazed

14. Dried bits of juices, fat and pieces of meat are
    removed from a cooking utensil for use in sauces
    and gravies by . . . .

    deglazing

Index